The
Polliwog
Fields

Masters Productions Publishing
Seattle, Washington
Copyright © 2019 by Jeremy T. Owen
All rights reserved.

The reader should not consider this book anything other than a work of literature.

Visit my websites at:
www.ThePolliwogFields.com
www.Jtowen.com

Printed in the United States of America
Masters Productions Publishing
First Edition Printing: March 2020

Cover Art by Lance Buckley
Illustrations by Jeremy T. Owen

Acknowledgments

This book could never have been completed without the constant support of my family and friends. The reality checks from my beloved wife, Julianne; the fantasy checks from my dear mother, Dixie. My brother Jarod's ability to laugh at himself and double down with stories we swore we would never tell. My sister Jenni's constant reminders of the good in the bad. Brother Jimmy's voice and humor always one-upping me with each line I wrote. Thank you to Jason Napolitano for your selfless effort, time, and advice. Thanks to Mary Rogers, the bravest English teacher ever! Thanks to so many of you who have passed on from this life but came back to be in my book. Here is to all of you, my friends, my family, and my host of ghosts.

The Polliwog Fields

To Black Bird

Table of Contents

Foreword

Myth is much more important and true than history. History is just journalism and you know how reliable that is.
—Joseph Campbell

The quote above pretty much sums up my feeling about myth in a nutshell.

Unfortunately, the word today is much maligned and misused by most people to mean a story that is false or fabricated. I think this use of the word is not only wrong, but that it is dangerous. The idea that "truth" is only found in the facts strips us of our God-given ability to feel and imagine, and to discern truths that lie below the glassy and antiseptic surface of the so-called "facts."

The real truth, which is the only truth worth knowing, can't really be expressed by facts, it only speaks to one on a heart level. Don't get me wrong; when I speak of myth in connection with this book, I am not saying that there are no facts in the book, because most of the book is based on the historical details of Jeremy's lived life. (I know because I was around for much of it, as we have known each other for more than thirty-five years now . . . good Lord, we are getting old . . . but I digress.) What I mean is that Jeremy has truly crafted a work of creative, childlike mythology in the sense that it transports one to another world and speaks to the soul. I consider myself lucky and honored to be included in *The Polliwog Fields.* (I am also a little jealous, because I do a fair amount of writing myself and I would be very proud to have written a book of this caliber.)

It is not an easy task to write a book in general. It is even more difficult to create something magical and heartfelt like this book. Since I have read it, I have been pondering what sort of person might have been able to pull off a work like this. After much speculation, thinking, and meditation, I have come up with the following rough sketch of the sort of individual that might be able to accomplish this task.

This individual would have to be born on Saint Patrick's Day, with just the right sort of ears and just the right amount of Irish trickster-like twinkle in his eyes. He would have to see things a little differently, feel things a little more strongly, and take on the weight of the world when he didn't feel he had the strength. Also, in addition to writing a great book, this individual would need to have the talent and the bing-bongs to hold a boozy, smoke-filled pub full of drunken knuckleheads spellbound with a simple guitar and his own whiskey-soaked poetry. Oh, also, he would need to have struggled with reading and learning during all his years of schooling. Oh yes, and lastly, this person would have to be honorable, funny, someone you could always count on if you need help, and he would have to be born into a beautiful family full of larger-than-life, big-hearted people who are filled with love and magical spirits.

Wow, that's a pretty tall order!

Good thing for all of us that Jeremy is all of those things and much more.

—Jason Napolitano

Preface

Well, we did some stuff. It was funny stuff. I wrote it down, and there ain't no defending it.

I should say, though, that I did my best to write the kind of book I would want to read. Maybe this was a way for me to spend a little more time with people and creatures that I knew not so long ago, and to let others see and meet them the way I did as a child.

My first memories are from the crib, watching my brother sleep in the room we both shared. Even before I could talk, I remember.

The words I have written here are how I remember my stories and how I hope they will be remembered. They happened, and to the little boy that was me, they are as true as any true story could ever be.

Growing up money poor meant we were adventure rich, and that meant we could do anything. Treasure hunts and dragon battles were always good distractions before noon, then it was off to the polliwog fields to look for real magic. We found it too! Giant volcanoes, great white sharks, pink boa constrictors, clam bears, monsters from deep in the forests of the Pacific Northwest—all were just outside our back door.

I can't promise you won't pee a little, but what I can promise is that the magic you will read about in this book is real magic. The treasure is real. The creatures are real, and the places are real too. Go there, use this book as your map, find them for yourself, and if you do, remember to be respectful. Oh, and tell Clam Bear I say hello.

—J. T. Owen

As my father sings,
As trees begin to sway,
As the river makes its
lazy turn to the sea,
I am born.

Prologue

And my father sings:

> *The house needs paint*
> *The kids need shoes*
> *I keep trying to win*
> *But I always lose.*
>
> *I know I got help from up above*
> *'Cause God built my house*
> *With wall-to-wall love.*

I had been hearing this song for months. It was our song. It was a song that had become a part of me, even before I was me.

> *Some bills ain't been paid*
> *In more than a year*
> *I keep telling my wife*
> *We have nothing to fear.*
>
> *When the furnace needs wood*
> *And the food ain't enough*
> *We must be thankful for a home*
> *With wall-to-wall love.*

And just like that, I took my first breath and gazed upon my brand-new world. The nurse looked down at me and said, "Oh my!" Then she handed me off to my mother's waiting arms.

My eyes were open, bright, curious, and green. Only, my eyes were not what the nurse was looking at. What she was looking at, or really, trying not to look at, were my ears! They weren't too big or too small, and there was one on either side of my head just like there was supposed to be. It was just that they were a bit different. They were the kind of ears that came to two small but perfect little points. You know, standard issue for fairy folk and the like.

In the year 1970, on the third floor of Saint Mary's Hospital in the small coastal town of Astoria, Oregon, I was born. It was on a rainy Saint Patrick's Day when my exhausted mother smiled and said to me, "Well, hello there, Mr. Leprechaun." I think maybe I smiled too.

My mom's name was Dixie, and my dad's name was Jim. I had a three-year-old brother named Jimmy, a four-year-old sister named Jenni, and a stray dog named Hobo. My name was going to be Jeremy, and soon enough I would have a little brother named Jarod. Together we were all about to go on some amazing adventures.

And my father sings:

The mailbox blew down again today
Jenni wants another dog
She found another stray.

Jimmy broke a window
On the house just down the street
I got to tell my wife again
There won't be much to eat.

I wish my kids could have
Something sweet.

Chapter 1

Nineteenth Street

The house my dad was singing about, just then when I was being born, was on Nineteenth Street. It was the second-to-the-last house at the top of our small hill, a hill that itself was on the side of a not-so-small hill. Our house was little, green, sort of plain, and a bit run-down, but we didn't mind because it was ours. From our front porch we could see our whole neighborhood—our whole world, really. If we looked hard, we could see all the way to the Astoria-Megler bridge, and some days clear out to the Pacific Ocean. From our back porch we could see the forest and the trail that wound its way through the woods clear up to the Astor Column, a tall lighthouse-looking thing you saw on all the postcards when you came to visit our tiny town.

The houses on our street were different colors and different sizes, and had different amounts of strangeness to them. There was a little pink house surrounded by pink plastic flamingos and pink roses that were tended by a little old lady who liked to talk about how pink the roses were.

Next to that was a big brown house with shutters that were always closed, a door that was always open, and a very old dog asleep on the porch. A dog that we were sure had never moved—not even once.

On our street we had a tall, thin house and a chubby, fat house. We even had a little crooked yellow house, which belonged to a little old man named Mr. Periwinkle, who was also kind of bent and crooked himself. He liked to collect rocks, all kinds of rocks—minerals, agates, and crystals that shone like rainbows in the sun. His walkway and porch looked like they were lined with magic, and we half expected fairies to pop

1

out at any moment. We used to say that Mr. Periwinkle's crooked little house might collapse all around him, and he would have to live in a pile of rocks.

Next door to Mr. Periwinkle's crooked house of magic stones lived a couple called the McDowells. Their house was blue and very straight, but only medium strange. Mr. McDowell was the local mortician, so we were afraid of him. His wife was a kind, quiet old woman whom my brothers and I would shamelessly shake down for cinnamon toast and applesauce every time we got a chance. We would hit that old lady up twice a day if we could get away with it, and we did. Brother Jimmy would lay it on thick about how very hungry we were, and the poor old woman got worried half sick about us. I can still see the look on my mother's face when she tried to explain to the nice people from the city how she really did feed us, and that we really weren't going hungry. Jimmy must have been a natural-born con man, because we were the chubbiest little starving waifs that you ever did see.

The house next to ours was white and haunted! Well, maybe the house wasn't haunted exactly, but it was all run-down and had a very long and overgrown driveway and a very mean orange cat. The cat was half bobcat, of that we were sure. Along with rats and mice, the big orange cat was also rumored to attack dogs both big and small, other cats, and any children that wandered too close to its creepy mailbox. The mailbox itself was also rumored to be haunted, and we were sure it was filled with cobwebs, spiders, and a mummy's hand that could reach out and grab you if you got too close.

The house below the haunted house was where our five cousins lived with a smelly old dog named Sally. Sally was the same kind of dog as Snoopy and just as nice, but real smelly—so, so smelly. Cousins Carrie, Debbie, Daintry, Sarah, and Ricko played with us most every day, and went on their own adventures too.

At the top of our hill was a big scary house that really should have been our haunted house if we hadn't had a haunted house already, but we did, so it was just the big scary house at the top of our hill. It was so scary that naturally our mother used to drag us along to visit the little old woman who lived up there. Mom would say, "She really loves little children." My brothers and I would look at each other and whisper, "So does the old lady in the gingerbread house." Mom would take our hands and walk us up to the old gray three-story super-creepy Victorian house—you know, the same one you see in all the monster movies. We would step onto the creaking porch, clang the big metal knocker, and wait for bats to fly out, but they didn't. The old lady was the kind of old that meant we would usually have to let ourselves in. Sometimes she would float down the stairs on a machine that looked and sounded like it was going to come to life and get us all. Other times she would already be waiting for us inside her iron lung in a small room next to the kitchen. Yep, I said iron lung.

To tell the truth, the old woman really did love children and was very kind to us, but to a small child the whooshing sound coming from the big iron lung, the floating-down-the-stairs machine, the creaking front steps, and the old bony hand poking out the little window of the scary metal tube was about all a three-year-old imagination could take. Luckily, Mom would let us run outside and play after a short while, and thank God, there were lots of other kids for the nice lady to visit with after we escaped.

On any given day mom was babysitting about a million of us rug rats. There were more cousins hanging around than you could shake a stick at. Most times there were just too many kids to count or even remember. But mom did her best to keep us safe while we grew and learned to explore our strange new world.

While all us kids were running around like crazy, the parents were off doing parent stuff. The dads worked at the sawmill or in the woods logging, on fishing trawlers or gillnetter boats, or down at the docks. The moms stayed home and took care of the kids, went to work down at the tuna cannery, or worked with Grandma Bea at the Woolworth store.

When we weren't at home or out adventuring around the neighborhood, we were mostly hanging with Mom. We spent lots of time with her down at the grocery store, sitting in waiting rooms, at doctors' offices, or worst of all at the beauty shop, which smelled like a nasty combination of cigarettes, coffee, tuna, burnt hair, and the chemicals they burnt the hair with. It was small-town life for sure, and we were in the thick of it.

The Adventure Begins

The street that ran across at the bottom of our hill was called Irving Street, and it went from our block all the way down to Grandma's house on Fourteenth Street. Irving Street was old. It had potholes and old crusted, cracked sidewalks, and was lined with bent-up apple trees. It had a Catholic school about halfway to Grandma's, with a little park that had a slide and swings and a sandbox we could play in, but none of that mattered to us because we were cut off by the old cement bridge that ran across a deep gully half a block from the bottom of our hill.

The old bridge and the gully were, in fact, the very spot where, according to the older kids, the tale of the Billy Goats Gruff had actually taken place. It seems that even though the goats had moved on to live in the front yard of the beat-up gray house that we would pass coming into town, the troll, having grown very attached to his old bridge, had not.

It was rumored that crossing the bridge of a hungry troll without holding the hand of a child older than age twelve was a sure way to get troll-eaten. In fact, the only safe way we could get across the troll bridge at all was to grasp hands, hold our breath, and tiptoe very slowly over to the other side. If we were too loud, tripped, or—God forbid—stepped on a crack, we would have to make a run for it and pray like mad we made it to the blue house on the corner. That was the house where an old yellow dog lived, and the troll, as well as all of us kids, were afraid of him. The dog kept the troll from coming up the hill and getting us, but the troll kept all us kids from going down the hill to see Grandma. It was an uneasy sort of stalemate, one that wasn't going to last forever.

The Polliwog Fields

Our grandpa Chuck Owen had one of the finest collections of arrowheads you have ever seen. He displayed them in carefully organized picture frames that took him years to complete. The arrowheads were arranged neatly in circles, stars, and crisscross patterns. To us kids they looked like mystical signs and warrior faces with sharp teeth and claws. They looked rare and magical, and to us they were. All of the arrowheads, spear points, and hide scrapers were thousands of years old and razor sharp, and the best part was, they were everywhere. The frames of arrowheads were on every wall of every room of Grandpa Owen's house, and on the walls of our great-uncle John Van Horn's restaurant. There are still some to this very day in the Astoria Heritage Museum downtown in the old city hall.

Finding all those arrowheads, hide scrapers, spear points, wampum, beads, and bits of rolled copper took our grandpa a lifetime of searching. Sometimes we even got to go along with him for the treasure hunt. We spent many early mornings on cold, wet beaches all up and down the Oregon coast, where the only sounds to be heard were the lapping of water, the crunch of footsteps in the pebbles on the beach, and sometimes, if you were lucky, the whispered singing of the stones. Grandpa would hike up his pants a little and kneel down on his poncho next to the water's edge. He would run his hands through the fine gravel like a mystical shaman casting a spell in the colorful pebbles that painted the beach at our feet. We would watch him, squatting in our little rubber boots and wearing our bright knit hats with little yarn balls on top. Grandpa would say, "Listen for the arrowheads to call to you. Listen for the copper to sing. Watch for the beads to appear."

He would move his hands from side to side and in a circle almost like he was in a trance or casting a magic spell. Then he would turn his head off to the side as if he was hearing music far, far away. He would whisper, "Do you hear it? Do you hear it calling to you? Okay, now look real hard." We would squat there looking until our eyes almost popped out of our heads. Then, slowly, Grandpa would reach down and there, as if by magic, at the end of his fingers, a sapphire-blue Lewis and Clark trading bead would appear. Or maybe a rolled piece of copper. Or an arrowhead made of flint or sometimes even agate.

He would show it to us, let each of us hold it in our hands, then say quietly, "You see how the stones can talk to you?" Tucking the treasure into his shirt pocket, he would go back to casting his spells at the water's edge.

On our trips to find arrowheads we found other kinds of treasures too. The first creature of tooth and scale I ever had the pleasure of meeting was laid out across the railroad tracks we followed down to Aldridge Point. I was maybe three or so years old and, like most three-or-so-year-olds, I was running out ahead of where I was supposed to be. The sun was shining, but there was still a chill in the early morning air. There in the dappled bits of sunlight, draped across the railroad ties, was the most beautiful beastie I had ever seen. It glowed like a little rainbow as the sun bounced from one coil to the next. It had wide, dark saddles, rough scales from its nose to its tail, and it was longer than I was tall. I squatted down and said a hello to my sluggish new friend.

My mother called out, asking me what it was I had found. Without answering her, I scooped it up and began to make my way back down the tracks, thinking that this would be a great present for my dear mother. I gripped the snake about a foot from its head and was holding it as high as I could muster. The snake's tail still dragged along the ground behind me, glinting in the morning sun. The snake didn't much like being dragged, so its coils began to move up and wrap about my waist and thigh. This made it hard to walk, and I struggled to make my way back, mostly because the coils of my new friend began to grip me tighter as I went. The sight of her child dragging a massive snake, which by this time had started wrapping itself all about my chest and hands, had my mother more than a bit concerned. She gasped out, "Oh God, oh God, please!"

Then she yelled to my dad. I remember Dad and Uncle Chucky, white as ghosts, running up the tracks to save me! When they got within a few feet and discovered that there was no rattle, and that my new friend didn't seem to be too much bothered by my rough handling, they let me go ahead and present it to my visibly shaken mother. Mom, being so relieved that it wasn't in fact a rattlesnake, but instead a wayward gopher snake from east of the mountains. She did her best to graciously accept the gift of my new scaly chum.

"Oh, thank you. Umm, what a wonderful gift he is."

She looked over to Dad and Uncle Chucky for help, but they were too busy laughing.

Mom said, "You know, Mr. Snake was probably out getting breakfast for his kids. I bet they miss him a whole bunch by now and are getting really hungry. Do you think maybe we should let him go back home to see them?"

Mom smiled, so I felt okay letting him slither off on his way.

At this age I had taken a keen interest in giving my mother a lot of "gifts," even if she did let some of them go. Aunt Sheryl had given Mom a housewarming plant not too long before, and Mom had been overjoyed to receive it. Only, the plant ended up wilting about a week later, and it eventually died. Understandably, I was quite concerned for Mom's loss. She explained to me how after a while sometimes plants start to die a little; she said that was okay and things can still have beauty even though they might not be as fresh as they once were. I took that to mean that Mom was going to need a new plant. Sometimes I decided she needed a new plant as many as three times a day, sometimes four.

These were only "plants" in the broadest sense of the term. They consisted of any sort of container that would hold dirt and any stick, twig, or weed I deemed gift-worthy at the time. I would bring our dear mother my newest treasure, perhaps an empty can of peas with a half-wilted dandelion stuck in it, and she would ooh and aah over it the way moms do, thank me for my kindness, and put it up on the windowsill or the porch railing where it would get some good sun so it wouldn't croak. Sometimes I would go so far as to tear out her good plants, declaring them to be dead, and replace them with old sticks or branches that I decided still had beauty. After a while our windowsills, porch railings, and what was left of Mom's flower beds began to take on a bit of an eclectic look, to say the least.

We just loved to give our mom gifts, and we spared no expense. Only we didn't have any money or any way to get money. Even if we did find some money it didn't matter, being that we were children whose only path to the store was blocked by a troll. This meant that most of our gifts were in the form of the treasures we came across during our daily adventuring. Colorful snail shells and bits of sky-blue robin's eggs were rather hoity-toity-type gifts. Rocks that we swore had spoken

10

to us and had declared themselves to be spear points, hide scrapers, or perhaps even pure gold itself made nice gifts for Mom as well. However, real magic was the best gift of all, so that was what we were always on the lookout for. To us, "real magic" meant black gold, magic beans—you know, the mystical treasures we sometimes called polliwogs. Polliwogs were the wriggly little sprites that could really and for truly magically change themselves into frogs—glorious, glorious, magical frogs.

We loved frogs so much that Dad let us keep one for a pet. Mr. Bullfrog lived in an old cooler at first. Then later we got a used glass fish tank so we could watch Mr. Bullfrog swim around in the water. We fed him flies, beetles, and the worms we collected on our daily adventures, to keep him fat and happy. Dad found some frog eggs down at the slough, and we put them in there with Mr. Bullfrog, hoping to grow our own polliwogs. Still, even though we were now a polliwog farming business, that didn't stop us from going on safari to harvest new and exotic polliwogs from the wild.

When we did catch new polliwogs, we would declare just what kind of polliwogs we thought them to be: bullfrogs, treefrogs, red-legged frogs, tailed frogs, Western toads, or even the rare spadefoot toads. Sometimes we even declared them to be the small catfish that we had seen at Coffenbury Lake. My mother would do her best to have us put the little creatures back where we found them. So of course, we would do our best to sneak them back home. We would put them in great gallon jars or Mom's good glasses for the best viewing. Then we would place the jars next to our beds, or on the windowsill if we felt they were going to be the kind of frogs that would like the window. If and when Mom caught us, we would explain how these were some very rare kinds of polliwogs, and how naturally they were a gift just for her, so we should keep them. She would humor us and put them up on the windowsill above the kitchen sink for a day or two. Then they went into the tank with Mr. Bullfrog, when we still had Mr. Bullfrog, or back out into the ditch that ran along the end of our block, where most of them had come from in the first place.

When Mom wasn't being lavished with our gifts or replenishing the local polliwog population, she was tending to what must have seemed like a million and a half kids, all of us coming and going to and from the house, asking for snacks and Dixie cups of Kool-Aid that was preferably made by anybody but my mother, who for reasons unknown to us didn't quite understand just how much sugar was supposed to go in with the flavor packet, resulting in countless tiny glasses of what could only be described as sour disappointment. Jimmy and Ricko sat on the back porch with a bag of sugar that they had liberated from Auntie Jerry's pantry. If they were feeling in a generous mood, you might get a spoonful or two. That is, if you had something good to trade. Many a wheeler-dealer was born on that back porch.

"How about three polliwogs and a mudpuppy?"

"Umm, four polliwogs and two mudpuppies!"

"You got yourself a deal!"

Yup, I sold my soul to the company store.

There was always some sort of calamity afoot. One of us had either lost a tooth or gained a tooth, twisted a limb, fallen out of a tree, or gotten bumped, scratched, cut, scraped, or poked in the eye. There were a lot of fingers poked in a lot of eyes back then, along with fat lips, bit lips, split lips, and rug burns, mostly self-inflicted. All of this made for an owie assembly line that Henry Ford himself would have been proud of. Aunt Jerry, Mom, and the older kids were constantly picking us up, dusting us off, giving us a hug and a kiss,

12

then sending us on our way. We were like little tiny polliwog miners, clocking in and clocking out of the polliwog fields, getting patched up, fed a cookie, given a Dixie cup full of Kool-Aid, and sent back out into the fields to earn our keep.

I had just limped in from the back forty, where I had nearly lost a hand to an invisible sliver in my thumb. Cousin Carrie was administering first aid in the form of an unnecessary Band-Aid when little brother Jarod came staggering up the walkway with a code-red. He had been out in the polliwog trenches for half the morning, pulling in a few rather fine examples that any child would have been proud of. He was making his way back home, with his prizes held high, when suddenly he was brought down by unseen forces. He went down hard, right next to the fire hydrant and so close to the haunted mailbox that we thought he was a goner for sure. Jarod staggered to his feet with an elbow scrape that could have taken his arm off clean to the shoulder if he had been a lesser boy. He was screaming in agony and moving like Frankenstein's monster with his left elbow locked straight out, one arm holding up the other so he wouldn't lose the limb entirely. At the sound of it, the sea of casualties slowly parted to let him pass. It was all Jarod could do to crawl up to the front of the assembly line. Mom rushed forward and fell to her knees so she could administer a healing kiss to the massive boo-boo, the kind of kiss only mothers can give.

Like the Lady of the Lake from the King Arthur story, she bestowed her grace upon the wounded limb with the tender touch of her lips. We all believed that we were witnessing a true miracle. The instant Mom's lips touched the rusty wound, Jarod's look of agony changed completely. First it went to horror and then slowly it melted into pure joy. Then Jarod went even deeper, slipping into utter hysterical laughter. As he gasped to

13

catch his breath, a look of confusion began to wash over my mother's face. Jarod was trying to speak. Slowly he cried out to the masses, who had begun to kneel before the miracle that was now upon us. The silence was nearly crushing. Jarod finally croaked out the words that we thought might be his last: "Poo-poo . . . you just kissed poo-poo!"

My poor mother dropped Jarod like a hot rock and immediately made for the kitchen sink to wash off her mouth. The masses of children looked on in horror as Auntie Jerry, who was trying not to laugh herself, cleaned off Jarod's elbow. Everybody was quiet at first, but then bit by bit kids started giggling. When Auntie Jerry started to laugh, that was it, we all cracked up.

Mom took it rather well, considering. After a good scrubbing and having composed herself, Mom grabbed the nearest glass and poured it full of milk. Then she got herself a cookie, sat down, and tried to put the whole episode behind her. After a few minutes, Mom had finished the last of her cookie and was taking the final swallow from her glass of milk. Only, something strange came over her as she stared into the bottom of her glass. There, now half rehydrated and floating in little black bits, were half a dozen of last week's polliwogs, long forgotten on the windowsill. They had dried to a crisp in the sun. At the sight, Mom began heaving: "Whooack, whooack." She sounded a little bit like a muffled duck quacking. She ran to the bathroom, where she let those polliwogs go too. Mom came back out, tears welling up and utterly defeated for the day. What else could she do but get in line with the rest of us and hope that just maybe her sister Jerry could hug and kiss away her boo-boos too.

The Boy in the Bubble

Like all children, I spent time in a plastic bubble. Okay, maybe not all children, but all the children I knew. Brother Jimmy and cousins Ricko, Daintry, and Sarah were all my bubble-buddies. Each of us spent close to a week in a bubble, or bubbles, really. In a way, it was the first campout we ever got to have together. We each got our own little oxygen tent to play in, with our own little bed inside. All our tents were side by side in the big hospital room like a tiny army camp, but we didn't get to have a fire. When we asked if we could make a campfire the nurses got very concerned. They tried to explain how having a fire would be a very bad idea in an oxygen tent.

Dr. Honnell came in and said we had all gotten pneumonia, which was something you can get when you're outside and wet all the time. Dr. Honnell said one of us caught it and brought it home and gave it to everybody else. It must have been Jimmy, or Ricko. Mom said we probably caught it out in the polliwog fields, but I told her we only caught polliwogs in the polliwog fields and this time we left them all outside like we were supposed to. That was a fib, of course; there were some polliwogs in a jar under my bed back home even then.

There were no TVs in our room, so Mom read us Dr. Seuss out loud, told us stories, and played cards with us. I don't remember exactly what game we played, but I feel like we would have played canasta, because canasta seems to me like a bubble-boy kind of card game, and it was fun to say "canasta." It was probably Go Fish, though.

I pretended to be a seahorse and ran around on all fours in my tent, which was now a fishbowl. Everyone else pretended to be regular fish and just sort of lay there, because nobody much felt like playing fish. The tent machines were making loud hissing noises, and it was hard to hear each other talking through the bubbles. So pretending to be a seahorse seemed like the thing to do, because seahorses don't talk anyways.

Mom told us that this was what the old lady in the iron lung felt like all the time, and she was stuck in there. I asked Mom to take her a stuffed fish and put it in the iron lung with her, so she could be a seahorse and wouldn't be lonely in the iron lung anymore. Mom said she would.

Mom, Dad, Auntie, and Uncle got to be very worried about losing Daintry and me; we had to stay an extra week after the other kids got to go home. I didn't see how they could lose us, though, because we were zipped up inside those bubbles, and they wouldn't even let us out to go pee or nothin'. Plus, we were coughing so loud everybody knew exactly where we were the whole time.

The Hatch

We got better after a couple of weeks and nobody got lost, so that was good too. On my last day in the bubble, I was feeling hungry for good food—not the stuff we had to eat when we were sick. Dr. Honnell let me pick out anything on the menu that I wanted to eat, so I did. I picked out chicken noodle soup, chocolate pudding, and a cup of coffee with creamer and sugar. The nurses laughed when they took my order.

Dr. Honnell sat and talked with me while we waited for my food to come. I asked him about the scar he had on his head, and he told me how he got the scar when he was an army doctor, from a thing that exploded. He said a piece of the explosion was still in his head. Mom said our doctor was a real miracle, and to me that meant he was magic. I was surprised when the nurse really did bring me the coffee; I ate all I could and drank my coffee too.

When I was done eating, Dr. Honnell said I was all better, and it was okay for me to go back home now after I got dressed. I climbed out of my bubble so Mom could help me get dressed. I don't know, maybe it was all the coffee or the posters on the walls that showed the different body parts of people and stuff. But for whatever reason, I chose that moment to take a keen interest in my little round jingly bits. Mom was getting my clothes laid out for me, and I was looking down and sort of pulling on them. She noticed the pained expression on my face, and said, "Hey, be careful, you're going to hurt yourself!" Mom asked me if there was something wrong, and I said, "No, it's just that, well, what are those things?" Mom laughed, then explained to me that those were called my testicles. I said, "Oh." Then I asked her, "What are they for?" She explained how their main purpose was for when I got to

17

be older, they would be used for making babies. I thought about it for a bit, I looked down, then back up at Mom, and asked, "Are they gonna hatch?" Mom laughed. "No, they are not going to hatch."

We said good-bye to Dr. Honnell and the nurses, who were still laughing too, then we packed up and headed back home to Nineteenth Street.

Our world had changed in just that short time. Sleepy frogs had gone off to take their long nap in the mud. The leaves had turned from greens to oranges and reds. Summer had sailed far, far away. Now it was the time of mushrooms, frosts, pumpkins, and candy!

The Dragon's Tail

Soon it would be Halloween, the most magical time of the year for adventuring. We got to dress up and be anything we wanted to be, go out at night, carry lanterns, play tricks, get treats, and run around like crazy, making ghost sounds and howling at the moon.

Each year Mom, Grandma Bea, and Aunt Jerry made all our costumes by hand. By the time I was three years old they had ten-plus kids to sew costumes for. All that fitting, cutting, and sewing was no small feat, that's for sure.

Growing up, we were what Mom called "money poor." Money poor meant we made stuff by hand whenever we could. Dad said that when you made your own things, they were called custom-made, and custom-made meant they were extra special and just for you. Jimmy was a friendly pirate with an eye patch and a drawn-on mustache. Jenni was a hobo with a bundle on a stick and a coffee-grounds beard, and Jarod was a spooky little ghost. I was a dragon, but not just any dragon. I was a real dragon!

Mom used an old oatmeal container to fashion a fearsome dragon snout and dragon teeth. She sewed a full head-to-toe dragon suit out of thick green corduroy that went right down to three little claws on my dragon footie feet, and fearsome green spikes all the way down to the tip of my dragon tail. If ever a mom sewed love-packed magic into a costume, this was it for sure. When I put on my dragon skin, I was every bit a dragon. I could feel the dragon magic that all dragons feel, from the horn on my nose down to the claws on my toes. There was so much dragon magic in me that I had to be careful not to spill any fire out of my mouth and accidentally burn all the people around me. I was super strong and super fast, and could probably jump over our

19

car if I wanted to. I couldn't fly, though, because Aunt Jerry didn't have time to sew my wings on, but she told me that was for the best because she didn't want me to float away.

It was a great responsibility to be a real dragon. I knew I had a big decision ahead of me, and that I would have to choose very wisely. You see, there were many different kinds of dragons in the world, so I had to think hard about what kind of dragon I was going to become. I knew I wasn't the kind of dragon that guarded treasure or princesses or ate villagers . . . well, maybe our rotten neighbor Scottie Steckler and his snotty little sister. I wasn't the kind of dragon that knights were always doing battle with. So I thought, and I thought, and I thought, and then I thought some more. After all that thinking I finally decided I was going to be the kind of dragon that we needed the most: the kind of dragon that ate trolls.

I had worn my dragon suit for three days in a row. By then, I had mastered nearly all my dragon skills. I went out in the woods, where I found a stick that looked like a cross between a wizard's staff and Tiny Tim's crutch. It seemed to me to be the kind of stick that trolls would fear if you waved it at them. I brought it home and practiced waving it at imaginary creatures and scaring them away. When I was ready, I took a deep breath, screwed my courage up tight, grabbed my stick, and started down the hill toward the troll bridge. I made sure no one was looking, because I didn't want anybody to get hurt during the fierce battle ahead.

I carefully made my way past the haunted mailbox and Mr. Periwinkle's magic-rock house. I was all the way to the yard with the big yellow dog when I heard footsteps crunch on the gravel behind me. I turned to see brother Jimmy running to catch up.

He said, "Hey! Where do you think you're going?"

I turned. "I'm a dragon and I'm going to kill the troll!"

He could see in my eyes that I meant it. He said, "I'd better go with you . . . just in case." He waved up at the top of the hill to Mom, who was looking out the window to make sure we were okay. We headed down to the road, where Jimmy had to hold my hand so that we could cross the street.

We stopped for a minute, took a deep breath, then stepped toward the troll bridge. The closer we got the tighter I held Jimmy's hand, until our knuckles were nearly white. Finally we got to the spot where the bridge began. Jimmy said, "I better go first and make sure it's okay."

I looked up at Jimmy and nodded my head.

Jimmy yelled, "Come out, come out, come out!" And he slowly stepped onto the bridge.

We listened and looked over the edge but heard nothing.

Jimmy yelled again. "I have a troll-eating dragon up here. So come out and be eaten, troll!"

He stomped hard on the bridge and jumped back to where I was. We were both shaking a bit, but ready to fight . . . or run away super fast.

I put on my biggest dragon voice. "Mr. Troll, come out and face a dragon! Come out and be eaten, troll!"

But he didn't come out.

We slowly walked out to the middle of the bridge and yelled again. "Mr. Troll, where are you? Mr. Troll?"

Still nothing.

I turned to Jimmy. "Maybe he's not home."

Jimmy glanced over the side of the bridge. "Or maybe he's just afraid of dragons."

"Yeah, maybe he is afraid, or maybe he's sick or something." I yelled, "Mr. Troll, are you sick or something? If you don't feel good, we don't have to fight, and I won't eat you, okay? So you can come out now, Mr. Troll."

Still nothing.

Jimmy looked at me and whispered, "Put down the stick."

I put the stick down. "I'm putting my stick down; you can come out now, Mr. Troll!" But still there was nothing.

I yelled, "We want to be friends now, and we don't want you to scare us anymore when we walk to Grandma's house, or the park, or the store."

That time we thought we heard something from under the bridge.

We waited.

I yelled again. "Okay, we're friends now, so I'm going to give you my stick. It's a good one; you can use it for a crutch, or a wizard stick, or for hopping over a ditch. Here it comes, watch your head!"

I dropped the stick over the edge of the troll bridge. There was another noise.

I yelled, "Okay, we're leaving, I hope you feel better soon. I'll ask my mom if we have any troll medicine."

Jimmy said, "Let's go."

He grabbed my hand and we crossed the street again. As we walked back up the hill, I asked Jimmy if he thought the troll was going to be okay.

He told me, "Yeah, trolls are tough."

Trick or Treat

The next week was Halloween, and we all went out trick-or-treating dressed in our Halloween finest. We walked to Grandma's, then trick-or-treated our way back home. We got all kinds of goodies, not just store-bought candy. We got real treats that people spent an entire week making for us. We got popcorn balls, caramel apples, and big pieces of fudge. Dad handed out deer jerky and Indian candy—that's sweet smoked salmon bits that melt in your mouth. Mom made lemon bars. The Bartoldus house had a giant pot of hot apple cider that you could dip a cup in. Everybody gathered together at the bottom of the block, and nobody was even worried one bit about the troll. Well, nobody but me, anyways. As we passed over the bridge on our way home, I lagged behind just a bit. When no one was looking, I took out my popcorn ball and let it roll down over the edge of the troll bridge, down to Mr. Troll. Jimmy yelled for me to come and hold his hand, and I ran to catch up.

I woke up the next morning and found half a popcorn ball tucked under my pillow. I was happy that Mr. Troll must have been feeling better.

The Sunset Empire Room

Great-Uncle John Van Horn was just that, he was great! Uncle was the head of our family like in the mob movies, except he didn't make anybody go sleep with the fishes. He would make you fish'n'chips, though. Uncle John and Aunt Cathy owned the Sunset Empire Room downtown across from the plywood mill that was on the water at the east end of town. The Sunset was a family-style restaurant with steaks, hamburgers, seafood, and oh yeah, fish'n'chips. More than *a* family restaurant, it was *our* family restaurant. So much so that on our way in or out of town us kids would always beg to stop in to say hi to everyone we knew who hung out there. If we were lucky, we would get a Shirley Temple, some of the cook's giant croutons, and a pocketful of soft dinner mints to go.

We loved the Sunset, and we loved all the people we saw there. We would see Grandma Mary, who was always pinching Jimmy's cheek and saying, "Jimmy. You're such a good boy!" even when Jimmy wasn't being a good boy at all. Uncle Billy and Aunt Margaret would be washing dishes, busing tables, or running around taking orders. Margie, Aunt Mary Alice, and Aunt Marie all worked behind the bar. Sometimes they would sneak us peanuts and pretzels, and then give us a wink that meant we shouldn't tell anybody.

There was a bear of a man called Indian Jim, who always had a cigarette dangling out of the corner of his mouth and spoke in a deep baritone voice that rolled like thunder across the bar. Us kids would climb up him like an oak tree to give him hugs whenever we saw him. The cook was named Sam, and her auburn hair was always up in a hairnet. She had horn-rimmed glasses with a string that went around her neck. Sam had an apron that she tied at her waist, and she smelled like the best french fries in the world whenever we gave her a hug. Sam put up with an endless stream of kids running in and out of her kitchen and was always kind to us in a gruff sort of way.

Chucky Chow was a little old Chinese man who always had a smile for us but spoke very broken English. We didn't know this at the time, but Chucky was a scientist; he invented imitation crab meat, the kind everybody eats in their sushi rolls now. Any family that Chucky may have had back then must have lived very far away, so we never met them. He once showed me an old black-and-white photograph of a woman and a small girl that I think maybe were his family, but he never talked about them. Most of the people we saw at the Sunset had little or no family in town, or anywhere at all sometimes. But they were all family to us. As kids do, we loved them with all our hearts, and I miss them even now.

On Fridays sometimes Mom would bring us down to the Sunset, and all the kids would crowd around the open door between the restaurant area and the bar. From there we could see the stage where Dad played guitar and sang. Dad would play while all the people danced, drank cocktails and beer, and talked about their days. We would try our best to stay awake until ten o'clock because that's when Uncle John would let Dad play songs he wasn't supposed to play while families were still eating. Dad would play "Spiders and Snakes," "Dead Skunk in the Middle of the Road," "The Finger Song," and any other funny gross song we asked for. He would play special songs as well. He would sing "Happy Birthday" if anyone was having a birthday, and he sang kid songs just for us kids too.

Dad was an original member of the Mickey Mouse Club as a little kid, and still had his mouse ears. He would put them on and sing the Mickey Mouse song for us, and we would all sing along. "Mickey Mouse, Donald Duck, Mickey Mouse, Donald Duck," and then we would hold our banners forever high, high, high. Dad would sing the songs that he wrote too: "Wall-to-Wall Love," "It's Not That Way Anymore," and "If Love Was a Can of Lard, I'd Keep You Greased Up All Day Long." That one was for Mom, and it would make her blush whenever Dad sang it. Dad would sing "The Bluebird Song" for Jenni, and he would start it off the same way every time. He would say, "With all my love, this is for my daughter, my little dancer, never forget how much I love you. You are the little bluebird in my soul." Then he'd sing, and she would cry every time. Sometimes he would cry a little too.

Some of my favorite songs were "The Dog Song" (Dad wrote that one for me), "Reuben James," "King of the Road," and "Mr. Bojangles," and because my name is Jeremy, my favorite was "Jeremiah Was a Bullfrog." That's also why Dad gave me the nickname Bullfrog, but he always called me Frog for short.

Our most favorite thing about the Sunset was the family Christmas Eve party. That was when Uncle John would close down the restaurant to the public, and then just friends and family were invited in to celebrate our holiday. Uncle John played Santa Claus most every year and handed out the gifts to all the kids. We got to go into the bar part of the restaurant that normally we weren't allowed to go into at all. All us kids played pool, drank Shirley Temples, and danced on the dance floor as Dad performed all our favorite Christmas songs. Everybody waited the whole night for him to sing a special song to Chucky Chow. Dad would sing "Blue Christmas" in his best Chinese. Chucky would smile as big as could be, proud, knowing that the song was just for him.

Us kids would all open and play with our Christmas Eve gifts until our eyelids grew too heavy to hold open anymore. Eventually we would drop off to sleep like little piles of puppies in random corners of the restaurant and up on the stage. We would drift away with crumpled wrapping paper for our pillows and piles of coats for our blankets, and when we awoke, we had been magically transported home into a warm bed and it would be Christmas morning.

The Sunset made us feel special. Special to be a part of a family that came in all shapes, sizes, and colors. Special because our dad was the one everybody came to see and be entertained by. Special because it was ours in a way few things ever were or ever would be again.

Chapter 2

Ensatinas

After a long, rainy, wet Astoria winter, we were itching to get back out into the polliwog fields, only it was a bit too early for polliwogs. So instead we headed off to look for other kinds of forest folk. March and April are a good time of the year to look for newts because that's when they go a-marching. Later we found out our marching newts weren't really newts at all, but a pinkish kind of salamanders called ensatinas. They were pinkish brown for the most part, and see-through on the smaller parts. If you picked them up, they were quick to ooze white goo, and they would drop their tails off if you scared them or they got too warm, so we kept them cold as best we could. We believed the white goo was the kind of poison you could put on arrowheads and blowgun darts if you were in the jungle, but I think that's just something the older kids made up.

Turns out, a lot of what we had learned about our world was a bunch of stuff the people we knew just made up, or someone they knew just made up. Actual newts were the creatures that we called fire belly salamanders, and although all newts are salamanders, not all salamanders get to be newts. The actual newt-newts were dry, rough and brown on top, and bright orange-yellow on their bellies. They were always friendly, bold little characters, and you could keep one in your pocket for half a day if you needed to.

Every year when the newts heard the first croak of spring they would begin to march. Newts, along with all manner of "slither and squiggle" forest folk and water sprites, would troop out of the forest, through the fields and across the roads, making their way back to the ponds, springs, or streams that they themselves had crawled out of not so long ago. Newts are fearless creatures and don't hesitate to march right out in the open. It's amazing to see how nothing challenges them on their way back home. Crows and snakes go around them, and even the cat from the haunted house next door would let them be. When they do arrive back at their shore, something unbelievable happens.

Our other grandpa, Grandpa Roy, told us the story of how the newts walk back into the water. With as much magic as forest fairies, bridge trolls, and river elves put together, they slowly begin to transform themselves. They sprout great ornate fins on their backs and tails, and they become young and strong again. Their magic is so strong they can even regrow a whole arm if it gets lost in battle. Grandpa said that if you ever find them in the water that's when you call them "pond dragons." Grandpa told us to always be kind to pond dragons, to never take them from their pond or stream, and how it was bad luck if you did. He said they were one of the few magical creatures left in our world that still let us see their magic. Grandpa said we needed to respect that. He told us that the pond dragons come back to their ponds to do dragon battle, and that if we were to sit quietly, ask permission from the pond dragon king and be respectful, they would appear and let us watch them fight for their queen and maybe even grant a wish or two.

Jarod and I spent the rest of that day down by the pond. We sat dreaming of dragon battles and of the thousand different wishes we would make to the pond dragon king. Wishes for gold and treasure, candy and magical powers. To be able to fly, to be invisible, to be knights and giants, or monsters, to breathe underwater and maybe even swim with the pond dragons themselves.

The legend of the pond dragon battles and of their great magic became one of those stories that grandpas tell little kids to make them be quiet and pass the time over by the pond, far away from where grandpas are trying to get their work done.

Even though some of us kids thought Grandpa Roy was pulling our legs about the dragon battles and their magic, Jarod and I knew different. We would still go down to the pond, sit quietly, and ask the pond dragon king's permission very respectfully, you know, just in case.

Cutthroat

.om before I can remember, I was fishin'—even before I was me at all, I was fishin'. That was because since Mom was fishin', and I was sort of swimming around in her belly while she fished, I was fishin' too. As we grew, every spring Mom and Dad would take us down the rocky trails that run alongside the Young's River Falls, pathways that themselves had been a part of the river just a month or so before.

For our fishing poles, Dad would take out his knife, select two or three long straight saplings of Indian plum or river willow, then cut and strip the leaves and branches and let them fall at his feet to float off down the river. We would gather driftwood for a fire, keeping aside any pieces that came to a Y to be used as pole holders or for cooking our fish. There was a big old hollow log that lay just a few feet back from the trail. In it we had stashed everything we needed for fishing. Hooks, line, weights, and bobbers were all wrapped up along with salt and pepper and were tucked way in the back of the log cache.

Dad would unwind fifteen or twenty feet of line from the small spool of six-pound test he kept in his shirt pocket. Mom would tie one end of the line to the tip of the sapling pole, and on the other end Dad would put two or three small split-shot weights about a foot and a half up the line from a number 12 hook. Dad would bait up the hook with a small piece of worm that we had dug out of our garden or any of a half dozen locations we referred to as the "worm farms."

When we were still too young to walk, Mom would set up the playpen alongside the river. Dad would put our fresh-cut fishing poles in the playpen with us, and we would fish from there. As we got older, we went from crib-fishermen to being bait-catchers. The four of

32

us kids would flip over rocks and logs to expose all manner of worms, tiny freshwater lobsters we called crawdads, snails, and such. We would scoop up as many as we could, then run back to a holding pond that the older kids had fashioned of rocks and clay from the riverbank. The ponds resembled dinosaur nests with their big ring of rocks surrounding a few smaller stones in the center for creatures to hide under and stay out of the sun. They would fill it with water as best they could, and in it we kept all things bait: periwinkle snails, crawdads, and small fish we called bullheads, which were really freshwater sculpins. There were giant salmon flies as long as your finger that hid under the loose bark of dried-up trees at the water's edge, and the artsy caddis-fly larvae in their ornate little houses made of sticks and stones hidden in shallow pools dappled in sunlight and shadow.

I can't remember a single fishing trip where there wasn't some sort of prison break, resulting in catastrophic losses to our miniature zoos. The practice of placing three- and four-year-olds in charge of our most important resource may have needed some rethinking. Traditions being what they were, we made the best of it. No one ever got in trouble for napping on the job, especially if it was actually their nap time. Though once, Jarod fell asleep with his bare foot in the holding pond and woke up with a crawdad pinched onto his big toe. He ran around in circles screaming and kicking his foot high up in the air as far as he could, trying to flick the monster off his little piggy. Dad almost had to hogtie him to get him to hold still so Mom could pry the tiny lobster off his toe.

Sometimes, in addition to gathering bait, we even caught a fish or two. Generally, we were after native cutthroat trout—sometimes rainbows, but mostly cutthroat. Looking down into the dark pools from above, the fish were invisible. Our only way to know if they were even there was to roll bright-red huckleberries down the sides of the boulders that lined the pool's edge. We'd watch them as they slowly sank into the darkness, waiting for the berries to blink out of sight as they were snapped up by hungry mouths. Deep in the river the cutthroat were invisible, but once on our lines, they were an explosion of colors. They were a deep green on top, speckled with big black dots that ran down from their nose and spilled onto their tail. Sides of silver flashed hard as they leapt from the water. Each twist was a wash of green, indigo, then back to silver as they shook a spray of water off in the sun, then dove deep before jumping again. Their gill plates of pink and gunmetal blue hid the two red lines that ran down their throats and gave them their name. The fish were dispatched and cleaned as quickly and respectfully as possible. The leftovers were given to the crawdads, and the trout were brought back to Dad and Grandpa Owen for cooking. That is, if Grandpa Owen had made the trip.

When he did, we were going to learn something new, even if it was the same lesson we learned last time, only better this time. Each fish got skewered with three small sticks—usually ones that Dad and Grandpa had been whittling on most the morning, or if they weren't in a whittling mood, split cedar did the job. The skewer sticks were woven through the meat at the middle and both ends of each fish. Dad or Grandpa, or sometimes Dad *and* Grandpa, would talk out loud as they prepared the fish.

"The trick here is to find a sapling that is not too thick and doesn't have any big branches coming off it."

Dad would do the work as Grandpa kept a close eye on him for quality control.

"You have to choose a sapling about as big around as a broomstick and almost as long."

Taking out his Buck knife, Dad would carefully, very carefully, split the sapling in half about two-thirds of the way down, making a giant pair of tongs.

"Now, don't tear the bark, we'll use that soon enough."

Sometimes he tore it; if he did, it was always the sapling's fault.

"Okay, kids, here comes the magic!"

He would peel the bark down one side of the tongs to just below where the split stopped, then use the bark strip to wrap and tie the pole so it wouldn't split any more. The wrapping made a good handle for holding. The skewered fish—as many as three of them, if they were small—were then slid into the giant tongs, and Dad would usually let one of us hold the split end together, securing the fish, while he tied it shut with the other piece of bark. Then he would say, "Fish sticks, anyone?" (It wasn't funny then either.) Then the fish were brushed liberally with River Sauce, a "secret family recipe" that Dad would tell to everybody he met on the river or on the way to the river, or if you just asked, really. This was the recipe:

Ingredients:
2 cups of soy sauce
4 tablespoons of Worcestershire sauce
1/4 cup of dark brown sugar
5 good-size cloves of garlic, mashed, not sliced
3 spicy cloves
3 bay leaves
1 cup of hazelnuts, chopped and roasted in the
    oven to a medium brown
4 tablespoons of butter

Directions:
Put everything in a saucepan and boil for five minutes. Then strain, pick out the cloves and bay leaves

35

and chuck 'em, but save the hazelnuts. Let the strained sauce cool, put it in a jar, and pack it up to go fishing.

Now for my favorite part.

Throw the hazelnuts back into the pan.

Add 1 cup of brown sugar and 4 tablespoons of butter, and bring the works to a boil.

Pour out onto wax paper and let cool.

Break into nut brittle and hide it from the children's grubby little meat hooks, if you want to have some for the fishing trip.

After the fish got sauced (yup, that was a Dad joke too), we would lean the fish sticks over the fire and wedge them between some rocks, or we would use the fishing-pole holders we had collected before.

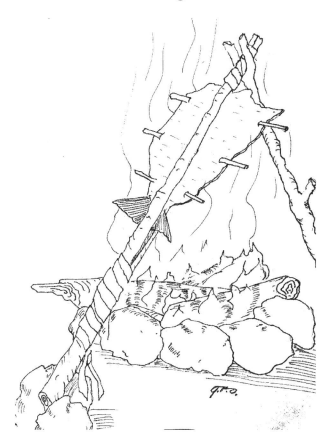

Dad would holler back from where he was fishing, "Try to keep them in the smoke! Keeps the flies off!" I think that was true, but it also made the fish taste good, so we did our best to keep them in the smoke. The kind of smoke was important. We had to use the best-tasting wood for the fire, or it could ruin the fish. Cedar or alder was our first choice, but maple or the inside of a cottonwood tree was tasty too. The dark outside of the cottonwood made you choke, so we tried not to use it at all. Fruit trees like apple or cherry were the best of the best but were hard to find most times, so mainly we used cedar or alder.

When Dad was a kid, he spent summers in Alaska with his great-uncle Bill Hanlon, who taught him about hunting, fishing, and stuff. He ran around with the indian kids, and had adventures of his own. He even got famous in the newspaper for finding some thousand-year-old paintings on a big rock that the village kids used for a slide. He ate salmon sticks, and little crabs that they cooked like popcorn in a fire on the beach. Dad even tried Eskimo ice cream once; he made a face and said he could still taste it from when he was ten. Dad said we were part Aleut from Grandma Mary's side of the family. Once, Mom even folded up a piece of paper and showed us just how much Indian we were. I have to admit, I was a bit disappointed to find out I was only a corner of a napkin of Indian, but I was still proud of it just the same. I decided that it was enough Indian for me to do the Indian stuff Dad taught me about.

Dad did lots of Indian stuff himself. Once I saw Dad talking to a deer. I was over looking for pond dragons when I was supposed to be guarding the bait. Dad was standing by the car when he turned and walked out into a grassy field. He had gotten about halfway out in the grass when a doe stepped out of the forest. The doe just walked right up to him. When she got close, Dad got down on one knee and the deer came over to look at him. Then the deer sat like a dog right in front of him. Dad very slowly reached out his hand, putting it on the side of the deer's face. He just held it there for a minute. Dad said something I couldn't hear, and then the deer got up and walked back into the forest. Dad walked back down to the fishing hole where I was supposed to be but wasn't.

I never did ask what they talked about. After that, though, I always believed that animals have more to say than we have the ability, or patience, to listen to.

The Clam Bear

Our great-aunt Maud was in her late eighties when she passed away. She was a small, plump, happy old lady, who always gave us gingersnaps and pieces of butterscotch. We arrived very early in the morning for her funeral. It was at a small church overlooking the Willapa River near the small town of Raymond, Washington. We piled out of the car and helped Mom carry in the casseroles and photo albums while Jarod slept. Jenni and Jimmy helped Mom set up all the stuff in the church, while I got underfoot. After I knocked over one of the flower arrangements, Mom suggested that I go outside and check on Jarod.

I went out and looked at him. He was still hard asleep in the front seat, half slumped down and dangling from the seat belts like a drunken marionette. His hair was all matted with sweat, and he had drooled down the side of his face into Mom's open purse, and some went into one of the cup holders as well. I made a face and decided it was best just to let him sleep.

Wandering around outside the church for a bit, I came to a swing set that only had one swing left on it, so not really a set so much. I sat there in the swing, dragging my toes in the dirt, drifting from side to side and back and forth, drawing little patterns in the dust with the toes of my good shoes. They were shoes that I didn't like anyways, because they were shiny, and I thought they looked like girl's shoes. I leaned back as far as I could and watched the tops of the spruce trees sway as I spun. After a bit I started to get a little sick and had to stop.

I went over and sat in a patch of sunlight on a hilltop overlooking the river until I didn't feel green anymore. Grandpa Owen had taught us how to find good places to look for arrowheads on rivers, so I was scanning the river shore, looking for the kind of places that might have held villages or camps where hunters made or lost spear points and the like. As far as I could see it was mostly small gravel beaches hemmed in with cattails, a good place to find the smallest arrowheads, called bird points. I imagined the Indian villages of wickiups five hundred years ago as I watched some ducks drift down from above the treetops and ski onto the river's surface.

The ducks bobbed along for a short stretch, blooping underwater now and then and coming up with a mouthful of muck. When they rounded the end of a big log jutting out from the beach, they spooked. Their wings made a clapping sound as they flew off and out of sight. I watched them as they went. Then something caught my eye. Seems I wasn't the only one watching them go.

A shape below me in the cattails moved. It sort of turned, as if to get a look at the birds as they went. It was a blackish-brown shape and appeared at first to be a really big dog. When the birds were gone, its attention went back to the beach. I sat up a little taller to get a better look at the beastie. I liked dogs and they were fun to play with, and wet dogs were the best.

I couldn't see its face, but I could tell it was digging for something. It was half hidden in the cattails, all hunched over with its back to me. It was throwing sand and gravel off to the side as it dug. It wasn't until it began to shuffle up the beach a couple of feet that I could see it had lost its tail. Poor thing didn't even have a little one.

Its hair was long, wet, and matted with sand and muck. I moved a little closer, thinking maybe it wasn't a dog after all, maybe it was something else altogether. I had never seen a bear before, but Dad told us they could be anywhere and that they would eat whatever they could find. So it totally made sense to me when I saw

40

the first clam flip out onto the beach beside the big furry mass.

 I watched awhile as the clams began to pile up. I had never heard of dogs or bears digging for clams, but that was what it was doing for sure. So after some more thought, I decided it must be a clam bear. I watched him for a few more minutes, until he finished digging up his clams. When he was done, he did a little shuffle with his back legs and sort of rocked up onto his huge feet. I saw his toes; they were not dog feet. They were big flat feet, really big—yup, they were definitely clam bear type feet.

 The clam bear reached out and moved the clams into a small pile. He leaned over the pile and brought both arms together, scooping up the clams and holding them to his chest. Then he rocked back onto those giant feet and got taller and taller and taller. He stood up as tall as the cattails grew. He turned and walked up the beach, stepping over the big log jutting out from the shore. He never turned or looked back over his shoulder or made a sound except a little crunch of the gravel as he went. He just made his way along the beach through the cattails into the shadows of the spruce trees, then disappeared, clams and all. When he was gone, I ran inside and told everyone, "I just saw a clam bear digging clams!" Mom said that was nice and that I should wait outside for my cousins because they would be there soon, so I did.

The Barleys' Pig

After the funeral we went out to visit the Barley clan. They lived on a mountain that we called Barley Mountain, but really it was somewhere around the Big Creek Forest. The Barleys had a double-wide trailer and a pack of German shepherds that ran wild all over the place. From time to time we would get to stay over and play with all the Barley boys. There were Joey and Bo, who taught us how to milk their cow; they would even squirt milk straight from the udder into our mouths. We chased chickens with Chip, Brad, and Shane, and learned to shoot a .22 rifle with our cousin Tommy. There was always something fun to do with them up on their hill. There was no electricity in the trailer, so we didn't watch TV shows; instead we looked for snakes, played in the fields of tall grass, ran around with all the dogs, and were just as wild as kids could be.

In the fall, a big machine would come out to make hay bales from the tall grass that we played in. As the machine baled the hay and rumbled along, we all followed behind it, watching the dogs run and chase the mice, moles, and voles. The dogs ran after the mice, behind the dogs ran us kids, and behind us kids waddled a giant pink pig.

The pig was more of a pog, really, or a dig. Well, she was a six-hundred-pound pink pig that thought she was a dog. The pog ate with the dogs, slept with the dogs, and ran with the dogs—well, waddled. You could even call her like a dog and she would come running over and sit and everything. You could say, "Lie down," and she would. She could even roll over when she was small, but now that she was a fatty, she just sort of wobbled back and forth for the treats we gave her. When she was wobbling, and if you were quick, you could hop onto her back and she would take off like a shot down the hill. We would fly through the hay fields, with the pack of German shepherds all around us. When she got to the tall grass it was as if we were on a pink magic carpet skimming across the grass tops, sailing on a sea of gold, the dogs leaping like dolphins all around us as we went. Quail burst into the air like they were shot out of cannons or spouted out of imaginary whales. Eventually she would slow down and let us roll off into the tall grass. The dogs would lick us and play like they were puppies again. We would all lie in the warm dry grass, looking up at the sun, breathing hard and smiling. Yes, pigs and dogs can smile. I know, because I have seen them smiling in the tall grasses of summer.

Not too far from the trailer there was a well, but not the kind of well that has a rope and bucket. This was the kind of well that didn't even look like a well at all. This well looked like a deep pool in a crack in the ground that fed a little stream that ran off into the hay fields below. The water was cold and clean and was the best water you ever drank. When we got to the well, we knelt beside it, cupping our hands and dipped them into the cool water. We would all take turns drinking at the well, that is until the pig caught up with us. She did not take turns. She drank what she wanted, then flopped down in the shallow part of the pool to cool herself off. She would roll around in the mud for a while, making a big mess of the whole thing, then waddle on back to the trailer. We would have to wait a bit for the mud and pig sweat to clear away so we could drink some more.

I had been to the well many times after pig surfing our way through the fields of hay. The water was always cool and refreshing, and this time was no different. Once again, after the pog waddled off and the pool settled, I bent down to take another drink. That's when I saw something move in the pool. At first, I thought it was a little fish, and then I thought it might be a new kind of frog. I could just make out a little face looking back at me. It shook its head, and with a flip and a flash it disappeared in a cloud of mud deep inside the well.

I jumped up and yelled, "What was that?"

Cousin Bo told me that I probably saw a pond dragon. Jarod and I were so excited. Jarod pulled me down beside him and whispered in my ear, "Wishes!" We looked at each other, then back at the well. We were both thinking the same thing: maybe somehow pond dragons and wishing wells were connected.

After that day, we always peeked into the well to try and get another look at one. Sometimes we would see the swirls in the muddy part of the water, but pond dragons are tricky, and their magic was always just out of reach.

Breakfast for Kitty

When we stayed the night with the Barley boys, we were always stacked in like cordwood. There would be two to a bed and four to a floor. Luckily for us the dogs stayed outside with the pig, but inside there were some cats—big, scary cats. These were what Dad called "wherever cats." They could be mean, really mean, so we just had to let them be *wherever* they wanted to be. If they came up to you, they were not looking to be petted. They would take the food right off your plate and fight you for it if you tried to get it back. So you had to eat fast around the wherever cats.

At night as we slept, we could hear a billion crickets in the hay fields. They chirped so loud it seemed like an ocean's roar of crickets was all around us. There were big-eyed owls making their hooty hoots from up in the trees, and off in the distance floated the three notes of a fat little bird we called a whip-poor-will. The coyotes would call in long, thin howls from far out in the fields, and then yip sharp barks when they were just outside the window. When they got too close the dogs and the pig would thunder out from under the trailer and chase them back into the darkness to keep us safe while we slept. Most days we would sleep until early morning, when the elk bugling or the sound of the dogs stirring would wake us up. Most mornings, that is, only this morning it wasn't the elk or dogs or the crickets or even the coyotes that woke me up, it was Jimmy. He was kicking me and whispering something in the dark. I listened hard. . . .

"Get somebody!"

I sat up and rubbed my eyes and peered into the darkness. Jimmy was lying extra still on the floor next to Jarod. I could just see the outline of the biggest and meanest of the wherever cats sitting there on Jimmy's

45

chest. I moved over to where I could see a bit better. Jimmy's eyes were as big as Frisbees as he lay there frozen, staring at the trailer lion perched on his chest.

The king wherever cat had caught a fresh mouse and decided to use Jimmy as a breakfast table. There wasn't much I could do about it, so I woke up Bo. I pointed at the big cat eating the mouse on Jimmy's chest. Bo looked at Jimmy, reached over, picked up a boot, and threw it at the monster cat, which ran off into the living room with what was left of its breakfast. Jimmy peeled off his T-shirt and used it to wipe the blood from his chest. He looked at me as if to say *What now?* I shrugged my shoulders and whispered, "Maybe it's good luck or something." Then I pulled my blankets up around my face and went back to sleep.

Chapter 3

Cedar Street

With four kids and only two rooms, the house on Nineteenth Street had grown too small for all our adventures. When I was four, with tears in our eyes we packed up Mr. Bullfrog, said good-bye to our friends, hugged our cousins, and moved down the hill to our new house on Cedar Street. Our new house was a tall house with three stories and two chimneys on top. It sat about halfway down the block overlooking the Columbia River at the east end of town.

There was a park at the beginning of the block that all the kids got to play in. There was a small store just across US Route 30 that we would all walk to and buy penny candy back when the penny candy cost three pennies and not really one. A train ran along the water on the other side of the park and sounded its whistle two or three times a day as it passed. We could always hear the sea lions barking off in the distance, all day every day; they didn't pass, they were just there. The new house wasn't on a hill or by a bridge, and it didn't have any trolls. A few times Jimmy did walk me back up to our old bridge so I could throw apples off the side down to the troll, just because I was worried about him.

The Club

Brother Jimmy and cousins Steven and Johnny were older than Jarod, cousin David, and me. They could walk up to the store on their own. They got to help Dad carry the groceries in and could cross the street when they wanted to. They would ride their bikes and play down by the river whenever they felt like it. Sometimes they would even sneak a sip of Dad's beer if he wasn't looking. They even had their own club. You know, the kind of club that little kids weren't allowed into. Their club had no clubhouse, no secret handshake, no special benefits of any kind. It was simply "The Club," and you were in The Club or you were out. I was always out. You see, I was always out because I couldn't get in, and I couldn't get in because there were ongoing, ever-increasing, insurmountable initiations to get through. Initiations that I had yet to complete.

It seemed like the whole purpose of The Club was to figure out ways of keeping me out of The Club. The initiations started out simple enough; I had to jump from one bed to the other bed, a span of about six feet. When I made that, it got harder. Next, I had to jump from one bed to the other, then to the top of the dresser and back to the first bed. When I made that, I had to ride my tricycle down the basement stairs. . . . I didn't make that. The Club did receive some harsh sanctions from Mom for nearly crippling a potential member.

The next week I spent an hour shut in a toy box with six smelly garter snakes. The joke was on them, though, because I took a nap for most of that time. After the snakes, I had to catch ten large garden spiders and let them crawl up my arms. I named them funny names, so they weren't scary anymore. Then I had to catch five big black bumblebees that we called Queen Bees with my bare hands and put them in a jar without being stung. I had to walk up the banister with no hands and climb over the top railing. At one point a little brown bat had come in through the broken window in my sister Jenni's room. I had to dress up like a ghost and go into her room to try and catch it, but I couldn't.

Finally, irritated that I got through every challenge they could think of, Jimmy told me I had to jump out the second-story bedroom window onto an old garage roof that was so rotten it was more holes than roof.

I soon found myself perched on the windowsill peering down at the old rotting roof next to our house. The garage was long overgrown with blackberry vines, ivy, and stickers and prickles, and was half fallen in on the far side. As I squatted and wondered if I could make the leap, Jimmy said, "Come on, Peter Pan; think a happy thought!" With that he gave me some gentle encouragement, and by that, I mean he pushed me out the window! I sort of sprung off the sill like a frog. I flew out over the sidewalk and passed over the picket fence. For a moment, a very brief moment that is, I thought, "If I believe, if I really truly believe, then just maybe I . . ."

Then I bounced off the side of the rotting garage and disappeared six feet deep into the thorns, bushes, and vines. Jarod immediately ran off and squealed to Mom. Mom, Dad, and Jenni all came running to see if I was dead. I wasn't.

I was, however, hanging upside down by one ankle in the brambles. It took almost half an hour before Dad could cut a trail with his machete back through the brambles to rescue me. The entire time Mom kept telling me, "You're gonna be okay!" and saying that I shouldn't cry.

She told me how I was just in the briar patch, and I should think of Br'er Rabbit and how he loved the briar patch. By the time Dad finally got to me, I had already calmed down and managed to wiggle my way loose from the branches and slip down into the thicket below. I really was quite comfortable there. I had made a neat little hollow and padded it with ivy vines and leaves. The thorns on the blackberries were much higher up, so it wasn't pokey, and it wasn't too dark or scary in there either. When Dad eventually rescued me and carried me out past the other boys, I asked them, "Hey guys, did I do it? Am I in the club?"

Steven replied, "Yeah, man . . . but um, well, we got a new club now, though."

He was right. They did have a new club. They were all in the Getting a Spanking and Can't Play Outside for a Week Club. It was also called restriction!

That week I started my own club, one with just us little kids; we even had our own secret fort. It was just down Dad's fresh-cut trail and a bit past the old rotting garage, out where it wasn't too dark, too pokey, or too scary. It was safe and it was sound, nestled there in the heart of the briar patch.

The Man-Eating Couch

We had a Hide-A-Bed-style couch in our living room, it was awesome. We used it for all kinds of fun. We would unfold it and watch TV family style, all of us piled high and eating popcorn. We would drape blankets over the sides to make forts underneath, or sometimes it would be a cave for us to search for golden bats. It was a boat when we needed to be safe from imaginary crocodiles, or a giant rock to escape the living room lava flows that showed up from time to time.

Saturday mornings it would still be unfolded from family movie night, and we would all watch cartoons on it while Dad slept in, snoring up a storm there on the couch. We would try watching TV all day if we could. We would try, that is, but Mom would have no part of it. She would snap off the boob tube and click on the record player. We would all scatter at the sound of Helen Reddy and the vacuum cleaner. All of us except Dad, that is; he would play possum. We tried to get away, but it was no good. Mom would corner the rest of us like trapped rats, then we would all be put on a forced march up the stairs and down the hall to our rooms, where we were sentenced to clean them up before we could go out and play as God had intended little children to do. Our sentence included cleaning the hamster cage.

We had a lot of hamsters back then, thirteen or more at times. So first we had to do a hamster count. Then we would clean the cage and feed and water them. Or if the count was off, we would go looking for any missing hamsters. With four kids and thirteen-plus hamsters, it wasn't uncommon for us to find ourselves hamster-shy.

Mom needed to vacuum the popcorn off the living room floor because she was trying to get ready for

51

a dinner party, and Dad was supposed to be helping her. Only, Dad continued to play possum. He was a pro at possum-playing. Mom asked him three or four times to get up so she could clean under the couch, but in true possum form he just lay there. Later Dad would tell me that it was all about commitment to the craft.

During the hamster count, Jenni noticed one of our piggies had gone to market. She sent Jarod and me off to start looking for it in its last known location. Mom went off to grab the vacuum. When she did, Dad snuck off to the bathroom. Then Dad made a rookie mistake by flushing the toilet when he was all done. Realizing his error, Dad raced back to the couch before Mom could fold it up. Only, Mom saw him coming and tried to get there first. Dad made a flying leap for it, landing sideways on the couch with a big flop. They both started laughing at the same time; Mom was laughing hard and trying not to wet herself, as she sometimes did. She caught her breath and said, "Fine, I'll just close it up with you inside it!" She flipped up the first section of the couch as a joke, and quick as a flash and with a flip flop floop, Dad was gone! Mom got to laughing harder and harder and harder, saying, "Oh my God, oh my God, we need to call the fire department! Oh my God!" Jimmy saw the whole thing, and Jenni came running in when she heard Mom say "fire department." She asked Jimmy what happened.

He yelled, "Dad is in the couch!"

They stood there staring and wondering what to do.

Mom said, "Can you breathe? *Can you breathe?*"

They heard the couch say in a very calm, low voice, "Yes, I can breathe. Do not call the fire department!"

That was all Mom's poor bladder could take. At that very moment the furry little escape artist made his move from the kitchen into the living room with Jarod and me in hot pursuit. We skidded to a halt and stood in front of the television as we watched Mom wet herself on the carpet, the same carpet she was supposed to be vacuuming. Jimmy and Jenni stood crying on either side of her. Even the hamster stopped for a moment before darting under, and then up into, the couch to snuggle with Dad.

Jenni was blubbering, "The couch ate my daddy."

Then the couch spoke again. It firmly said, "Get. Me. Out. Of. Here!"

We all pulled and pulled, and finally the couch threw Dad and the hamster back up. Dad didn't say anything; he just walked upstairs and closed the door to his room and went back to sleep. Jarod scooped up a very confused hamster and put him back where he belonged. After that day the rest of us were all a little less trusting of what we now called The Man-Eating Couch.

The Witch

It had been two weeks since we watched *The Wizard of Oz* and one week since the couch had eaten Dad. For many nights, I kept having the same horrible dream about the Wicked Witch. I would be running and running as the Wicked Witch flew behind me on her broom followed by her flying monkeys. The harder I tried to run, the slower I would go. It got to be so bad I would stay up as late as I could, afraid to go to sleep and be chased by the witch.

I was having the nightmare again when I woke up crying. I stepped off the bed onto the floor and I felt the witch's hand grab my ankle and pull me under the bed. I could feel her sharpened claws scratching my leg as I went under. When I finally pulled myself free, I had the scratch marks on my leg and everything. I jumped onto Jimmy's bed scared to death and sobbing. Jimmy carried me all the way downstairs to Mom even though I was too big for him to be carrying. Still crying, I showed Mom and Dad the scratches on my leg and told them how the witch got me.

Dad and Jimmy went back up to my room with a stick to check under the bed for witches and flying monkeys. Jimmy stood at the door as Dad knelt down to peek under the bed. Dad set the stick down and reached way back under the bed with his whole arm. When they came back down, Dad looked at Mom and said, "Springs and staples." Mom said, "You see, honey? Just springs and staples." But I didn't see. Where did the witch go? Where was she now? Why did she scratch me with springs and staples? Was she coming back? That was it; I refused to go back to my room, and I was too afraid to go to sleep on my own. This went on for days and days, and it wasn't getting any better.

Big brothers can be a lot of things to you when you're growing up. They can be bullies or heroes, friends or enemies, and sometimes all of those at once. This time my big brother was just the kind of big brother I needed most. Two days after the witch scratched my leg, Jimmy took me into the living room and sat me down next to the heater vent that ran straight down to our furnace. He said to me, "You know where that goes, right?"

I said, "To the furnace?"

He said, "Yeah, so you know anything that goes in there is burned up forever and ever, right?" I nodded.

He opened a small cigar box that had some wooden stick matches, a rubber band, and some tinfoil inside. He showed me a bit of black cloth and some yellow straw clipped from a broom. He held it up to show me. He said, "You see that?"

I asked, "What is it?"

He said, "I got her! That's the witch's broom, and this is her cape."

He broke the straw into little bits and wrapped it in the tiny piece of cloth. Then he took the matches and broke the heads off. He said, "You see that, those are fire, and a witch is trapped by fire."

He put the match heads in the cloth and wrapped it all up in the tinfoil, then folded the foil as many times as he could. Finally, he wrapped the rubber bands around the entire bundle. Jimmy pounded it with his fist. He looked at me and I pounded it too. He said, "Get mad!"

So I did. I punched and punched it real hard. He used the edge of a dime to turn the four corner screws on the heater vent. We both pulled the vent open.

Jimmy asked, "Ready?" I nodded, and then we threw her in and slammed the vent shut. We heard the bundle rattle down into the furnace.

Jimmy said, "She's dead. The witch is dead! Now she can't get you anymore."

We screwed the vent back tight, went into the living room, and sat on the couch. Jimmy put his arm around me, and he stayed with me until I fell asleep. I never had that dream again.

Pack Donkeys

When I wasn't with Jarod in the briar patch, playing Peter Pan, or burning witches, I was off exploring for secret treasure in the deep dark jungles of Astoria. The lost obsidian mines of Cedar Street were located just up the hill behind our house. Jenni and Jimmy had discovered the mines while out surveying our kingdom sometime the week before. Jarod and I overheard them plotting their treasure hunt and threatened to tell Mom if we didn't get to go along and bring home some of the spoils for ourselves.

After a short discussion, Jimmy and Jenni told us that they supposed they would need a couple of pack mules for the quest. So Jenni said we could be them. We were instructed that pack mules can't talk, so they can't tell anyone what they see or where they go or anything like that. Jarod and I talked it over, and we agreed to do it, but we had one condition. We needed to know what pack mules were.

Jenni sighed, rolled her eyes, and said, "They're donkeys, jackasses!"

After another short discussion, Jarod and I agreed that we would be donkeys, but we would not be jackasses. Jenni and Jimmy brought us down to the garage, where they outfitted us with their old school backpacks. For donkey ears we each tucked two socks into our headbands, which we made out of old bandannas. For tails, we tied a bit of rope onto our belts. Then we got loaded down with hammers and screwdrivers and a small thing called a pry bar. We figured it was for prying bars, if we found treasure that was locked behind bars. Then we each got two carrots from the garden, cause that's what they paid pack donkeys at the time for hauling quest treasure back home.

We set out on our quest just after nap time. We worked our way from the garden over to the rabbit hutch where we were supposed to be cleaning out the rabbit poo and putting it in the garden.

Jimmy whispered, "The coast is clear!"

Then the four of us slipped out of sight behind the rabbit hutch, up a small hill into the shadows of the forbidden pine forest that ran between the highway and the back of our house. The highway was the reason the pine forest was a forbidden forest instead of just a regular one. We knew we were not allowed to go in there, but the thought of mining magic gems or chunks of gold was just too great to resist.

Jenni insisted we would have to risk it. Jimmy agreed, and because Jarod and I were donkeys and couldn't talk, we just stomped our hooves to say yes. Then off into the forbidden forest we went. I was still wondering why we cared if the coast was clear, if we weren't going down to the beach, but I didn't know how to stomp that question out with my donkey hooves, so I just kept it to myself.

The mine was about halfway up the hill and almost a block west of our house along the ridge through the brush, stickers, ivy, and such. Jimmy and Jenni had hidden the treasure under some sword ferns, moss, and rocks after they found it the first time, so we had to dig it all up again before we could donkey-pack it back home. As Jimmy and Jenni started to uncover the treasure, it began to sparkle and shine like the jewels in the Snow White movie. When the sun hit the stones, they came to life. The light made them move like they had a fire inside. They were black, but not just the normal kind of black. It was some new kind of black, like a hole-in-the-ground black or a cave black or a wet black or maybe just a very, very old black. Jenni said this was black lava out of a real volcano from the Earth's heart. I asked where the volcano was now and why the rocks weren't hot and would they get hot later and will the volcano come back. Jenni gave me a big-sister look, and then I was reminded that donkeys can't talk and I was told to eat a carrot.

The pieces were large, too large for donkeys to carry, so Jimmy began to break chunks off with a hammer. As the rocks shattered, they broke like ice into all kinds of shapes and sizes. Now we could see even more colors than just black like before. Some pieces were smoky, and others went from gray to clear, then back to black. Some had streaks of red and brown like aggie marbles. Jenni and Jimmy worked away like little dwarfs, mining jewel after jewel, naming them as they went.

"This one is a Dragon's Eye, this one is a Dark Fairy's Heart, this one is the Healing Stone, this one is the Monster Stone because it keeps away all monsters."

Having had to deal with the witch, I put the Monster Stone in my pocket just in case. Jarod and I filled each other's packs with the gems and magic stones until we were in danger of rolling down the hill like turtles on our backs instead of donkeys. We packed up for the journey home and began to donkey along the hillside back the way we came, while Jenni and Jimmy covered up the rest of the treasure with ferns, moss, and ivy.

After a few trips to and from the mine, we each had enough treasure to fill a small treasure chest. Not the large ones that are on pirate ships; ours were the same size as a shoe box. Our treasure chests were made by Buster Brown Shoe Company.

We were mesmerized by the glimmering treasure. We took the stones out in the sun and watched them sparkle. We lined them up to make maps and secret symbols that could make fairies appear, make goblins disappear, and perhaps even summon the elusive pond dragons themselves. We were rich, rich I tell ya, magic rich and jewel rich. We were all dancing around and celebrating being rich when Jimmy ran his hands through the treasure, all greedy-pirate style. That's when we learned the treasure had one more magic trick to show us. Some of our favorite jewels were ones that the light could shine all the way through, and that meant they were razor thin and apparently razor sharp too. Suddenly Jimmy was bleeding everywhere, and he was bleeding a lot. He ran to get a bandage, but before he was even on the porch, the donkeys began to squeal like little piggies right to Mom.

Sadly, that was the end of our mining days. The overlords seized the treasure before any of the rest of us accidentally made another blood sacrifice and summoned the creatures from the dark wood to run amuck in the yard. Jenni and Jimmy were sentenced to clean the dungeons, for entering the forbidden forest and for using their little brothers as pack animals. The overlords saw to it that the donkeys were set free in the yard, where they got to eat as many carrots as they wanted to.

After a real bad infection Jimmy's finger healed up, but not for two whole weeks. This was because the overlords took away all the magic stones that could have fixed it in a day. Even the most powerful stone of all, the sacred Monster Stone, capable of warding off all monsters, was lost forever. Though some say that they have heard whispers from deep, deep, inside the briar patch that quite possibly the Monster Stone could have quietly slipped through a small tear in the stitches of a little boy's teddy bear and that maybe, just maybe, it's still there, inside his old worn-out bear, on a shelf, in his room, to this very day.

All the Candy in the World

There was a strange hint of chocolate in the air as we entered our bedroom. This was the third time in a month I had come into our room and thought I smelled the sweet scent of a candy bar. It was a bit like going over to Grandma's house the day after she baked cookies but by the time we got there the cookies were all gone because they were for a bake sale or something like that. All that was left was the ghost of a memory of a cookie.

I asked Jimmy, "Hey, do you smell something?"

He said, "Yeah, I smell candy!"

I knew it! We looked everywhere; we took the whole room apart. We looked inside piggy banks, under the beds, between the mattresses and the wall, but there was nothing, not even a candy-bar wrapper.

Over the next few weeks, I kept up the search. I looked from the attic to the basement, from the car to the pantry, but nothing! The closest thing I came across was some little brown Tic Tac–looking things, but I think those came from the hamsters.

Maybe it was just that we had seen *Charlie and the Chocolate Factory* a few weeks back at the Liberty Theater, so candy was on my brain. You see, for us, Halloween was our only real source of candy, and it was so far in the past and at the same time so far in the future that it could just as well have been held on the planet Mars. Besides, Halloween candy could only be rationed out to last a week, two tops. My supply of Halloween candy had evaporated by day five. Sure, summertime had its own delights, including marshmallows, watermelon, and a glorious never-ending selection from the Popsicle man. Only we were still money poor, so those delights were few and far between.

Dad would bring us home fresh Brownsmead peas from the next town over; giant paper sacks of peas still in the shell that opened with a crisp pop and tasted as sweet as any bit of candy, to be sure. We had fresh baby carrots from the garden and blueberries that stained our fingers black. Oh, and jars upon jars of Aunt Terri's peaches, pears, and the best of all, cherries—all purple, plump, and soft, dripping in the sweetest sweet syrup ever!

Those jars of pure happiness came from Hood River, Oregon. Hood River is where Aunties Jerry and Teri, Mom, and Grandma Bea would all crowd into Aunt Teri's kitchen, cutting, snipping, and canning all the treats we would have for the whole rest of the year. Hood River was a hot place, not like Astoria at all. I got to spend part of every summer there from the time I was just one and a half years old.

The first time my Auntie Teri took me to stay with her was when I was getting usurped. "Usurped" is a word from a Shakespeare play; it means that when you get back home from Aunt Teri's there is going to be a new baby, who will take away half of your stuff and all of your mom's attention . . . for the rest of your life.

Anyways, while I was being tossed aside like yesterday's toddler, Aunt Teri was doing her best to make me feel like I was her favorite, and that was because I was, in fact, her favorite. That's right; it's in a book now, so it has to be true. I win, cousins . . . check and mate! To be fair, Auntie had a way that made each of us nieces and nephews feel like we were her favorite, so the confusion for the rest of you is understandable.

When I wasn't basking in the joy of being Auntie's favorite or wallowing in the sadness of being usurped by my soon-to-be little brother Jarod, summer after summer I was off adventuring with cousins Matty and Mikey. We ate fruit in abandoned orchards until our bellies were about to explode, played with giant orchard beetles as big as your hand, and walked down to the little store to get treats.

The summer when I was three, Mom gave me five whole dollars to take to Auntie's. I had never had five whole dollars before, so the possibilities seemed endless. Okay, let's be honest, there really was only one possibility, and it was candy! Matt and Mike walked me down the block past the abandoned orchard and down a long hill. There we stopped to gather some apples that had fallen to the ground. We let the apples roll down the hill out in front of us as we walked. We watched them pick up speed until they bounced off the road, exploded against a tree, or disappeared into the tall grass that covered the hill. We started to chase the apples as they went faster and faster, until finally the three of us came stumbling into the little store in a cloud of dust and half out of breath. The little store was a small-town kind of one-room five-and-dime thing with all the stuff a kid could ever want. It had weird food in jars on the sales counter—pickled eggs, pickled pig's feet, and pickled pickles. We didn't eat the stuff in jars because we only came for the candy.

The candy section was five rows high and had every kind of candy I had ever seen. Marathon bars and Chic-O-Sticks, Smarties, Necco Wafers, wax lips, Fun Dips, Ring Pops, Bottle Caps, and Pop Rocks that exploded in your mouth. I picked out as much candy as I could hold in my little hands, went up to the counter, and gave the man my five dollars. He smiled and gave me back my change. Matty explained that I could pick out more candy if I wanted to, because I had only spent two dollars. So I did. I went back and forth from the counter to the candy rack as Matty taught me how much each piece of candy cost, how to add it up, and how to pay the man behind the counter. This would be the only math lesson in my whole life that ever really mattered. We made our way back up to the house with a sack of candy as big as my head. I thought it would last me forever. Only it didn't. I returned home a little older, a little wiser, and a lot chubbier.

But that was long, long ago, in the times of plenty. Now we were back home in the middle of the most severe candy drought I had ever known. Like I said, I had been looking for the source of the ghost candy smell for weeks. Then came Saturday morning. I lay there slowly drifting back from dreamland, my eyes just starting to creep open. That's when I noticed some movement across the room. It was a sneaky type of movement. It was Jarod, and he was sneaking! He was doing something weird over at the bookshelf next to his bed. This bookshelf was off-limits to everybody. It had some books, yeah, but mostly it was for Jarod's mint-condition, still-in-the-box toys. Toys Jarod himself had declared to be off-limits, so nobody got to play with them, not even Jarod! If we touched them or moved them or got them out of order, Jarod would completely flip out, so we never went near them.

As I lay there Jarod was doing something with one of the bigger boxes. My God! He was opening it! He reached his hand inside the box and pulled out a candy bar with a picture of a little bat on it. He carefully closed the box and placed it back exactly where it had been. Jarod quietly slipped the candy bar into his pajama pocket. I couldn't believe it! I don't know what was crazier, that he still had candy from Halloween, or that he had actually sacrificed his mint-condition Chutes and Ladders game to make a hiding place for the candy. But either way, clearly we were dealing with a sick mind here.

I sat up in bed and yelled, "I knew it! I knew it, I knew it, I knew it!" Jarod jumped like he had been hit by a bolt of lightning. He landed and froze, like maybe that would save him, only it didn't! The Kit Kat was out of the bag, baby.

I said, "Hey, where did you get all that candy?" even though I knew.

Jarod said, "It's mine, and you can't have any! You didn't save any of your candy, and now you don't have none. You just ate all your candy at once."

All of that was true, so very true; I did eat all of my candy, and some of Jimmy's candy. I even snuck some of the candy out of Jenni's dresser drawer when she wasn't looking. I also ate all the chocolate chips out of the pantry, then blamed it on the hamsters. I had a problem, and I knew it. So I did the only thing I could do. I made a deal with the devil. Yup, I made a super swear that if Jarod shared his candy with me now, then when we grew up I would give him "all the candy in the world!"

It took a good half hour of finagling before he actually agreed to my master plan. I made the super swear, and Jarod reluctantly gave me a Marathon Bar. Now, in my defense, I had a candy addiction, and I thought he would forget about the swear in a few days like most little kids do. Boy, was I wrong. I made that super swear when I was four and a half years old and Jarod was almost four. It has been over forty years now, and he is still trying to collect.

To this day, anytime we are at the store, Jarod picks out a piece of candy and, without a word, he just puts it on the store counter expecting me to pay for it. And I do.

Gone with the Schwinn

I learned to ride a bike at age four and a half. My iron
pony was a little green Schwinn. It got hand-me-downed
quite a few times before it eventually got to me. Auntie
Jerry, uncle Dick, and the Bartoldus cousins brought it
over to our house, where we had good sidewalks for
learning how to ride a bike. That meant we had good
soft grass on either side of the sidewalk, making for a
nice crash pad should you need one. All my cousins
tried and tried to teach me to ride that morning, but I
wasn't having much luck. After three spills and a near
concussion, I had all but decided to give the bike back.
After a while the other kids found less futile things to go
do, and peeled off one by one. But not cousin Debbie;
she just wouldn't give up on me. After all those earlier
crashes, it took a lot of convincing to get me to try
again. I'm not sure, maybe it was the concussion, but I
finally agreed that if she super-duper-duper promised
not to let go of the seat, I would try one last time.

We started out at the top of the driveway, next to
the garage. Debbie braced the back wheel between her
knees and helped me up onto the purple and white seat
with the big letter *S* on it. The seat had been dropped
down to as low as it would go, but still only one of my
feet touched the ground at a time. I placed my feet
firmly on the pedals and gripped the handlebars so hard
that my little knuckles turned all white. This time
Debbie told me not to pedal around and around, but
instead to push my feet down one at a time.

She called out, "One, two, three, go!"

I pushed one pedal down as hard as I could, then
the other. Pointing my handlebars off in the direction of
the sidewalk, I pushed and pushed. Left foot, right foot,
left foot, right foot. It was working! I yelled, "Don't let
go!"

Debbie said, "I won't." And she didn't. She ran with me as we went by house after house, stretching two blocks into three. She said, "You're doing it. You're doing it all by yourself!"

Still with just one finger left on the seat, she said, "Are you ready for me to let go?"

I yelled, "Okay!" I heard her footsteps slow, then stop running, and I knew I was doing it for real. As I sailed along with the wind in my face, I thought of how free I felt. I thought about how I did it, I really did it. Then, suddenly, I thought about Shel Silverstein.

You see, there is a book by Shel Silverstein called *Where the Sidewalk Ends*. I always think of Debbie when I hear his name or one of his poems. She taught me so much that day. How not to give up and how to believe in myself and how to trust in someone you love. I have kept those lessons for the rest of my life. I just wish she had taught me one more thing that day. I wish she had taught me how to use the brakes.

She said it calmly at first: "Okay, stop."

"OKAY STOP!"

Only I couldn't make it stop!

She yelled, "Pedal backwards!"

But I just couldn't make my legs do what they were supposed to do. Every time I tried to make my feet pedal backwards, I just seemed to push harder forwards. That made me go faster and faster still. Debbie ran faster and faster as well. That's when I saw it. I was headed right for the Shel Silverstein!

Where the sidewalk ended in our neighborhood was at a gully where all the people in the neighborhood dumped lawn clippings, branches, rotting fruit, and all sorts of worse things that smelled, oozed, and attracted flies. It was there that raccoons and possums and skunks were seen coming and going each day at dusk and dawn. It was there that I landed crisscrossed and crumpled in a heap. It was also there that Debbie scooped me up, brushed me off, and made sure I was okay. We walked back home together, pushing the bike. I asked her, "Next, could you teach me how to stop?" She thought that would be a good idea too.

Wink Chicken

In addition to our thirteen-plus hamsters, we had some rabbits. We had a lot of rabbits! We had brown rabbits and white rabbits and rabbits that had three and four colors. They all lived in a hutch in the backyard that Dad and Uncle John fixed up for them. Sometimes we had as many as twenty-four rabbits at a time in the hutch. Us kids had to fill the water bottles and feed the rabbits their food pellets and kitchen leftovers Mom put in the rabbit pail.

Every few weeks we would have to shovel the rabbit poo onto the garden and mix it into the soil so we could grow vegetables—the same vegetables that we took to the kitchen, that Mom put in the pail that we took to the rabbits, that the rabbits made into poo that we put in the garden. We thought that was real funny.

A lot of time and effort went into fixing up that hutch, but Dad and Uncle must have done a really bad job, because rabbits were always getting out. Every time they escaped, we would have to go and look everywhere for them, but unlike the hamsters, none of them ever turned up.

Even though all the poop work was smelly, we were proud to have rabbits and even prouder to have a garden. We planted corn and peas and carrots. We pulled weeds and picked slugs out, we flicked aphids off, and we hoed. We liked hoeing so much that even when there were no rows left to hoe, sometimes we would go over to Mom's flower bed and hoe the snot out of her petunias just for fun.

Not only did we have to do all the work to make the garden grow, Dad told us we had to protect it from the "raiders." Dad said, "If we're not careful, raiders will come and steal all of our vegetables." To us, raiders meant only one thing: *Pirates!* Immediately, we pictured

70

greedy pirates filling their treasure chests with our carrots, beets, and peas. We guessed that was why Mom was always telling us to eat our vegetables, 'cause they were valuable. Jarod and I liked that idea so much that we took to cutting our carrots very thin, so they looked like piles of gold coins on our plates. We would bite them on one side of our mouths, like gold miners, to make sure they were real carrots.

To protect our treasure, Mom helped us make a scarecrow to put out in the garden. This was the first time we had heard of a thing called a scarecrow. We decided it had something to do with the crow's nest on the pirate ship, a ship that in our imaginations was sitting at the mouth of the Columbia River, just out of sight, waiting to come steal our peas. Jarod and I had quite the talk about why pirates had a crow's nest but no crows and did have parrots but no parrot's nests. Jarod said that being pirates, maybe they stole the crow's nest and gave it to the parrots. But that still didn't explain why we were building a scarecrow and not a scare-parrot. When we started making the scarecrow, we thought it was going to be something fierce, a creature that would send pirates running in fear and make parrots fly away. Only, when we were finished, our scarecrow did not look like it was going to be able to battle pirates, or rabbits for that matter. It looked more like our chubby little old neighbor lady Mrs. Beatty out in her garden with her floppy hat, holding a broom. We wondered if pirates were afraid of brooms. Jarod said maybe, like us, they didn't like cleaning their rooms. Just in case they got past the little old Mrs. Beatty scarecrow, we took to keeping sharpened sticks under our beds, and we lay awake at night talking about what we would do when the pirates came to raid us.

The old Mrs. Beatty scarecrow must have fallen asleep on the job, because we woke one morning to find we had been attacked during the night. We looked out the bedroom window and saw giant footprints going across the yard, leading to the garden. We ran down the stairs with our sticks, screaming like maniacs.

"Raiders! Raiders!"

We shook Dad awake and told him the raiders had attacked our garden. He rolled out of bed and stumbled out into the yard to survey the damage. He sort of gritted his teeth and said, with a snort, "We have a mole!"

We had never heard of a mole, but from the size of the footprints, it must have been a giant one. We asked Dad why the scarecrow didn't work. Dad told us, "Moles aren't afraid of scarecrows."

He said that moles had fur and big claws and were almost blind. So it made sense to us that the mole didn't see the scarecrow. While we all ate breakfast, Dad took the hose out and filled the footprints with water. Mom said the water would stop the mole, so we just figured Dad was making quicksand. Then it would get stuck when it came back. We kept our sharpened sticks at the ready, in case we trapped one.

A few tense days later, Dad told us we were all safe because the neighbor's beagle had gotten the mole. We were extra nice to that little dog after we found out it could take on a monster like a mole.

Dad invited the neighbors over for a barbecue where Mom made potato salad and dad made Wink Chicken. Whenever we had Wink Chicken, Dad would say, "We are having chicken tonight," and then he would wink at Mom. Dad would go out back, and we all got to go watch TV really loud. The day of the picnic Dad fired up the barbecue and started cooking the Wink Chicken. Mom and us kids set out all the paper plates, sporks, and napkins. The neighbors brought pie and a great big watermelon that was ice cold. We sat down to eat, said thanks to God and the mole-getting dog, and then each of us four kids got a drumstick. It was a great celebration. We were saved from the mole and harvested the garden, all before the pirates came to raid us!

On a sad note, another rabbit had run away that day. We looked and looked for him, but we never did find the little guy.

Chapter 4

The Great Divide

In 1975, Mom and Dad got a divorce. Aunt Jerry said it was because Dad was a tramp.

Who Is Going to Cook for Us Now?

We had just left the family dog with our grandparents and begun our drive out of town and away from everything and everyone we had ever known. All four of us kids were crying as Mom drove us off toward our future in a faraway unknown place called Seattle. As we drove, she tried her best to comfort us by saying the sort of things moms say as you drive off during a divorce. But we just kept crying. When she told us that Dad still loved us, and that we would see him at Christmas, we kept crying. Mom was quiet for a bit, and then she looked at Jenni, who was sitting in the passenger seat, and said, "It's okay to miss your dad."

Jenni sobbed, "I know."

Mom said, "You'll get to come stay for the summer."

We all cried a bit louder.

Mom said, "You'll still get to see your grandparents when you come to visit."

Jenni sobbed, "I know."

Mom asked, "Is it because of the dog? Is that why you're crying?"

Jenni said, "No, that's not why we are crying."

Mom said, "Oh. Well, do you want to tell me what it is?"

Jenni just shook her head no and kept crying. We all kept crying. Now Mom was starting to cry too. She asked if it was because we were leaving all our friends. Jenni shook her head no again. Mom kept asking questions. She asked all kinds of questions. Most of the questions were about things we hadn't thought of yet, and it just made everything worse.

Finally Mom said, "Please just tell me why you're crying."

Jenni, still sobbing, looked back at us, and then at her feet. She mumbled something.

Mom said, "What, honey?"

Then Jenni just blurted it out. "Who is going to cook for us now?"

Mom said, "What, um. Don't worry, kids, I'll cook for you now!" Then we all cried even louder.

You see, Dad cooked. Mom made food, too, but Dad was our cook. He had worked at our uncle's restaurant, so he knew how to cook restaurant style. He made Polynesian drumsticks, beef Stroganoff, breaded elk steak and eggs, spiced crawdads, deer jerky, pan-fried trout, sautéed wild mushrooms, Wink Chicken, Chex mix, and navy-bean soup. Did I mention Chex mix? Sure, we were gonna miss our dad, but for God's sake, we were really going to miss our cook!

At five years of age, I was nowhere near prepared for the culinary drought we were about to face. There were some bleak years ahead, to be sure. It wasn't only because Mom didn't have the restaurant expertise that Dad did, but somehow by the time we got from Astoria to Seattle, Jarod had caught the celiac disease.

This was the kind of disease where you needed to take all the flavor out of all the food you ate. Then you had to remove any sort of moisture it had if it was meat. On top of that it was super important that any of the animals you were going to be eating had been living and eating far better food than you were. That was called free-range. Free-range is what we were before we got sentenced to go to school. Free-range organic turkey was on the menu more than it should have been. It tasted like wood, but not the good wood we used for smoking fish. It tasted like park-bench wood. When we finished the park-bench turkey, we had to eat a thing called tofu. At the time, no one had ever heard of tofu, and we didn't know how to cook with it, so *bluglllh*. That's the sound you make when you barf because somebody

76

made you eat tofu. As a kid, having to eat tofu made you feel a little bit like God didn't like you anymore. Jarod did get to eat these little rice crackers that tasted great, only the rest of us kids weren't allowed to have any, so we stole them when he wasn't looking.

It was a Sunday morning and we were having a bowl of cereal, sort of. It was puffed corn cereal-ish stuff from a big wooden barrel in the health-food section. Eating it was like eating a bowl of Styrofoam chunks. It even squeaked when we chewed on it. I was staring at my bowl of Styrofoam, poking at it with my spoon and watching it bloop back up, when I noticed Jimmy was standing at the end of the hallway. He motioned for me to come over to him, so I set my bowl of Styrofoam down and went over to see what Jimmy wanted. He held his finger to his lips for me to be quiet, and then motioned for me to follow him. Knowing my Styrofoam would still be floating when I got back, I followed him.

I followed Jimmy through the laundry room and we slipped out the back into the yard. We jumped the fence and made our way two blocks over to a little blue house behind the big brown church. There was a kid in my class named Marcus that lived there. His dad was the preacher at the church, so they got to live in the little house out back. Sometimes on a Sunday, we would go over and play with Marcus's electric car track while we waited for his parents to finish cleaning up at the church.

Jimmy and I went to the back door and knocked, but nobody answered the door. We waited a bit. After a minute or so, Jimmy shrugged and tried the door handle. It was open, so we went inside. We sat at the kitchen table waiting some more to see if Marcus would show up to play. After a while, Jimmy went over and opened up the cupboards. He took down a box of Lucky Charms. Then he got some bowls out, and the milk, and we ate two bowls of cereal each. After we finished, Jimmy cleaned the bowls and put away the cereal. We waited a few more minutes, and then Jimmy said, "Well, I guess he ain't coming. Let's go." As we walked back home, I asked Jimmy about taking the cereal. Jimmy told me it was okay as long as we did our dishes and put everything away, since they always gave us some snacks when we came over anyways. That made sense to me, and since I had never had Lucky Charms or Trix or Cocoa Puffs before, I didn't think too hard about it.

After that day, we spent a lot of Sundays waiting for Marcus to come home, but he never did. I guess maybe it was because around that same time Marcus started getting into a lot of trouble. His dad kept having Marcus do extra chores at the church almost every Sunday. His dad said Marcus was in trouble for not telling the truth, and for something that was called gluttony. We didn't know what gluttony was, but poor Marcus must have had a bad case of it.

Art?

We still visited Astoria for summer vacation and Christmas break, funerals, graduations, new babies (both accidental and planned), and sometimes just because. Usually we stayed where Dad was staying, and then eventually we drifted off to visit one relative or another around town. Those summers we were still free-range children. After being locked up in school for a whole year, I can tell you this much: free-range is better for sure.

My first day of school did not go well. I had spent virtually every moment of my life with Jarod by my side. Now for the first time I was on my own. Mom walked me to my classroom and stood at the door as I found my seat.

The teacher said, "Now, class, please introduce yourself to the person sitting behind you." So I did. That's how I met David Clark. He would be my only friend at school for the entire first year. He would also be my dear friend for the rest of my life.

I was a quiet, rather uneasy child at school, and I spent a lot of time off by myself. Mostly, I sat up on the monkey bars or on the swing set and watched the other children play. When David wasn't up on the monkey bars with me, he ran around with the other kids playing and getting into a bit of trouble. For me, each recess was the same. I would climb to my spot at the top of the monkey bars, where I would sit and watch the mayhem.

I didn't play or make friends; mostly I just waited. I waited for lunch. I waited for recess to end. I waited for the day to be over. I waited to go home, and most of all I waited for Jarod. I waited for Jarod to be old enough to come to my school, so I would have someone to play with. While I was waiting, Jarod was off at preschool, where he was having just as much trouble fitting in as I was. Only it didn't seem to bother Jarod as much, because he had always been the kind of kid who marched to the beat of his own drummer. Well, he was really more like the kind of kid who would browbeat the drummer until the drummer played exactly the song Jarod wanted to march to.

For the fall open house, Jarod's class put on an art show that we all got to go and see. The theme was friends and family. Each child was asked to pick a friend or family member and make a drawing of them for the show. It was to be a full life-size drawing. The teacher had each kid lie down on a big piece of butcher paper so she could trace their outline. They cut out the shape of their outline, then colored it in to represent their friend or family person. Each child taped their artwork up on the walls of the hallways that you passed through as you came into the preschool. Jarod wasn't really the kind of kid that spent a lot of time with pen or brush, so we were all excited to see his first masterpiece.

Jarod had chosen Dad to be his friend or family person. This was probably because we didn't see Dad as much as we used to and because Dad and Jarod spent most their time together when Jarod wasn't off adventuring with me.

There were some fine works of art at the show. You know, for four-year-olds, it was mostly dads and moms with the occasional grandma or grandpa. Along with a few best friends and one or two kiss-up drawings of the teacher. We munched our cookies and perused the gallery. We meandered from hallway to hallway, and everything seemed to be going very well. Then we noticed that a few of the kids passing by us were snickering and pointing Jarod out to their parents. Jarod didn't seem to notice, he just hurried us along toward the hallway where his drawing was displayed. We couldn't help noticing the crowd gathered outside Jarod's classroom. There were a lot of parents doing their best to explain to the children about art, about what was art and what wasn't art. We reached the place where Jarod's masterpiece hung beside a visibly shaken preschool teacher who was currently under assault for her decision to let Jarod participate in the art show. The teacher looked at my mother, who then looked at the masterpiece, then at her proud son. She simply said, "I like the way you drew his eyes."

Jarod's portrait of our father was accurate, to be sure. He drew Dad's long brown-black hair, his beard and mustache too. But unlike the other dad drawings, which showed them with ties and briefcases or lunch pails and hard hats, our dad was wearing the first suit he had ever owned: his birthday suit. Jarod had taken a brown crayon and drawn in Dad's armpit hair and some wispy chest hair to match. He had also gone to some great length, no pun intended, to cut out the shape of Dad's little man and his little man's friends. Whereupon he drew another little beard, so they wouldn't get cold.

Jenni shrieked, "Oh my God!" and left the room immediately.

Jimmy crossed his arms and just said, "Nice." Then he went off to get more cookies. I stood with Jarod, amazed at how nothing anybody said seemed to bother him. He was proud of his dad, and proud that his drawing was accurate, and not one person could take that away from him. I didn't have that kind of confidence around the other children at my school, but I was proud of him too.

A Dragon Prayer

It's true that Jarod and I were obsessed with those magical little polliwogs. So if we weren't out trying to catch 'em, we were plotting how we could get our next polliwog fix. We would lie awake at night in our bunk beds talking all things polliwog. We would talk about the best places we had ever caught polliwogs, who caught the most or the best kinds. Mostly we talked about the places we hadn't been polliwoging yet. I was still listing off my polliwog greatest hits when Jarod veered off subject. "Do you think he's real?"

I said, "Who's real?"

"The king."

I stuck my head over the edge of the bunk bed, my hair puffed out like a dandelion. "What king?"

Jarod said, "The pond dragon king."

I said, "Oh, the pond dragon king."

Jarod sat up. "Yeah, do you think he's real?"

I replied, "Grandpa Roy says he's real."

"Do you think he can grant wishes too?"

I thought for a minute. "If he can grow back arms, and transform to be young again, then I'm sure he can grant wishes. If they're good wishes."

Jarod looked worried. "I hope so, but we've never seen him, and I'm starting to think maybe he isn't real."

The blood was starting to run to my head. I said, "There are lots of things we've never seen that are real. We've never seen a polar bear, but they're real. We just have to keep being respectful. We'll see him."

Jarod said, "I think we need a magic chant."

"What do you mean?"

"Like a prayer or something we can say when we go to the pond, so they'll know we're real respectful, like Grandpa said"

I told him, "Good idea. We can make one tomorrow. Now go to sleep, I'm tired." We said good night and drifted off to sleep.

We spent most of the next day playing with Legos and working on our pond dragon prayer. After a few tries, it went like this:

> Hello, pond dragons,
> We fold our hands and bow our heads
> 'Cause we believe what Grandpa said,
> That you are true and for real.
> So with respect we will kneel
> And ask that we could get to see
> The dragon battles of pond and sea.

I don't think pond dragons are in the sea, but Jenni helped us make all the words rhyme together, and she said the pond dragons wouldn't mind any.

The next day, Jarod and I were itching to get out and put our new prayer to the test. We ran down to a pond we had seen about a half mile from our house. It looked like the kind of pond that pond dragons would do battle in. It was located on an old county road, in a large field that had the most beautiful white horse in it. The horse was so beautiful I used to think it was really a unicorn that stayed there to protect the pond dragons' pond. Only, unicorns don't show their magic to people anymore, so they just look like a beautiful horse instead.

The field was surrounded by a fence, but it wasn't the kind of fence that had a gate to go through or you could climb on. This fence was made of wire that you could sort of go under if you found a low spot. We walked along the road until we found a place to duck across. We picked some long green grass that the horse couldn't reach and gave it to her so she would like us. We went over to the pond, and with as much respect as we could muster, we said our pond dragon prayer. We said it twice just to be sure. We sat and looked into the pond real hard. The horse ate the grass we gave her, then came over and bugged us for some more. I went back over to the fence and got some more grass, then came back and sat down by Jarod to keep being respectful.

The horse came over and stood next to us. At first we thought it was being respectful too. For a second I thought it might talk. I stood up to listen to what it was about to say. The horse came closer, looked me in the eye, and with its big nose pushed me into the pond. I fell back and landed in about a foot of water and was soaking wet. I crawled back on shore spitting pond water. Jarod looked at me, then at the now muddy pond, and said, "That's not very respectful." He meant me, not the horse.

I replied, "Yeah, let's go home." We went back to the low spot to slip under the wire, only this time I grabbed the wire to move it out of the way.

We had heard of an electric fence, but this was the first time we had ever seen one, or in my case felt one. My brain went *Zaazaazaazaazaazaazaa!* My eyes got super big, and I think I could smell hair burning. I was frozen to the fence and couldn't let go. All my muscles were tight. I couldn't even talk. The fence just kept zapping and zapping and zapping me. Jarod could see I was in real trouble. He ran over and tried to pull me off the fence, but when he touched me, he got zapped too. After that he did the only thing he could do. He got a running start, jumped up, and kicked me right in the gut so hard he knocked me off the fence. I staggered back and fell into the pond. I caught my breath, then we found a better spot and this time we safely crawled under the wire. As we walked back home Jarod said, "There were probably no pond dragons in that pond anyway." I think he said it just to make me feel better.

Comeuppance

When I wasn't off expanding my mind with Jarod's fine art or going on quests for the magic of pond dragons and polliwogs, I didn't know what to do. I mean, I knew how to hang out with Jarod and stuff, but all these school kids were too much. So I mostly just sat back and watched all the other kids do what kids do. I had a good view of their mayhem from my spot high atop the monkey bars. Most days it was the same old thing—kids yelling, kids running, kids crying. It was a long time before anything happened that was out of the ordinary.

One morning, just after first recess started, I noticed a bit of commotion in the nook between two hedges that were just out of sight of anyone not perched upon the monkey bars. There were four little boys crouched and whispering to each other. They were peeking out, watching for what was about to happen. Nothing seemed out of the ordinary at first. Kids were running and yelling the way they always did. The recess teacher, Mrs. Porter, was ringed by children like she was in *The Sound of Music*. The boys were playing soccer, and the girls were skipping rope.

A kid named Jacob slowly made his way through the middle of all the mayhem. He seemed to be in a bit of a trance as he went. Jacob slipped quietly through the safe zone and down into the Valley of the Bullies. Down there Meagan, the puller of hair, Rachel, the girl who bites, and Brick, the biggest, ugliest bully of all, sat with their hoard of stolen snacks, toys, balls, and jump ropes. It was a massive pile of plunder that they had taken away from all of the weaker kids. This pile was a symbol of their power over the masses, a constant reminder of what would happen if you dared step out of place or stood up for yourself. Jacob approached slowly at first. Then without even looking them in the eye, he went for the soccer ball his dad gave him for his birthday. He snatched up the ball from off the side of the pile and began to walk back the way he came.

Brick said, "Hey, get back here!"

Jacob kept walking, only a little faster now. Brick stood up and began to follow him, yelling out again, "I said, get back here!"

Jacob stopped, turned and squinted, stuck his finger up in the air, and made two quick flicking motions as if to say *Come and get it*. Then he ran past the monkey bars and ducked between the two hedges, where the other three boys were waiting. I heard him gasp out, "Get ready."

Brick lumbered back between the hedges ready, willing, and able to give Jacob the thrashing of his little life and reclaim the re-stolen soccer ball. He stepped toward Jacob, who was no longer holding the soccer ball. Instead, he had one hand hidden behind his back. When Brick stepped forward, the other three boys slipped behind him unnoticed.

Brick said to Jacob, "You're dead!"

Jacob just sort of grinned. Then suddenly all four boys landed on top of Brick and collapsed him to the ground. They pinned his hands and feet and Jacob leaped onto his chest. Brick was horrified when he realized he was helpless to stop what was about to happen. Jacob slowly brought his hand out from behind his back, scary-movie style. He was holding a pair of the green left-handed round-nosed safety scissors that we used at art time. Jacob looked Brick square in the eye and said, in the way that only a five-year-old with lispy *R*'s and a vendetta could, "Now, suckew, youwa gonna be bald!"

The other kids stuffed a mitten over Brick's face so he couldn't scream as Jacob chopped Brick's 1970s-style bowl cut into something that looked like what happens to a Barbie doll after it goes under the lawn mower. The boys let go and took their ball over to the soccer field. Brick sat in the grass for a moment, then gathered up his hair and went into the boys' bathroom for a while. Brick didn't cry, and never told on the boys that I know of. He kept being a bully, though, just not to them anymore. After his hair grew back, it was like nothing had happened at all.

I kept waiting, sitting on those monkey bars every day for the rest of that year. Eventually school was over, summer came back, and we were set free to go on more adventures.

Chapter 5

Walking the Dog

Our Saint Bernard's full name was Anheuser-Busch Natural Light; we called him Busher for short. Dad used to say he was every bit of two hundred pounds of dog, ten pounds of drool, and five pounds of smell. He was protective when he needed to be and a pain in the butt when he wanted to be. At different times he lived on the porch, in the house, or in the back seat of the family car. Of course, it was the back seat of the great big 1958 Ford station wagon, not the dinky-sized Toyota.

I think Dad had the Ford wagon to haul his instruments from gig to gig, but mainly it just seemed to haul a lot of kids and a very stinky dog.

The first few times we came to stay with Dad, he lived in a rambler with a woman named Linda and her daughter, Penny. That's where he was staying when he got our Saint Bernard. Busher was a large puppy when we got him at Christmas, but by the time we came down for the summer vacation, a puppy he was not. We three boys were supposed to walk the big dog each afternoon to do his business, much to the chagrin of the neighbors, because there were no poop bags or stuff like that. Back then, dogs just sort of went where they went. You see, back in the day, walking your dog was a poop lottery of sorts. When our giant dog dropped one in your yard, you won the Megabucks, baby! It took Jimmy all of ten minutes to convince me I could walk Busher all by myself while he watched TV. Eventually I believed him. I mean, I really believed him. Jimmy had me thinking I could walk three Saint Bernards at once if I really wanted to.

I was barefoot that summer. I had lost my shoes the week before when I left them on the bumper of the station wagon. When we drove off after a day of catfishing up at the Brownsmead slough, my shoes bounced off into the ditch somewhere on the way home. I had also left my bag of clothes at Grandma's house when we first came down to visit, so in addition to being barefoot, all I had to wear was hand-me-down shorts and a T-shirt that said Orange Crush on it. I hiked up my shorts, made a slipknot out of the dog leash, and wrapped it around my wrist. I wanted to make sure that when Busher pulled, I wouldn't lose hold of him. Oh, I didn't lose him!

The walk started out great; we made it all the way to the mailbox before Busher caught the scent of a female Saint Bernard three blocks down. He had probably been thinking about her for days. Now this was his chance. Without so much as a how-do-you-do, Busher bolted.

In the cartoon version of this, I fly like a kite flapping in the wind behind the big dog as he runs along the streets (goofy music plays), then I gently float onto the soft grass as the two dogs meet at the fence with big throbbing hearts in their eyes. Only, in the reality version of this, Busher ran for a full three blocks straight down the middle of the street, past all the good people who were washing their cars, mowing their lawns, and minding their own business. Suddenly out of nowhere comes a two-hundred-pound Saint Bernard, half running and half humping the air, with a forty-five-pound child tethered to his collar screaming bloody murder as he was dragged all the way down the block.

The pavement was tearing holes in what was already a limited wardrobe, to say the least. As we got to the house where the female dog was, Bush took the corner wide. I skidded a bit, then hit the curb and sort of bounced. I flew up and up in a wide arc onto the lawn and landed with a thud. As I went, my shorts, being three sizes too big, flew off and sailed past me. The huge dog hit the cedar fence with such force he knocked it clean down. I just lay there crying, facedown in the grass, bleeding, with my bare assets covered in road rash. I was still attached to the dogs as they got acquainted. The owner of the other dog drug out the hose to try to stop the party, but it was a waste of time and water. Ol' Busher didn't even notice the spray. I eventually caught my breath, and the little girl from the house next door brought me my shorts. Sniffling and too beat up to be embarrassed, I let the giant dog walk me home. When I got back to our house, Jimmy promised to walk Busher for the rest of the summer, if I didn't tell Dad. I didn't.

The Dart

Jarod and I were born sixteen months apart, and from that moment on we would be forever known by the phrase "Jeremy'n'Jarod. Now, which one are you?"

We were opposites in many ways, but the same in all the ways that counted. We were brothers as close as twins. We both liked frogs and Legos and, of course, adventures. We spent many an hour together focused on all three. Having only ever had one little brother, I naturally assumed that all little brothers were as special as mine—smart, funny, quirky, and painfully uncoordinated. Jarod never quite got the hang of some of life's basics, like catching a ball or running in a straight line, yet he mastered complex strategies without ever even trying. He could see how board games were going to play out a hundred moves ahead, but at the same time he couldn't nod his head for a yes or a no. He just moved it around like a little bobblehead for either one. Most people never knew quite what his answer was, but I always did.

We did everything together—slept in the same room, played the same games. We shared the same toys, whether we liked to or not. We even got the same presents. Each Christmas under the tree there would be our gifts, labeled "To Jeremy'n'Jarod." On paper, I'm sure it made sense for aunts and uncles to get us one gift that we could play with together, since we were going to play together anyways. You see, the thing was, I was a bit of a slob, and Jarod wanted his toys to be in mint condition and still in the original box, if at all possible. Oh, and yes, everybody made *Odd Couple* Felix and Oscar jokes about us. That was bad enough, but there was the minor detail that playing certain games with Jarod could be downright hazardous to one's health.

Somebody made the mistake of getting Jarod and me a dartboard, the kind with real darts. Then Mom made the bigger mistake of letting us play with it! To her credit, she made sure we followed strict safety guidelines so no one accidentally walked into the line of fire. When one of us was throwing, the rest of us had to sit on the floor in the back of the room in the "safety zone." We each got three darts to throw, and there was a little chalkboard we kept score on.

After we got all set up, Jimmy went first and, being older, he did really good. He got all three darts in the board and almost hit the bull's-eye. I took my turn next and hit the target with all my darts, too, but didn't get anywhere near the bull's-eye.

We let Jarod stand a bit closer to the board, so he would have a better chance of hitting it. His first dart went off to the right side of the dartboard and stuck in Jimmy's Evel Knievel poster. Jimmy gave Jarod a look. I gave him a point on the chalkboard. His second dart bounced off the lamp and landed on the floor next to the gerbil cage. We had told Jarod that if it didn't stick in the board or the wall you were allowed a do-over. His do-over throw stuck in the lamp shade. It was close enough, so I gave him another point. With his last dart, he was really determined to hit that bull's-eye. He took his time and aimed very carefully. Then he gave it a really big windup and let it fly. When he did, he stepped forward and threw hard, following through like a major-league pitcher. Only, unlike a major-league pitcher, he didn't let go when he was supposed to.

Now, at the moment of the great throw, I was sitting directly behind Jarod with the scoreboard on my lap. I was in that area Mom had named the "safety zone"—you know, against the wall, back where she said we were supposed to be safe from the darts. I sort of *heard* the thud of the dart hitting its mark. I looked over to see where the dart had landed. Only, it was about then I began to feel the sickening pain running up my leg. Jarod was staring hard at the dartboard to see if he had hit the bull's-eye or not. He had not! As the pain grew more intense, my mouth just fell open in horror. I couldn't seem to make a sound come out at all. Not seeing where his dart went, Jarod began to look around the room for it. I slowly set down the scoreboard and held my knee with both hands as I stared at the bright-red dart fins that were now a part of my leg. It had gone in under my kneecap and was about as far in as a dart can go. I was sure we would need to go to the emergency room to have it removed. Jimmy looked at me and at my leg and put his hand over his mouth. He was about to come help me, but it was too late. Jarod spied where the dart had landed. He just reached over and yanked the dart out of my knee and walked back over to the tape on the floor and lined up for another shot. With my mouth still wide open I gasped out, "What the heck?" Jarod simply said, "Well, that one didn't count." He wound up to throw again, and Jimmy and I dove for cover. This time the dart stuck in the wall. I did not give him a point. Mom washed my leg off with peroxide and put a little Band-Aid on my wound. She took away the dartboard from us until we were older. Jimmy and I didn't argue.

Tie Your Shoes

Cousin Ricko helped me climb my first apple tree. He drug out Auntie's washtub, turned it upside down so he could stand on it, and boosted me up to the first branch. We sat up in that tree picking and eating sun-warmed apples until we were as fat as puppies. The Green Grannies were so juicy they would drip down your arm, and made a glorious crunching sound when you took a bite. After we were full, we got some sticks about two feet long and we shoved the bruised or rotten apples about halfway down on them. We would whip 'em as hard as we could, and they would fly clear up and over the treetops. Most of them did, anyway. Some of them may have broken a window or two.

When they weren't breaking windows, the apples were also good for making pies. Only we didn't know how to make pies. Instead, we cut them in half and put cinnamon and sugar on top and pressed them into the top of the woodstove with a potato masher. They would sizzle and fill the whole house with the smell of sweet boyhood dreams.

As we ate our cinnamon masher-apples, we played songs on Ricko's record player. We played "The Night Chicago Died" and "Bad, Bad Leroy Brown" over and over. Ricko even taught me to move my feet to the song "Seasons in the Sun." He was a good cousin to have, and would even give me his hand-me-downs before he needed to.

Ricko and I went back outside to where Jenni and cousin Sarah were up in the apple tree singing "See, see, my playmate, come out and play with me." We were getting more apples when I tripped over my shoelaces and fell down. Ricko picked me up, dusted me off, and told me to tie my shoe. Only I didn't, I just looked down at the untied laces. He could see I was embarrassed, and asked me if I knew how to tie shoes yet, in a way that didn't make me feel bad.

On that day, Ricko taught me to whip apples, to dance, and most important of all, he taught me to tie my shoes. I had been having trouble at my new school for lots of reasons, but the one that bothered me most was not knowing how to tie my shoes. Mom tried to teach me, but I just couldn't get it down. Ricko took me to the top of the stairs that led down to the basement where we had been woodstove-frying apples all morning.

Ricko sat on the top step and said, "This is how you do it."

He crossed the laces, slipped one under the other, and pulled tight.

I said, "I know that part."

He said, "Okay, make a loop like this in one hand, keep it tight. Now that's the blue bunny's ear. Got it? Hold it tight so the blue bunny doesn't get away. Now grab another bunny's ear."

He made a loop with the second lace. "Okay, that's the red bunny, don't let go. Ready? The blue bunny chases the red bunny around the tree and jumps through the hole. Now you pull their ears until they squeak."

I did what he said, and my shoe was tied. "I did it!"

We took a step down and tried again. Each step down, Ricko repeated the story of the rabbits chasing each other around the tree. By the time we were at the bottom of the stairs, I knew the whole story by heart. Now that I knew how to tie my shoes, I used this story to teach Jarod how to tie his, and one day after I was all grown up, I would use this story to teach my own kids as well.

The Hunt for Mr. Hershal

Papa was a rolling stone. After Mom and Dad got the divorce, Dad moved around a lot, as musicians tend to do. Almost every visit during the summers and vacations we stayed in a new place, where we met new people and found new things to do. The summer when I was seven years old, Dad lived in a house once owned by an old couple named the Hershals. Mrs. Hershal had gone crazier than a bag of cats, and who could blame her? Mr. Hershal had disappeared some time back, never to be seen again. There were rumors all over town that the missus had done him in and buried him somewhere in the yard, or the woods, or maybe the field behind the house. So if she wasn't crazy before, all the talk probably didn't help too much. When we were moving in, old Mrs. Hershal explained to us that the neighbor kid, who she said was "a little off," kept sneaking onto her property at night to whittle on her house with his pocket knives. She would point out any little nick in the paint or a bit of rot on the porch, looking sharply out of the corner of her eye and growling through clenched teeth, "Pocket knives!"

Mrs. Hershal had also moved all the trees on her property to the middle of the yard, explaining that someone was oiling the trees, so she had moved them where she could keep an eye on them. This made a small forest in the center of the yard, fenced in by hay bales, railroad ties, and hog wire. Those trees were going nowhere, that's for sure. All of us kids had our theories about what had happened to poor old Mr. Hershal, and we decided it was up to us to find him. That meant when we weren't out sneaking past trolls, collecting polliwog gold, or riding the Barleys' pig, we were off looking for Mr. Hershal. All geared up with pails, shovels, and a wagon, or a wheelbarrow if we were feeling really lucky, we would head out around the property with whatever supplies we could muster. Our food stores usually consisted of bologna and mustard sandwiches or a can of Spam and a butter knife and maybe some deer jerky if Grandpa Owen brought some when he came to watch us. We would line up for inspection and Grandpa would tell us what part of the grid we were going to excavate that day, so he knew where to supervise us. Then off we would go.

Now, Grandpa Owen had supervision down to a science. He was a supervisory master. He could do it asleep, awake, from the front porch with a cigarette and coffee, or from the living room watching TV with a beer. Heck, he could even supervise in a lawn chair with a half-melted glass of iced tea and a big white cockatoo on his foot. We had received strict instructions to bring back any and all "clues" for inspection. We were to separate and wash any aluminum clues that had a five-cent deposit, bag them, and put those in a sack in Grandpa's car. He would look at those later and get back to us if they were pertinent to the case. The rest of our finds we separated out into piles, and Grandpa would tell us if it was trash or a clue. Occasionally we would dig up actual bones, along with our other kinds of clues. We would line up everything we found, in the yard on a big tarp. Grandpa would pull up his lawn chair and show us the difference between T-bones, deer ribs, elk jaws, raccoon skulls, and turkey drumsticks. After a full summer of digging, there was still no sign of Mr. Hershal.

We were all on our way back in from the polliwog fields with some red-leggers and a bullfrog when we saw two state trooper police cars pull into our driveway. As we walked up closer, we could hear the officers trying to gingerly broach the rather gruesome subject of the wayward Mr. Hershal. Dad, seeing he had them on the ropes, strung the officers along for a while just for fun. Finally, when he couldn't keep a straight face any longer, he said, "So you want to come and look for old Mr. Hershal, do ya? Well hell, we've been looking for him all summer. You're welcome to try."

They asked Dad what day would be the least intrusive on the family. Dad said, "Well, we should shoot for Saturday, if that will work for you."

The officers agreed, thanked Dad, and then were on their way.

Come that following Saturday, by the time the troopers arrived everybody we knew was already there. They brought their mothers and their grandmothers. There were cousins and friends and neighbors. Everybody came! We hadn't had a barbecue with this many people since the last Fourth of July family picnic.

When the officers arrived, they were quite amused to see all us kids lined up like little soldiers waiting for our orders. We were all decked out in the little outfits we had been working on the whole week. All of us except Jarod were dressed just like Indiana Jones; Jarod was dressed like Louis Leakey, the famous anthropologist. Jarod went on and on and tried to explain to us how his outfit was more "right" than ours because we were looking for bones and not for treasure, and that what we were doing was called anthropology and not archeology, but we just wanted him to shut up about it. We stood there with our pails and shovels ready to help dig for poor Mr. Hershal.

The officers tried to discourage us from helping, not wanting us kids to be traumatized just in case we did actually find Mr. Hershal's body, but we would have no part of it. We explained how we knew all the best places to look, and we showed the officers the map of where we had already dug and where we had not already dug. We even showed them the pile of clues we had accumulated and explained how if they found anything with a five-cent deposit, they would need to wash it and put it in a bag in Grandpa's car. Dad and Grandpa just sat and chuckled at the officers' plight and of course didn't lift a finger to help them explain the situation to us.

The officers, seeing that this was clearly our dig and that they were our guests, eventually let us lead them around with the cadaver dogs, at least until we got bored and went off to join the barbecue. After an hour or so the officers got bored like us, and came over and got some barbecue as well. We didn't find Mr. Hershal that day or any other day, but we did get to play Frisbee with the cadaver dogs, which was very cool.

It was about three years later that Mr. Hershal was finally found by hikers, some ten miles away in a state park just across the bay. There was no foul play that anyone could see. I was told that he was suffering from dementia and simply wandered off and died of exposure, but I know better ... I say it was pocket knives!

Jarodese

Jarod had been playing quietly for longer than normal. This usually meant that he was either planning to take over the world or someone had upset him.

I asked, "Hey, what are you doing?"

Jarod said, "I'm thinking."

Now I knew he was upset, because Jarod didn't have to think about taking over the world, that came naturally.

I asked, "About what?"

Jarod paused. "About being ashamed."

Yup, he was upset. I said, "What are you ashamed of?"

Jarod said, "Nothing." Then he went back to playing with his Legos.

"Wait, then why are you thinking about being ashamed?"

He took a breath. "Because people keep telling me I should be ashamed of myself, but I'm not."

Jarod looked at me and asked, "Are you ashamed of yourself?"

I looked down. "Um, not right now."

Jarod said, "But sometimes, you are ashamed of yourself?"

I said, "Yeah, I guess so."

I could see this was going nowhere, so I jumped ahead and asked, "What happened at school?"

Jarod said, "The girl that sits next to me in class smelled like pee again, so at recess I told her that if she pees on herself, she needs to wash it off, so she doesn't smell like pee anymore. She started crying and said I should be ashamed of myself. Then she ran off and told the teacher. My teacher said that I should think about what I did. So I am. But what I'm thinking is, if anybody should be ashamed, it should be Amy. She's the one who peed on herself, not me."

I told Jarod that he was right about not needing to be ashamed, and he could stop thinking about it now. You see, I spoke "Jarodese." Jarod had a way of saying things that made people look at him funny, or sometimes he put words together in ways that didn't make sense to anybody who didn't speak Jarodese. Jimmy and I guessed that the part of his brain that was supposed to say "Hey, maybe I shouldn't say that," or "Most people would say it like this" was busy doing something else, usually plotting the takeover of the world.

Most times as Jarod talked, I would help him, weaving our words in and out of each other's as he spoke. I would add the nice stuff that people expected to hear, to sort of unscramble the Jarodese. It was something we had always done, and I didn't even know we were doing it. I guess it made things easier, so that the other kids didn't feel stupid and cry, then go tell the teacher on him.

It wasn't just me and Jarod; all four of us kids had trouble with school and letters. For us, the letter *b* and the letter *d* looked the same. Most times, *m* and *n* had either too many, or not enough, humps for us to make out what they were supposed to be. Because of that we got free tutors to help us get better grades, only we were mad that we had to have a tutor at all. Also, they made the mistake of separating Jarod and me. So, unfortunately, Jarod's tutor had no one to protect her from Jarod. You could hear the poor lady almost in tears saying, "Do you mean yes, or do you mean no?" Jarod's head would bobble around and around until by the end of the tutor time, the lady looked like she was never coming back. But she always did. My tutor eventually gave up on my *m*'s and *n*'s, too, and just let me tell funny stories that he would write down to make into a little book that I could show Mom.

I wasn't doing all that great, but Jarod was doing worse. His celiac disease was making his hearing bad, so he had a lot of trouble saying some of his words the way he was supposed to. Jarod couldn't hear the tutor telling him how to say the words that he couldn't hear so he could learn how to say them. We could tell Mom was getting worried because Jarod's words were getting worse, not better.

I thought about this a long time. Then I remembered the time we were looking for arrowheads with Grandpa Owen down at Aldridge Point. Grandpa showed us how to put our ears on the railroad tracks to listen for trains far, far away. He told us how if we pushed our heads against the track hard, we could hear the train through the bones in our heads. I decided that would work better than yelling at Jarod over and over. So each day while we played Legos or cards or drew pictures, we would lean in and press our heads against each other. I would say the words he was having trouble with, and Jarod would repeat them back to me. I would show him how my mouth moved to make the sounds, and he would copy it.

We were going over Jarod's word list. It wasn't a list from his teacher or his tutor; it was a list of words kids made fun of Jarod for saying wrong. We played cards as we went down the list.

"The word is 'elephant.' " I would lean back and show him my mouth and say the word again. Then I would lean in and rest my head on his head and repeat the word. Jarod would say the word back to me, and we would keep repeating the word back and forth, me and then Jarod, until I felt he had it.

"Elephant."

"Alephnt."

"Elephant."

"Elephnt."

"El-e-phant."

"Elephant, got any twos?"

"Good, go fish, next word."

Jarod drew a card. I looked at the next word on the list, looked Jarod in the eye, and said, "Caterpillar."

Jarod repeated, "Cartarpilewr." I leaned backed and showed him my mouth again. "Cat-er-pill-ar." Then I leaned in. We pressed our heads together hard and I repeated the word: "Caterpillar."

Jarod laughed. "Oh, caterpillar."

"Good, got any nines? Next word."

I leaned back and read off the list, "Broken."

I leaned in and repeated, "Broken."

Jarod said, "Go fish, any kings?"

I said again, "Broken," only Jarod didn't say the word this time. I repeated, "Broken."

I saw his tears on the cards before I understood what they were.

Jarod said, "Am I?"

"Are you what?"

"Bwoken."

I was mad and sad at the same time.

"No! You're not broken. You're different."

Jarod leaned back and I could see the tears in his eyes. He asked, "Do you think the pond dragon's magic could make me *not* different?"

I looked down. "I don't know, maybe. I don't know. . . . No kings. Go fish. . . . Next word."

Jeremy T. Owen

The Electric Grandma

A good fix for sadness was a trip to Grandma's house.
My other grandparents, the Woods grandparents (my
mom's parents), Grandma Bea and Grandpa Roy, that
is, lived over the bridge and through the woods. No,
really, they did, so over the bridge and through the
woods to Grandma's house we'd go. It was a little house
on the Wallooskee River. The Wallooskee is a river that
joins the Young's River that empties into the Columbia
River that empties into the Pacific Ocean. It was hard to
say where one river started and the other stopped.

There were woods to play in and carpets of
clover to play on. We had all kinds of berries to eat—
blackberries, orange salmonberries, red huckleberries,
blue crowberries, salal berries, and super-sour Oregon
grape berries with their pokey leaves and seeds you had
to spit out. There were berries we didn't eat, too—white
poison coffin berries that stayed on the plant all through
the winter and even the birds wouldn't eat, though
Indian Jim said the Indians would eat just one or two for
a greasy stomach. There were lots of cattails that you
could eat the hearts out of. They tasted like cucumbers if
you got them from the clean part of the river. They
tasted like poop smelled if you got them from the
mudflats, so you had to be really hungry to get them
down there. Nothing tasty ever came out of the mudflats
except maybe catfish and crawdads.

We liked to eat stuff and make stuff from the
outdoors when we could. When we got hot, we made
forest iced tea. Mom's brother, our uncle Dale, taught us
to use spring birch leaves from the tree with the white
paper bark. We would add the tips of spruce branches
for zing and flowers off the pineapple plant. That was a
little white-flowering plant that smelled just like a
pineapple when you crushed it up. It was really wild

104

chamomile, same as the chamomile tea that Grandma drank with Mom. We would boil it up in a big pot with lots of sugar, add some of Grandma's Red Rose tea, and put it all in a big jar out in the sun for a day.

Grandpa Roy kept banty chickens and a goat that he said "keeps the forest from overrunning the place." Each year Grandpa would plant a good-sized garden that the "damn deer" were always getting into. Grandma Bea would spend her time out in the flower beds pinching the heads off the rhododendrons and tending to her dragon lilies. She would make little bags out of her old pantyhose and fill them with family members' hair clippings. She then tied these to all the rose bushes to scare away the "blessed deer."

My grandparents were older and were in retirement by the time I was born. That's when Grandma got sick, and I almost didn't get to meet her at all. Mom was nine months pregnant with me the night Grandma had seven heart attacks in a row and almost left us for good. Uncle Dale was far away in the Dominican Republic when he called and told Mom he had some real vivid dreams that he was at the hospital and was floating up above Grandma in her room. Uncle wanted to know if something was wrong. Mom told Uncle Dale how Grandma was having all those heart attacks and how in between the heart attacks Grandma was yelling at Uncle to get down off of the ceiling!

She kept yelling, "Put some damn clothes on, Dale."

We don't know how Grandma could see Uncle floating up there all the way from the Dominican Republic, but she did. Later I asked Uncle why he was floating naked in Grandma's hospital room. He said it was just his soul that was naked, and that he wore pajamas and was pretty sure only Grandma could see him up there anyways. So Grandma kept dying over and over again, and poor Uncle Dale's naked soul kept

105

flying all over the place. At the same time, Mom was praying hard out in the hallway when she looked up to see the ghost of her Grandma Hattie floating there in front of her. Mom said it was a black-and-white ghost that looked like the old picture of her grandmother that she had as a kid.

The Hattie ghost said, "Get your mother out of here if you want her to live."

Mom didn't want to argue with the Hattie ghost, so she made Grandpa make the doctor take Grandma up to Madigan Army Hospital in a chopper to put a pacemaker in Grandma's chest. The copter flew up along the North Cascades past the Mount Saint Helens volcano, the same volcano that would explode a few years later when we were stacking firewood over at Grandpa Owen's house.

On the way to the hospital, Grandma hollered to the pilots, "Hey boys, can we buzz the mountain?"

They hollered back, "No, Mrs. Woods, we're in a hurry, but we'll tip the copter so you can see it!" And they did. That's how Grandma got her pacemaker.

Back then pacemakers needed to have their batteries replaced when they ran low. By the time I was five, Grandma was on her third set of batteries. She was our "electric grandma" and we could always tell when she was getting low on juice because she would wind down. We would come visit and find her out in her garden moving like a snail, and then off she would go to get a fresh battery. When she was all juiced up again, you'd better watch out, 'cause she had stuff to get done and chores for you too!

We all were out visiting just after Grandma received that third battery. She was back to her old self, and Grandpa was out working on the tractor mower. Grandma had given me some eggshells to take down and feed to the banty chickens. I sat in the sun beneath the huckleberry bushes with my back against an old cedar stump. I crushed up the eggshells and threw them to the chickens the way Grandpa had shown me. As I sat there, I started to cry. I sobbed and sobbed and sobbed. Without a sound, my mother appeared at my side. She squatted down and asked me why I was so sad. I told her I was sad because my grandparents were going to die soon. Mom smiled a sad smile and told me how dying was a natural part of life and how my grandparents would always live in my heart.

I said, "Yeah, I know."

I told her I understood that part, only it wasn't them being gone that made me so sad. Mom asked me what it was that did make me so sad. I said I was sad because I was so little, and that I would only ever be able to know my grandparents as a seven-year-old boy could. I wouldn't get the chance to talk to them, to really talk to them and get to know who they were. They would be gone before I was old enough for that. My mother smiled, rocked me, and called me a very old soul.

Mom took my hand, and we walked back up to the porch and had a glass of Uncle's iced tea. On that same porch I would sit, play checkers, learn canasta, eat sandwiches, peel potatoes, talk, and get to know my beloved grandparents over the next thirty-one years of my life.

Rip Tide

August 16, 1977, was a bright summer's day on the Oregon coast. Grandpa Roy, Jarod, and I had been out on the sand dunes collecting tiny wild strawberries in little Styrofoam cups for most of the morning. The little strawberry plants grew like secrets in the dunes, hidden in and out of the bunch grass and in spidery patches here and there. That meant we had to look extra hard to find them. The fog had finally lifted off the dunes, and seagulls were flying in as the beach began to warm. The air smelled of strawberries and saltwater. Grandpa sat on a clump of dune grass plinking strawberries into his coffee can as Jarod and I ran around stuffing our little faces with the warmest, sweetest, most strawberry-est strawberries that have ever strawed or berried.

Grandpa told us that if we could pick enough strawberries, Grandma would bake us a pie. You haven't tasted strawberries until you have eaten sun-warmed wild strawberries off the Pacific Ocean sand dunes. Sadly, we didn't make it back with any berries to bake a pie. As with all of our berry-picking endeavors in the past, we returned with sticky fingers, stained faces, full bellies, and empty containers. Grandma Bea would always pretend to be surprised when we came back empty-handed, but was never disappointed with our lack of production. Somehow she always seemed to scrape together a pie for us.

We grabbed a quick lunch and snatched up our pails and shovels. Then Grandpa Roy and Grandma Bea walked us down to play with the other kids in the tide pools on the beach. As we walked along Grandpa would sing "The Old Gray Mare" and "I Don't Care, and I Don't Mind." He would tell us not to stick our toes in the warm tar that would bubble up on the old cracked road leading down to the beach. Of course, the second

108

Grandpa wasn't looking we always would. Grandpa Roy must have cleaned off over ten thousand tiny toes in his day. He would dip an old rag in gasoline and start scrubbing little piggies free of tar.

This little piggy didn't listen to Grandpa, this little piggy wouldn't do what he was told, this little piggy stepped in tar anyway, this little piggy is black as coal.

Jimmy, Jenni, Carrie, and Daintry were all looking for starfish in the tide pools that form at the base of Haystack Rock. The rest of us were playing in the surf, trying to catch the sand fiddlers as they buzzed around our feet. Sand fiddlers play where the water crashes onto the beach and explodes into foam. With each wave the fiddlers would appear, rush around like mad, and then zip back into the sandy bottom and bury themselves until the next wave would crash. Some people called them mole crabs, but I liked sand fiddlers better; that name made them seem happier.

We also looked for live sand dollars—like the kind you get at the gift shop, only they were furry and still moving. If you put a live sand dollar on the sand, it would disappear in no time at all. There were all kinds of sea stars in the tide pools, and on the sandy part of the beach too. We found blood stars, sand stars, and vermilion stars, bat stars and giant sun stars and purple sea stars, along with orange sea stars that are the same kind of starfish as purple sea stars, only they eat different stuff so they're not purple but orange instead.

There were moon snails so big you needed both hands to hold them up. We scooped up all kinds of fish from the pools when we could catch them. If we found any clingfish, we would try to stick them on each other's ponchos with the suction cup they have on their belly. When you grabbed a clingfish, sometimes you would get the whole rock they were clinging to as well.

It was amazing how a little armored fish no bigger than your thumb could hold up a rock as big as a football.

We found blennies, which look like little brown and green eels but are really fish. My most favorite of all the fish we caught were the sailfin sculpins, with dorsal fins as tall as they were long. They bounced around like little cocker spaniels and fought over their spots in the rock pools. We looked for pond dragons, too, until cousin Sarah told me that tide pools are not the same as ponds, in that they are much too salty for frogs and such.

While we played, Grandpa Roy would always make sure we were safe out by the water, saying, "Never turn your back to the ocean!" Then he would tell us about the rip tide and how it could carry swimmers away quick as a flash. Grandma Bea would listen and nod along. I found out later that Grandma used to swim for miles in the ocean every day. I would picture my little round Grandma swimming out in the ocean with the killer whales and great white sharks, until Mom showed me a picture of Grandma swimming when she was younger. I told Grandpa that Grandma looked just like one of those girls painted on the side of an airplane in World War II. Grandpa smiled and poked me with his elbow and gave me a wink that made Grandma blush red.

After a few hours of playing, it was getting late in the afternoon. The wind began to blow, making it too cold for us to play in the surf. Grandpa Roy whistled really loud with his two fingers, and we all packed up and headed back to the cabin that Auntie Jerry had rented for the week. Most of the older kids ran up ahead, and we smaller kids walked along with Grandma and Grandpa as he sang. The clouds started to come in off the ocean, and it got real gray as we got close to the cabin. I could see Mikey, Ricko, Matty and Jimmy on the porch of the cabin; they were sitting on chairs and looking in the doorway.

Before we even got to the stairs, we could hear the sounds of sadness. The radio announcer was saying how the world was never going to be the same. Everyone was sitting on the floor holding each other and watching the radio. The man said, "Elvis Aaron Presley, age forty-two, died today. There will never be another like him." Sadly, the radio man was right. We all cried as we listened, and eventually we fell asleep on the floor in front of the radio. I remember a lot about that day. I remember the sweet taste of summer strawberries, the roar of the ocean, the roughness of my grandfather's callused hands, the feel of warm tar squished between my toes, the loss of a King, and the distant sound of sadness.

Black Bird

There was a small black-and-white jumping spider crawling across the porch as we sat listening to Dad play guitar and sing. I got up, walked over, and stepped on it. My dad watched me kill the little spider, and when I sat back down, he stopped playing, set aside his guitar, and asked me why I did that.

I said, "Well it's a spider. Spiders bite!"

He then asked, "Did that spider bite you?"

I said, "No."

Dad looked down at the broken spider. "Okay then, I want you to fix it. Put it back together. Don't come in until it's working like it was before."

Dad stepped inside, leaving me there alone with the broken shell of the little creature. I sat down on the porch and tried to think if there was a way to undo what I had done; maybe there was a way to fix it, or some magic I hadn't been taught. I got down on my belly and looked at the pile of pieces. Even if I could reassemble all the parts, I wondered how I could make it go again. I looked at the bottom of my shoe. There was a piece there too. It wasn't too long before I became overwhelmed with the task and began to cry. Dad came back out a few minutes later to find me in tears.

He looked at me. "Why the tears?"

I told him, "I couldn't do it; I just didn't know how."

He said, "I know, son, only God can do that. Not even your pond dragons can fix a broken spider."

Dad sat with me and the spider, and he told me that taking an animal's life, no matter how big or how small that animal is, is something you can't take back. That there are times in your life when you will need to take a life, maybe to eat or to protect yourself or to protect others or even to end suffering, and that I should remember how every life you take becomes a part of you. If you're respectful and have need, you will be at peace with that part of yourself. If you take life needlessly or disrespectfully, you will have to carry it with you. Then one day you will need to find an answer for why you did what you did.

I asked, "Did you ever kill something that way?"

He said, "Yes, when I was young."

I asked, "Do you carry it with you?"

Dad looked down, took a deep breath, and said, "Yes I do."

***

High upon a perch sat a red-winged blackbird, the blackest of all the birds we children knew. Blackbird feathers are very neat and smooth, not ruffled like a crow's or shaggy like a raven's. When lit by the sun, they could shine so bright that they were hard to look at. The three of us boys could hear the blackbird calling through the cattails all morning. We had been chasing him for most of an hour, losing him and then finding him again as he called. Dad once told me his call meant "I am here. I am here" in the blackbird tongue.

The sun had risen high enough to melt the mist off the water and take the chill from the air. Suddenly the blackbird landed low on a cattail not more than ten feet away. His call was much louder now; he was almost screaming. The others were saying, "Take the shot! Take the shot!" And the blackbird held still until I did. His feet gripped the cattail tightly, both wings stretched out wide, frozen for a moment in time, showing the crimson and orange patches on his shoulders. A spray of red arced across his tail feathers. There was no sound as he folded his wings and slowly slipped from the cattail, landing eyes closed in the mud. His clean black feathers were now soiled and ruined.

Sometimes when my mind wanders off to dreams, I find myself thinking back to that day running through the cattails trying to find the blackbird. Only it's me who is calling, "I am here. I am here."

Chapter 6

Around and Around

Dad's little brother, Uncle Billy, and his little sister, Aunt Margaret, were just teenagers when we used to go over to Fourteenth Street for the Fourth of July. Uncle Bill would let us play with his toy soldiers, but only if we waited for him to play too. He would help us light sparklers so we didn't get our fingers burnt, but of course one of us always did. Bill would show us where in the yard to catch the best salamanders and how to chase the Brownlie girls with them. He was a good uncle like that.

Bill was cool. He got to use the push mower with the spinning blades to cut the grass every Fourth of July, and was usually still cutting it when we arrived. He could make the blades spin through the grass with a slicing whir sound that still makes me think of summer.

Grandpa Owen had a big piece of quartz in the rockery that we liked to look at, so Uncle Bill would lift it out and show it to us. He would tell us how it came from deep inside the earth, how the crystal formed over a million years. Then he would help us put it back carefully, so as not to squish anyone living under it.

Uncle Chuck and Great-Uncle John ran the barbecue and cooked up all the goodies for us. The neighborhood kids and families flowed out of their houses into the streets to talk and eat hot dogs and Popsicles. Dad and his brother John played basketball at the hoop that someone had nailed to the telephone pole in the middle of the block. They always played hard until they were covered in sweat and/or got a bloody nose or a fat lip by accident. Aunt Margaret would take all the little kids two yards over to where Mrs. Jenkins had an old-fashioned German washing machine in her front yard. It was an open-topped thing that you put the wet clothes in and spun by hand until the water flew out, before putting the clothes on the line for drying. Margaret would put us kids in the washer, one or two at a time, and give us a ride until we would spill out laughing and dizzy, stumbling and rolling around the yard. She would lead us back down to Grandma's house, all holding hands, like a daisy chain of tiny bobbleheads still spinning from our time in the washing machine.

Raining Frogs

As we got older, our polliwogin' skills matured beyond the challenge of what even the stealthiest polliwogs could provide. We eventually put aside our childish ways, and one by one we left the pursuit that had consumed our younger selves for so many years. We came in from the polliwog fields for the last time, not even knowing that it would be the last time. The endless pursuit of polliwogs faded into the yellowed pages of our memories. As children do, we had moved on, we had become something else, something more. We, like our fathers before us, were transformed. In the same way the polliwogs themselves were transformed; we had become something new. We were older now; we were wiser. Now we were frog men.

Grandpa Roy said that bullfrogs were territorial. Mom and Dad got us a big black set of encyclopedias. Mostly it was for looking up the things that grandpas say. We called it the Encyclopedia Gramptanica. According to the Gramptanica, "territorial" meant that bullfrogs would defend their part of the pond against other bullfrogs. They would use their croak. They would show off, make chase, do jump attacks, and even wrestle—freestyle, we thought. In other words, bullfrogs were awesome. The only thing that could have made them more awesome would be if they had a king of the bullfrogs, too, and they did. We called him the Bully King, and every one of us claimed to have seen him nearly every time we went to Coffenbury Lake. We all wanted to catch him and all of his bullfrog friends too. We weren't going to eat them or sell them or anything like that. We caught bullfrogs for the pure joy of catching bullfrogs. We played with frogs like some kids played with puppies.

Hand nets were for amateurs and babies. We were frog men now, and we had a dozen different ways for catching frogs. We would stealth 'em, corral 'em, jig 'em with a worm tied on a fishing line, use the old three-man rush, the belly crawl, the log float, the Geronimo, aka the Screaming Johnny, and the list went on and on.

We were always trying to come up with a new signature style move that would set us apart from lesser frog men. We were true artists. Jimmy was pretty much the god of the frog men, when it came to sheer numbers, that is. So Jarod and I were always trying to find an edge, if only to just keep pace. I was watching the PBS channel one day when I saw a scientist stun a side-blotched lizard with a rubber-band gun. It didn't hurt the little guy, he just froze long enough to be scooped up and put in a jar. Then I saw another show where some Indians would slap the water with a big stick and stun the fish they were after. Then they scooped them up as well. With this in mind, Jarod and I made our way down to the slough to try out this new scientifically derived idea of mine.

We got ourselves an old laundry-soap bucket and a scoop made from a bent coat hanger and the left foot of an unopened pack of Mom's pantyhose. Lucky us: on the way down to the water, we found a loose fence board that we were sure nobody would miss. It was a two-man job, frog stunning. Jarod held the bucket and the scoop as we crawled over to the water's edge.

Insects buzzed and the frogs were croaking at full volume as the light began to fade that summer evening. I saw a red-legger in the water, just off the other side of a small log jutting out on our side of the slough. I slowly moved into position, rocking back and forth with the wind so I looked like a tree branch swaying. I eased the board above my head bit by bit as I swayed, until I had the board at full height and ready to swat the water next to the frog. Only, the frog was too far out, so I needed to step out onto the log just a bit more.

I slowly edged out, still moving like I was a branch, but now the board was getting really heavy. By the time I got close enough for the swat, I was no longer trying to shake like a branch, I was just shaking trying to hold the board up. I gave Jarod a look, so he knew to be ready with the bucket and the scoop. I held my breath and swung the board hard, aiming for the water next to the frog. But as the board came down my foot slipped. The frog jumped, and the board landed square on the frog's head. The splash in the water made all the insects and frogs instantly go quiet. Well, not all of them. The frog I smacked with the board began to scream, *Eeeer-eererereee!*

Jarod looked at me in horror and started yelling, "Why? Why? Why?"

The frog kept screaming and kicking farther out into the water. *Eeeereererereeeeerrreerer!*

Jarod dropped the bucket and homemade scoop and covered his ears. The frog rolled over belly up, his legs out stiff, still screaming, *Eeerererererererererererr!*

Jarod said, "What do we do?"

I said, "I don't know. I don't know. Just run!"

We began to run home as the poor frog kept screaming off in the distance. We were both crying as we ran. We cried the whole way home. All these years later, if you make the sound *Eeererererererere,* Jarod goes stark white, shakes his head, looks at me, and says, "Why? Why?"

***

Every summer we had a picnic at Coffenbury Lake, nearly always at the west campground, back when it was still all dirt roads. We had our regular spot, where Uncle

John would run the barbecue and Dad would play guitar and sing. We would run and play, swim and fish, and get to see everyone we hadn't seen in a while. At some point, usually after three hot dogs, two cans of pop, and four marshmallows—okay, five—we would grab our buckets and hike the entire loop around the lake trying to catch the Bully King.

One year would be remembered as the most epic frog-a-thon in history.

The previous summer, Jimmy and Steven had swept the field with five bullfrogs apiece. Johnny caught three, David caught two, and Jarod and I caught one each. It was quite a haul of bullies, but this year we were older and wiser, and Jarod and I had a feeling that this was going to be our time to shine. The east side of the lake was closed because the parking lot was being paved, so this year the trail around the lake was blocked off due to *con*struction, only Jimmy reopened it on account of *de*struction. That is to say, Jimmy and Steven kicked a hole in the construction fence that we all slipped through, and with that we were off.

We hadn't gone twenty feet when Jimmy bagged his first frog. He just bent down and came up holding a frog that could have been the king himself. It wasn't looking good for the rest of us. He tossed it in my bucket with a soft plop. I said, "Hey!" He gave me that big-brother look that meant *You're lucky to be tagging along at all*. I thought to myself, *Dang, bucket boy again*. I took a deep breath, covered the frog with a beach towel, and looked at Jarod. Only he wasn't looking at me, he was looking past me. Suddenly he zoomed by me like a crazed spider monkey. He went full Screaming Johnny, straight into the lily pads. After splashing around a bit Jarod came up with a face full of mud and a frog's legs sticking out from between his fingers. He sloshed out of the lake, walked over,

120

dropped it in the bucket, and said, "Your turn." My little brother was not taking this lying down.

It wasn't long before we had each caught a frog or two. Frogs were everywhere! Even so, Jarod and I kept our eyes peeled, just in case a pond dragon surfaced or slipped off a log into the deep. Our troop had only made it a third of the way around the lake, and we had already almost passed last year's frog count. We were catching so many frogs, we started throwing the small frogs back to make room for bigger ones. We lost track of whose were whose. It was a freaking frenzy of frogs, mud, polliwogs, salamanders, and bugs. We were all lost in what would be the most memorable frog day of our lives, only not for the reason you would think.

As we came around the back side of the lake, we had spread out from each other a bit and were silently sneaking along with our heavy buckets in hand. We worked our way past the lily pads and toward the beach; there the frogs thinned out and were getting harder to catch. Normally this part of the beach was packed with people, but since this side of the lake was closed it was totally empty. We made our way up to the spot where a big hedge ran down to the shore next to the swimming dock. Jimmy and Steven were just up ahead of Jarod and me. David was back down the beach a bit, and Johnny was back farther than that. I heard something; it was sort of a hissing sound.

I looked over to Jarod and whispered, "Do you hear that?"

Jarod said, "Hear what?"

Then we both heard it.

This time we saw Jimmy and Steven motioning in our direction and saying, "Psst."

They were pointing up onto the shore at something we couldn't quite see from where we were. We crept down the beach so we could see what it was they were looking at. Our sudden movement caught

David's attention, so he grabbed his bucket and snuck over to us to see what was up. By the time we three crawled over by Jimmy and Steven, they were practically having a fit. We set our buckets down and stood up enough to see what it was they were laughing at. There up on the beach was a man. He was a tall man. Umm, he was also a very naked man. He was a very tall, very, very naked man. He was peeking through the hedge, and he was doing something. Tugging on Steven's shirt, I whispered, "What's he doing?" Steven looked at me, trying not to laugh. He whispered, "He's twanging it."

I didn't know what that meant. "What?"

Steven shook his head. "You know, he's twanging it."

Jarod and I looked at each other, confused.

Steven rolled his eyes at us and whispered, "He's shaking hands with his little man!" We whispered back, "Oh!" so he would think we knew what he meant. Only we didn't.

A split second later, the day went from all sunshine and lollipops to the shores of Iwo Jima. Jimmy reached into his bucket and grabbed a half-pound bullfrog and handed it to Steven. Then he got one for himself. He gave the rest of us a look that could only have meant *Lock and load, boys, lock and load.*

Down the beach, Johnny suddenly stood up, like he heard imaginary bombers coming in low off the water. He grabbed his bucket and began to run toward us almost in slow motion. Our general cocked back his arm, then with a snap sent the first bullfrog flying. He held his other hand out to say *Hold, hold.* We lost the bullfrog in the sun for a fleeting moment, then it drifted back into sight, spinning in slow motion like a little froggy balloon. The naked guy must have heard the imaginary bombers as well, because he turned just as the bullfrog hit him square in the chest. Jimmy yelled, "Freak!" but all we heard was *"FIRE!"*

We all started unloading our frogs like grenades. Johnny, seeing what was happening, turned into some sort of super soldier. He began unloading his bullfrogs while still on the run. Frogs were rocketing in from all directions at once and landing everywhere. Some overshot the hedge, some landed in the bushes, and others tumbled onto the grass. Frogs were hopping, croaking, and squirming all over the place. From the other side of the hedge, suddenly two nude girls ran out, grasping their towels and screaming as frogs rained down all around them. Because it was the Fourth of July, Jarod and David snapped to attention and gave a small salute as the two girls ran past. Then, having never seen nude girls before and just because we could, we let them have it too.

Fireworks

We made our way back to the family barbecue with our now mostly empty buckets of bullfrogs. Since we had lost count of whose frogs were whose, we picked a champion based on who hit the naked guy with the most bullfrogs. Johnny won by two frogs.

After a big day catching bullfrogs and picking the goat's-head thorns that grow around the lake out of our bare feet, we loaded the station wagon with wet kids, wet clothes, all things sandy, and one super smelly Saint Bernard. Dad and Uncle Chuck had to spend quite a bit of time rigging up the old station wagon so we could drive back home. Seems that when all us boys marched off to frog war that morning, Dad had tied old Busher's leash to the car door, only no one told Bush. When he tried to go with us, he folded the car door back on itself, and now the door wouldn't close anymore. Luckily for the naked guy, Bush stayed back with what was left of the car, or that poor guy would have been traumatized by more than bullfrogs.

We rolled down both of the back windows and Dad threw a piece of rope in and out both sides of the car. He tied each end to the door handles, and that kept the doors from flying open, but it also made it so if we stopped quick, the rope would hit anyone sitting in the back seat right in the throat. That meant you had to sit real low in the seat so you didn't get your head cut off when dad put on the brakes.

We all headed out from the lake back to Aunt Marie's to light off fireworks. Those of us kids who didn't want their heads cut off by the rope in the backseat rode in the back of Grandpa Owen's pickup. First, we had to stop by the store to get ice. Since we had Grandpa's truck, we needed to pick up Aunt Marie's porch at the store too. The porch, or what was left of it, had been sitting in the handicap spot for a week or so. Seems that Dad had left Busher chained up to Auntie's front porch while he went to work, but Bush decided he wanted to go to work too. Dad got a call from his friend Haulis, who worked out at the store about five miles from Auntie's house.

"Hey Jimmy, I got your dog down here at my store."

"No way. I left him chained up to Marie's front porch."

"Don't worry, Jim, he's still chained to the porch."

Then Dad said . . . well, we don't need to hear what Dad said. Auntie needed her porch back, so we all loaded it up in the back of the pickup truck and drove it out to her house. Dad and Uncle Chuck hammered the porch back onto the house, but not before their friend Dicky walked out into thin air and fell on his butt.

Uncle John Van Horn had gone to the Indian reservation and brought back a trunkload of fireworks. Everyone we knew had pitched in, and Uncle bought out the store. There was every kind of firecracker and skyrocket a boy could dream of. Dad divvied up the goodies, and we each got a paper sack piled high with enough gunpowder-filled joy to keep us busy for the rest of the night. It wasn't dark yet, so we focused on firecrackers and screaming whistlers. At the time, Black Cats and Boomers were all the rage. If you pinched a Whistling Pete just right, it would go *pop* when you lit it off. We ran to the car and grabbed the pillowcase we had filled with old toy soldiers, half-broken toys, and anything else we thought would look cool if it went *KA-BOOM!* We dragged a couple buckets of water and a few sheets of old plywood up on top of the hill behind Auntie's house, where we could launch rockets and have a place to line up toy soldiers for the firecracker battle. Three hours later there wasn't a toy left standing, and the sun had become but a whisper on the horizon. The smell of hay, fireworks, and cardboard hung in a low cloud just above our heads.

The cardboard was what we used for toboggans to race down the back side of the dry, grassy hill. The buckets of water were for putting out any fireworks that set the grass on fire when they landed. We would run down, stomp out any fires we saw burning, and call for water if we needed any. After dark, we could see the fireworks show going off in the town of Seaside just a few miles away. We would all sit on our hill and watch the show until it finally lit the sky to full bright. Then we would listen for the cars to come racing down the highway to park out in front of our property. Dad would yell, "Here they come!"

We were so proud to have a big fireworks show that people wanted to watch. Great-Uncle John would make us wait for the cars to get all parked before we started our show. Then we would let fly. All the dads, uncles, and kids older than twelve would take turns lighting off skyrockets, Roman candles, and mortars, filling the sky with fiery colors and giving the boom of the Thunderbird a run for its money. We smaller kids watched the magic, roasted marshmallows, and desperately tried to stay awake so the night wouldn't have to end.

On a side note, I would like to say I'm sorry to the neighbor kids for launching all those skyrockets down the hill into the middle of your Fourth of July celebration; that was bad, and totally Jimmy's idea. Okay, I may have had a bit to do with the calculations of distance, direction, velocity, and compensating for wind—you know, standard eight-year-old stuff.

The Pool Kid

That summer we were staying at a rental house on Florence Street just up the hill from the Tapiola pool. It was the kind of neighborhood where the city required Busher to be on a chain, not just fenced in. This was in part because the four-foot chain-link fence was kind of flimsy for a dog of his size. The house had three floors to it. Dad and his friend Bike shared the main floor, and some woman who would disappear for weeks at a time lived on the bottom floor. There was a stoner guy who lived up on the top floor, but we never saw him much. The caliber of tenants was what one might call questionable at best. Still, the house had a big yard and was close to the pool, the park, and Aunt Jerry's house. You could walk a couple of blocks to Bob's little store, where we could cash in aluminum cans. A rather large pile of aluminum cans would accumulate out back of Dad's house between our visits. Each can had a five-cent deposit, so this was where we got our spending money, food money, and well, just money. It got to be a daily chore: rinse out the aluminum cans, stack the red wagon three rows deep, throw a garbage bag full of cans over your shoulder, and off to Bob's store we went.

We would wheel in our treasure, and old Bob would count out our cans one by one. When he was done, we would hand him a note from Dad. Then Bob would put Dad's stuff in a bag that we weren't supposed to look inside of. So we looked. It was beer and cigarettes and more beer. We picked out some groceries, and by groceries I mean whatever three boys under the age of twelve deemed to be food. We would load up our chips, pepperoni sticks, noodle ramen, a half gallon of milk, and a *Mad* magazine.

Jimmy would holler, "Ready, boys?"

Move 'em up, head 'em out
Head 'em out, move 'em up
Move 'em up, head 'em out
Rawhide!

and away we went. We wagon-trained our way back down the hill to the house, put the stuff away, and went off to find some trouble to get into.

There weren't many other kids close by to play with, but twice a day this little blond monster would pass the house going to and from his swimming lessons. Twice a day he would walk over and kick the gate until ol' Bush would run down to the end of his chain and bark like mad. Twice a day Jimmy would chase the little brat halfway down the block, and this went on for half the summer.

It was a couple of days after the Fourth of July party. Jimmy had just come back from chasing after that neighborhood brat who was teasing the dog again. That's when we heard the sound of a pickup truck idling in front of our driveway, followed by a *boom, boom, boom* on the door of the first-floor apartment. Two half-drunken idiots were looking for Sally or whatever her name was, in apartment number one. Only she wasn't answering the door, and they were getting madder and madder by the minute. Of course, we boys saw that as an opportunity to sit on the garage roof and gawk at the men below, who were now yelling at us and demanding we tell them where the lady had gone.

Jimmy, seeing the men were in distress, offered the helpful suggestion that they might try looking in each other's butts to see if she was in there. They did not see the obvious humor in this, nor did they find it helpful. Jarod and I were laughing hard when one of the men reached up and took ahold of my leg. This was a mistake on his part, and that's when all heck broke loose. Off in the distance, we could hear the screaming sound of the chain spooling out like a boat was dropping anchor. Next the sound of roaring thunder came rolling down the stairs, followed by the sharp *ping* of a chain snapping and a loud *thud* as it whipped back and hit the house.

To its credit, the city may have had a point when it required dad to chain Bush to the house as well as have him fenced in. Turns out the gate was indeed a symbolic gesture, as it folded back around itself with a loud clang. There was a quick flash of brown and white, then all two-hundred-plus pounds of Busher flew through the air and bit down hard on the guy's arm, and Busher didn't let go! He landed on all fours, growling. With the guy's arm still in his mouth, he slowly walked him backwards into the street. Busher opened his mouth just enough to let the man take a step back. Still growling, Bush said a loud *Bwooofff* and slobber flew everywhere. The guy panicked and started to run around the truck. This was his second mistake. Bush took this as an opportunity and, in true Bush style, with a glint in his eye, added a little insult to injury. We were howling with laughter. His buddy made it back to the truck and was pleading for us to call the dog off.

Jimmy yelled, "He'll stop in a minute. Just don't make him mad again, or he'll get you next."

Finally, the first man scrambled out from under the dog's warm embrace, jumped up into the back of the pickup truck, and slid in through the passenger-door window. He jumped over to the driver's side and rolled down the window to give us a piece of his mind. That was his last mistake.

Bush stood up on his hind legs, put both paws in the window of the truck, and nearly bit the guy's face off. The truck peeled out and tore off down the street. Bush chased it for half a block but was tired from all the loving and wandered back to the porch for a long nap.

The following morning we were all watching cartoons when I jumped up and ran into the bathroom for an emergency piddle. After the piddling, I emerged from the bathroom to find an empty house where a full house had been but moments before. I looked behind the couch to see if it was a surprise for me, but nobody was there. So I looked in the bedroom, then in the kitchen, then back in the living room again. My family had disappeared. They were nowhere in the house! I heard a noise out on the front porch, so I walked over to where I could see Dad, all red-faced and collapsing onto the stairs. Dad was only in his thirties, but I had heard stories of how my grandfather had lost his own father when he was my age.

I ran to Dad's side as he lay there convulsing. I yelled, "Dad, Dad, are you okay? Should I call 911?"

He gulped in a breath and squeaked out, "Frog! Go help your brothers."

I looked out onto the flat tar garage roof to see seven-year-old Jarod rolling in a ball back and forth, red-faced, with tears streaming from his eyes. On the opposite side of the roof, Jimmy was draped over the edge, gasping for breath. He was also stricken, writhing back and forth. As Jimmy's eyes met mine, he could see the panic in my eyes.

Through his tears, he gasped, "Come quick, man. You have got to see this!"

I hopped over the railing and stepped out onto the roof. Suddenly I heard a flapping sound and the frail voice of the seventy-nine-year-old lady from next door.

She was hollering, "Bad doggy! Bad doggy!"

I stepped to the edge of the roof, and the scene that presented itself to me would come to symbolize the word "justice" and make for a great story for the rest of my life.

After ol' Busher had broken his chain the day before and bent up the gate, we didn't want him to get in trouble or have anybody find out that he had bit the lowlife guy who grabbed my leg. So we did our best to bend the gate back into shape. We smacked the latch with a rock a few times until it shut okay, sort of, and then we found some wire bread ties and tried to fix the chain, so it at least looked to be in one piece.

That morning must have appeared to be just like another day to the neighborhood brat. I'm sure he did what he always did, kick the gate to get a rise out of ol' Bush. Only this time when little Ronny kicked the gate, the latch just slid down to the ground and ol' Bush just wandered on out after Ronny with big old hearts in his eyes. Even though Busher barked a lot at Ronny, he was a lover, not a biter. Unless you were a lowlife who tried to grab my leg.

Later, Jimmy told me Dad heard the commotion first. When he saw the kid, he started laughing so hard he collapsed on the stairs. Dad sent Jarod and Jimmy to pull the dog off Ronny, but they too were overcome with the hilarity of the situation. There he was, little skinny Ronny in his green swim trunks and white tennie runners, with his little blue towel rolled up under his left arm and his sack lunch gripped tight in his right hand. After all these months, ol' Busher was taking his frustrations out on Ronny in true Busher fashion, with a gleam in his eye and love in the air. That little old lady from next door was smacking the crud out of Busher with her cane as little Ronny's sack lunch was getting shook back and forth with every hump, shook-shook, shook-shook. I felt pretty bad, because I was Ronny's last hope. Surely little Ronny would need a miracle now. Only, God must have been busy that day or else on ol' Busher's side, because no miracle arrived. As I gazed down at Ronny's ordeal, I too was struck down, the same as Dad, Jarod, and Jimmy. Unable to move a muscle to help little Ronny, I just convulsed with laughter.

When Busher was done, little Ronny was a sad sight to be sure. He was crying and trying to get a hug from the little old lady, who sadly would suffer the same fate as Ronny a few days later. We really should have fixed that fence.

As Ronny stood there sniveling, Bush wolfed down the contents of little Ronny's sack lunch and then, just as happy as he could be, Bush made his way back into the house for a long nap on the couch. When we could breathe again, we told Dad about the day before and how Bush broke his chain and the fence and the latch and how we tried to fix it. To our surprise, Dad wasn't mad at all. He was proud of Bush and told us that it was a dog's job to protect us when he wasn't home. For the rest of the time we stayed at the house on Florence Street, little Ronny could only be viewed far off in the distance as he gave our block a wide berth on his way to the pool. We would see him from time to time at the swimming pool or the park, and of course we would gather the other children around and tell the tale of "The Boy Who Cried Bush."

Zombie Trout

Over the next few days, we used up all the fireworks we had left and got into as much trouble as we possibly could. We used our last six bottle rockets trying to stun fish down by the fish hatchery. By that, I mean *in* the fish hatchery. We waited until dark, and then we hid in the woods just up the hill from the big concrete tanks that held all the fish. We lit the rockets and tried to fire them down into the big hatchery pond. That was easier said than done. We hit tree branches with the first four rockets, and the fifth one was a dud. Jimmy decided to jump the fence and shoot the last rocket straight into the pond. He lit the fuse. We heard *hiss, whoosh, bloop, whoom* . . . and *boomp!* Then we waited, and we waited, and we waited. Hmm, nothing. Jimmy looked up at us and shrugged. It was then that Jimmy noticed a tank filled with the biggest rainbow trout we had ever seen. He signaled for us to come down to where he was, so Jarod and I belly-slid our way through the brush and leaves down to Jimmy. He made a face because we were being way too loud.

He whisper-yelled, "Get ready!"

Jarod and I looked at each other and tried to be ready. Suddenly Jarod got knocked off his feet and flew back into the brush. He wasn't ready! I turned back to look at Jimmy, only to catch a fish upside my head. I wasn't ready either. Two more fish flew over the fence and flopped around in the bushes. Jimmy climbed out of the hatchery and ran over to us.

He said, "Stop gawking and grab one!"

Jarod got ahold of one by the tail and started going down the trail. He was bobbling all over the place and looked like a drunken racehorse jockey trying to hold on for dear life. I got mine by the gills but couldn't hang on. I dropped it over and over again until I got it under my arm like a football. Jimmy grabbed the last two fish and came out of the bushes with his arms flopping around like noodles.

He yelled, "Go, go, go!"

We ran to catch up with Jarod, who looked to be in a death match with his big fish. I lost my footing as we ran past the pool, and accidentally launched my fish like a torpedo down the sidewalk, clipping Jarod's heel. He staggered sideways and spun out on his back in the grass beside me. His fish, which was now clearly dead, was on top of him. It looked like Jarod was being attacked by a zombie trout. My fish slid down the grassy hill toward the pool fence. I ran fast to catch up with it as it went zipping along. I tried to stop it with my foot but stepped on its tail and slipped, landed on my face, and came up with a mouthful of muck. I scrambled down to the fence, grabbed my fish, and ran back up the hill, where Jarod stood red-faced waiting for me.

I was about to say, "Okay, let's go," when Jarod began swinging his fish at me wildly. I didn't care why. I just ran to catch up to Jimmy, with Jarod, wielding the zombie trout like an ax murderer, chasing me the whole way.

When we got back to our house, Jimmy cleaned all the fish. We cooked up half of one in a pan with butter, garlic salt, and some flour to make a crispy skin. Dad didn't ask where we got the fish. But a few days later he told us a story of how he and Uncle Chuck snuck some fish out of the hatchery when he was a kid.

Barstool Cowboy

Dad slept a lot. He sang at the Sunset until 2 a.m., then most nights he would be home by 3. He slept late and would take a nap on the couch in the afternoons. When he wasn't sleeping, he played guitar and sang to us. He played so much guitar his fingers grew callused from the finger work. Not little calluses like from gardening, but big ones. The thick strings on his Gibson guitar wore deep grooves in his fingertips; they would grow so deep he couldn't press the strings down anymore. I would watch Dad file his fingertips down with a small metal file he kept in his guitar case. When he was done filing, he would hand me the file and I would put it back in the little guitar-case compartment that held extra strings and smelled like Grandma's musty coat closet. As Dad rehearsed and played all the songs we loved so much, I messed with his pitch pipe, counted guitar picks, and played his tambourine. It was in the back of the tambourine that I found a folded-up piece of paper with writing on it. I asked Dad what it was.

He looked at it. "Oh, that ain't nothing. Just something I was working on once upon a time."

I said, "Is it a song? Can you play it? Is it new? Can you play it?"

Dad could see I wasn't going to drop it until he played it for me. He only ever played it for me that once. Then he folded it back up, handed it to me, and said, "It's yours now. It's up to you to sing it."

I remember how Dad tuned up his guitar, started on a G chord, and sang smooth and clear. I can still hear it now.

And my father sings:

You know that I know
That I've hurt you

135

With my thoughtless, babbling brain
The things that I've said
They've twisted your head
Time and time again.

And I know that you think I'm a villain
The kind that's tied you to the tracks
That I'm twisting my 'stache
Waiting for trains to crash
But baby, I ain't nothing like that.

I think that I could be your hero
The kind that comes save the day
Yes, I think that I could be
All the things that I should be
If only you could see me that way.

Close your eyes.

chorus:

And this old barstool could be my white
horse
This old microphone be my gun
And my guitar's still a guitar
And this old bar's just an old bar
And my buckles as silver as my tongue.

Like the Lone Ranger
I'll gallop to your rescue
And at the last moment come rushing in
Saving you from the me
That you sometimes see
Because baby I ain't nothing like him.

Yes, I think that I could be your hero
If you give me just half a chance

The Polliwog Fields

Because I ain't trying to hurt you
Sully your virtue
Or steal the old deed to your ranch.

I'd like to ride with you into the sunset
Steal away the girl of my dreams
Fight at high noon
Catch you when you swoon
Close your eyes and you'll see what I
        mean.

(chorus)

Yes, saving you from the me
That you sometimes see
Because baby I don't want to be him.

Catch It If You Can

It was that kind of midafternoon late-summer day when the seagulls would fly in fast from the ocean. They would slow up and lightly drift down onto the baseball fields and the high school track. One after another, little flocks would circle down, eventually painting the green fields almost completely white.

Dad yelled through the wind and across the sound of the boat motor, "Are they dancing?"

If the seagulls were dancing, we would have good weather, but if they all huddled together and just sort of stood there, then bad weather was soon to follow.

Jimmy hollered back to dad, "Yep, I think they're doing the cancan!"

The gulls danced to fool the worms into thinking it was raining. The pitter-patter of their little feet felt like big raindrops to the worms, making them come up to the surface so they wouldn't drown in wet wormholes. Then the seagulls could snap them up.

It only worked when the ground was already wet. I think it was because the worms were already close to the surface and a little jumpy from the last rain. Jarod and I spent a lot of time trying to figure out how to make it fake-rain so we could catch worms for fishing, but we never could.

We were motoring up the river in a small open-topped motorboat. As we sputtered past the dancing gulls, the boat got a bit tippy with four kids, Dad, a full cooler, and a Saint Bernard at the helm. Yeah, the dog was in the driver's seat, and we couldn't get him out. So Dad had to steer from the back of the boat. That was the thing with Saint Bernards. If they were happy to sit still, then you should be happy to let them. Dad said that was our policy, so we stuck to it. Plus, in dog years Busher was old enough to drive, so we should be okay legal-wise.

We motored up the bay past where the gillnetters were hauling in their nets. Dad usually knew everyone we ran into, and these gillnetters knew him too. There was a guy named Otto who said we could stop and get some fish when we motored back by the dock on our way home. Dad said, "Thanks," and had Jimmy toss the man a can of beer. Otto tipped his hat, and we motored farther on up the bay.

We passed cattails and clumps of bunch grass and a beaver lodge that was bigger than a car. Dad said that the beavers lived inside with their entire family. After a lot of begging, Dad let us get out and try to find a baby beaver to take home as a pet. No one was home at the beaver lodge when we got out to look. As Jarod and I stood on the edge of the lodge peering down to where the sticks and branches disappeared into the murk, we thought we saw a swirl in the mud, and maybe a dragon's tail. We froze, held our breath, and waited to see if there were more, but nothing moved.

Dad yelled for us to get back in the boat, and we kept going up the bay past Uncle John Van Horn's place. We waved at the house as if they knew we were passing by, but they didn't. We kept on going and were halfway to where the Wallooskee River pours into Young's Bay. As the tide got lower and lower, the mudflats got bigger and wider, making it possible for us to get close to all the different birds that were still floating in the small pools that dotted the mudflats as far as we could see.

We were counting hawks and fish jumps and great blue herons and birds we called hell-divers, which were really called cormorants, water turkeys, or snake birds. There were horned grebes and non-horned grebes. Grebes do a tango in the spring and were the best-dancing birds we had in the river. They bowed to each other then they danced and danced. At the end of the dance, the grebes stood up on top of the water and ran across the river, for real. There were bufflehead ducks with their beautiful white crests, and loons, always in a pair, speckled with white and brown just like the pictures in the Encyclopedia Gramptanica.

It wasn't long before we saw some ducklings way off in the distance disappear into the cattails.

Jimmy said, "I bet we can catch a baby duck if we find some more!"

Dad said, "You think so?"

Jimmy said, "They can't fly yet. We could catch one for sure!" I noticed he was looking at me when he said the "we" part.

Dad laughed and said, "I'll tell you what. If you can catch one, you can keep it."

Jimmy peeled off his shoes and socks and gave me a look that meant I was supposed to do the same. So, I did. Jarod peeled his off too. Dad had us put on our life jackets and told us to stay in the puddles of water that dotted the mudflats so we wouldn't sink all the way in. We went for another five minutes before we saw something.

Jenni said, "What about a baby crane?"

Jimmy said, "That would be cool."

Jenni pointed up ahead on the mudflats where a family of cranes was standing in a pool of water. The littlest ones were only a foot or so tall. Before Dad could call us off, there was a *splash, sploosh, splash* as the three of us hit the water. Ol' Bush nearly tipped the boat trying to follow, but his leash was wrapped around a bow cleat just in case, you know, he tried to follow us. Jarod got about five steps in, gave me a look that said *Forget this*, and went back to the boat, where Dad scooped him in.

As Jimmy was trying to herd the foot-high chicks in my direction he was screaming, "Go that way! Go that way!"

The mud smelled like rotten eggs and was deeper now, up past our knees. Jimmy got up on a big log that lay across the mud, ran about five steps, and made a wild jump toward the chicks. He landed on his butt and spun out like a turtle on its back. As he went whizzing past me, he covered us both in some of the foulest water we had ever smelled and, unfortunately, tasted. I started to gag, and Dad and Jenni were nearly peeing themselves back in the boat.

Jimmy was still screaming, "Catch one! Catch one!" as the chicks ran past me and off into the distance.

I don't have to tell you how disappointed Jimmy was with my poor performance. He reminded me the whole rest of the day. Before Dad would let us back in the boat, he made us string a rope through our life jackets, and then he stood on the bow and dipped us up and down like tea bags until the mud washed off. The mud came off easy, but the stink did not! We continued to smell like rotten eggs all the way back to the dock and all the way home too.

Dad drove with the windows down. We took turns in the shower when we got back to the house. We were so smelly Dad rubbed tomato juice on us like you do for skunk spray, but he had to stop because it was just too spicy. I'm guessing that was because our tomato juice had the words "Bloody Mary Mix" written on the side. We washed that off too. Then Dad reached up in the medicine cabinet and pulled down a bottle with a sailing ship on the front. He said, "If you're going to stink you might as well stink like men."

He washed us down with a healthy dousing of Old Spice and had us sit on the porch to air out some. After we aired out enough for a car ride, we took the fish we got from Otto back at the dock to an old house with a long driveway. Dad told us to stay in the car, and he took the fish down to the house and left it on the porch. When he got back to the car, we asked why he gave away the fish we just got. He said that the man who lived there had more need of it than we did.

That was about the time the sawmill closed down, so there was more need than jobs. We spent the rest of the afternoon running up on people's porches, leaving fish, and running back to the car. Dad would honk and give a wave, then we would drive off. We asked him why we didn't stay and talk and play with some of the kids we knew. Dad said some of those people wouldn't take the fish if we did. Over the next few summers we would do this with fish, deer meat, and leftover fishing-boat groceries, whenever we could. Back when we lived on Nineteenth Street and were more money poor, we had often come home to find bags of groceries on our porch when we needed them too. I guess this was a way for us to repay that kindness as best we could.

Chapter 7

BGIV

Before the age of ten, I had been kicked, punched, stabbed, impaled, lacerated, knocked cold, and shot, all of which happened while playing the board game Monopoly. So, as you can imagine, family fun night was always approached cautiously and with trepidation, to put it mildly. Of all of us brothers, Jarod was particularly prone to a little-known syndrome called BGIV: Board Game Induced Violence. Jarod had always been the kind of kid who if you pushed too far was likely to bite you. Not so different from Dad's old stray dog Hobo—or a real hobo, when you think about it.

None of us had ever heard of autism at the time, so we just thought that Jarod, like that old dog or an old hobo, from time to time got worms or something and sort of snapped. All of us kids were kind of quirky in one way or another, and I think Grandpa Owen might have been right when he used to say he wasn't sure there was a prize piglet amongst us.

We used our quirks to entertain each other the best we could. Our friend Richie got his foot cut off by the train that runs past the river. When he was over, we would have one-legged or three-legged races, depending on how many kids we could round up. Mom used to say we should celebrate people's differences. We took that to mean that it was okay to make fun of each other as long as everybody got their equal share of being made fun of. If a kid had a lisp, he got to be Daffy Duck when we played Chase Daffy Duck. If a kid was a bed-wetter, he got to be the Swamp Thing when we played Chase the Swamp Thing.

If a kid was, let's say, autistic and my little brother, you could wait until he wasn't expecting it and sneak up behind him. Then you'd shove your thumb into his bellybutton and grab him around the waist with your other hand and hang on tight while counting aloud, "One Mississippi, two Mississippi, three Mississippi, four Mississippi." That way, you could see how long you could ride the bull while he tried to buck you off. We called it the "bellybutton scritch game." To be fair, he played too. It was a great source of pride for whoever was the champ at any given time.

Another game we played was pirates, complete with sword fights. We used Mom's darning needles for swords. That game wasn't played too much after we thought we lost one of the needles, only to find it dangling out of Jarod's right ear.

We played a game called "rock fight." The name sort of says it all. That one ended with my left ear all bloody and another trip to the emergency room. Rock fight was an outdoor game anyways. Since we lived in Astoria, and the word "Astoria" is more or less synonymous with the word "rain," we once again found ourselves stuck inside playing *board* games. Those are the games we played when we were *bored* and our adventuring was called on account of rain. We played Life, Sorry, Yahtzee, and poker with almost half the deck designated as wild cards. We played checkers, Hot Wheels cars, Legos and more Legos, and of course the dreaded Monopoly. Of all the games we played, Monopoly was the most dangerous, followed closely by Legos. Yes, it's true. Monopoly and Legos turned out to be more dangerous than yard darts, BB-gun wars, and a game we called Mumbly Peg, which was throwing knives at each other's feet. Yup, Monopoly was more dangerous than all those games put together.

Lego Warships

When we played Monopoly, Jarod always had to be the banker. When Jarod was the banker, the money was always lined up in perfect little rows. The accounts were always balanced, and everyone was paid on time, every time. He ran that bank like a little seventy-year-old Swiss bank manager. Looking back at it, the order of it all must have appealed to his autistic side. The rest of us were trying to win by hook or crook. We were all okay with stealing a few bucks from the till now and then when Jarod looked away. It wasn't like anyone was going to get hurt. Or would they?

You see, you never knew exactly what was going to set Jarod off, so it was hard to know when we were pushing him too far. Things that might upset other children didn't seem to bother him one bit. He wouldn't even notice you were being sarcastic to him or making fun of him. Whereas moving one of his toys or taking some blocks off his Lego warship could get downright dangerous.

One Saturday afternoon Jarod and I were playing Lego warships in our room. During the battle my warship crashed into Jarod's warship and knocked off one of his Lego cannons. I snatched up the fallen cannon and snapped it onto the deck of my warship. Now my warship had more cannons then his warship.

I proclaimed, "I have more cannons than you, so I win!"

Jarod simply set his warship down on the desk, picked up a long, pointy pair of haircutting scissors, and threw them at my head. In this game of Lego warship, the winner got to explain to Mom why the scissors were sticking through his hand. Then he wound up with the grand prize, stitches.

As we drove to the emergency room, Jarod explained in great detail why the scissors sticking out of my hand were not, in fact, his fault. First he pointed out that taking his cannon was against the Lego warship rules. He carefully explained how the cannon would have sunk all the way to the bottom of the Lego Ocean, so I wouldn't have been able to pick up the cannon even if I wanted to. He also noted that my cannons and his cannons were different kinds of cannons, so my cannonballs wouldn't work in his cannons. He said if I had tried to use the wrong cannonball in either cannon, the cannonball would have jammed in the cannon and caused the cannon to explode, destroying my warship altogether. So no matter what, he would win instead of me. My mother kept driving, sort of shaking her head as we went.

Finally, Mom asked in a calm, steady voice, "Is that why you stuck the scissors in your brother's hand?"

Jarod said, "No, that was his fault too. I threw the scissors at his head, and he blocked it with his hand."

Mom let out a loud sigh and said calmly, "I want you to apologize to your brother." There was a long silence as we drove, then Jarod looked over at me and whispered, "I think she's talking to you."

Mega Leapfrog

Not every game we played ended up in the emergency room. Most times Jarod and I got along like worms in dirt, communicating without speaking, playing and working together in a way only brothers who spend every moment of every day together can. We climbed trees, built forts, and rode our bikes all over the place. Jarod had a large plastic tricycle called a Big Wheel that he used to play Evel Knievel on. Evel Knievel was a super famous stuntman who would jump his motorcycle off or over stuff he probably should not have tried to jump off or over. They say that he broke every bone in his body doing those stunts, so he was totally our kind of hero. Inspired by Evel, we would build bigger and bigger jumps for Jarod. He would tear out on his Big Wheel, pedal furiously up the hill on our block and then, grabbing the hand brake, spin half a cookie in the gravel and come to a stop. Once there, he paused for a moment at the top of the hill and then, like a bat out of hell, raced fearlessly down. We would line up six kids deep behind the ramp. Jarod would come flying over us all—no helmet, no seat belt, just guts, gravel, and glory. He would slam down, grab the hand brake, spin a full three hundred and sixty degrees, and step out of a cloud of dirt like a superhero.

Then he would look back at us and just say, "Higher."

We would keep making the ramp bigger and bigger. Then some adult would come along and stop us and go rat us out to Mom. Once we "borrowed" a section of the neighbor's fence and laid it across our couch, which we had carried out onto the lawn, to create a much bigger ramp. After that time, the neighbors got wise and were quick to call Mom at work whenever they noticed us dragging our furniture outside.

We played other games too. We used to throw a piece of fishing line up and over the old maple tree branch that hung over the intersection at the bottom of our hill. The branch was about ten feet from the stop sign, a prime location for the other neighborhood kids to hide in the woods and egg cars as they passed. We got egged twice there ourselves. I got the idea that we could just tape an egg to the string, then run back up the hill and wait for a car to drive into the egg. What a sight! The drivers would jump out and run around all crazy like, yelling at the invisible kids that they knew were hiding just out of sight. The whole time we would be sitting two blocks away cracking up laughing. We got into a lot of mischief. Grandpa Woods said it was because we were too smart for our own good.

On a crisp, cold Monday morning Mom came running in after hearing the crash of the bedroom window breaking. She rushed into our room to find us still buried under layers of covers. Mom worriedly asked, "What happened?" I told her that Jenni had just opened the door to tell us it was time for school, and since our room heater was broken, it was very cold in our room. It must have been the heat from the other room hitting the cold window that caused the glass to break.

Mom said, "Okay," and we taped some cardboard over the broken window and went off to school. The next day Mom had to go to the emergency room after slicing her hand wide open when she was trying to fix the window. She was breaking out the remaining chunks of glass with a screwdriver when she cut her hand open. She later would tell us that Grandpa Roy had taught her better, and she should have wrapped a towel around her hand for safety. When mom got back from the hospital, we helped her fix the rest of the window and nobody got hurt—oh, except for Mom, of course.

What really happened was that Jarod and I were goofing off instead of getting ready for school like we were supposed to. We decided that we would play tackle to see who could get to the bathroom first. Our game of tackle escalated quickly into a wrestling match, which morphed into a game of mega leapfrog. Mega leapfrog is like normal leapfrog only with a running start and measuring the distance to see who can leap the farthest.

Jarod had put in an impressive leap, landing about a foot short of the toy box that sat in front of our bedroom window. I felt I could outdo that rather impressive jump. So I got some super speed going and shouted like He-Man, "By the Power of Grayskull!" and went for it.

As I sailed past Jarod's mark, I was feeling rather pleased with myself. Then I panicked because I was now sailing past the toy box, and that was bad. With a bang, my head crashed through the window, and suddenly I was staring down at the lawn mower in the backyard. It took a second to pull my head back inside. As I did a big chunk of glass crashed down, nearly making me even shorter than I am today. Jarod and I looked at each other, then we both leapt back under the covers like a couple of guilty prairie dogs, and Mom was none the wiser.

Autism for Jarod

Jarod liked things that were square. I think this was because they fit together so neatly. He liked blocks and Legos and the boxes that blocks and Legos came in, and of course more Legos. He would spend hours in our room making increasingly complex Lego space rockets, tanks, trains, and battleships. He would arrange them in an orderly fashion inside what we would come to call his "Evil Lair."

Jarod's lair was made by the Frigidaire refrigerator company. Maybe it was because its boxes are squarish, too, or because Jarod liked to pretend, he himself was still in mint condition. We don't know for sure, but for whatever reason, from age seven to nine Jarod practically lived in a refrigerator box. Don't get me wrong. He spruced it up with a couple of windows for light, and he placed a neatly folded blanket at one end and even put up some curtains. His little Lego workstation was in the back corner. He even had a little makeshift refrigerator for snacks. It was a pretty snazzy setup except that, being made of cardboard, the lair would sometimes suffer from a bit of wear and tear. The wear and tear it suffered was usually caused by either Jimmy or me roughhousing too close to it. Of course, when this happened, it would be all hands on deck, because Jarod was about to have a complete meltdown. This sent Mom and Jenni driving all over town, at all hours of the day or night, in search of a new lair. Jarod would be freaking out the entire time they were gone. Jimmy and I had to deal with Jarod the best we could. If Mom and Jenni took too long to find another refrigerator box Jimmy and I would have to stick Jarod inside a closet and go watch TV. I once asked Jimmy why we had to put him in the closet when he flipped out like that. Jimmy answered, "We don't *have* to, we *get* to!" It was quieter and seemed to calm him down till Mom got back with another box. Though Jimmy was joking, I think we were both a little worried that Jarod's "differentness" was still getting worse.

There were lots of things that would set Jarod off, and after a while we got pretty good at staying clear of the worst of those things. But every once in a while, something would slip through. Shawn Rossiter's birthday party had, like, a bazillion kids and was filled with lots and lots of noise and a clown that Jarod kept his eye on just in case the clown did any creepy clown stuff.

We all sang "Happy Birthday," ate cake, and played party games. In the backyard there was a big piñata tied to one of eight or nine large pine trees that ran along the forest edge behind the house. All the kids were excited to take their turn and try to break it open and get all the candy. They let the special children go first. That meant Jarod. We didn't have a plastic bat, so instead we used a softball bat that was lying around in the backyard. Jarod put on a blindfold, and we spun him around and around. When you think about it, given Jarod's general level of spasticness, spinning him around and around may have been overkill.

Everybody stood back, way back. Jarod got ready, he wound up, then with a quick snap he whipped the bat up over his head, but the bat didn't stop. It kept going all the way back and swung down hard behind Jarod. It made a loud *ker-slap* as it hit him right in the butt. He dropped the bat and jumped straight up in the air. His feet were already running before he came back down. When he landed, he took off like a shot, screaming out into the forest. Jarod still had the blindfold on as he rocketed off through the trees. Jimmy took off after him. But it was too late. We heard a dull thud off in the distance. That was quickly followed by a loud Jarod yelp, and then he came rocketing back in our direction, still wearing the blindfold. Jimmy tackled him, took off the blindfold, and held on to Jarod until he stopped running. Mom checked Jarod for dents and scratches, and then got him some ice cream so he would calm down.

After the party, Jimmy and I walked down to the Fred Meyer store to see if they had any refrigerator boxes to give us for Jarod. They didn't, but offered to save us one. We said thank you, and went and looked at the pet section and then at the fishing poles.

Jimmy and I were talking about what kind of fishing pole we would buy if we could and were walking out of the store when we heard some lady saying, "Would you care to donate to autism awareness?"

We immediately stopped in our tracks. We looked at each other, both thinking that this was the thing Mom said Jarod had. We slowly walked over to the woman's table and just sort of looked at her for a bit.

She said, "Autism. Get the word out!"

We were both shocked that an adult would do that to those poor kids. She kept talking about it, and we were getting mad at what she was saying.

She said, "Autistic people need your pity."

Then the woman said, "Help make people aware of autism!"

Man, we were getting mad as could be; finally, Jimmy just couldn't take it anymore and yelled, "Jesus Christ, lady, what would you want to do that for? They got it hard enough already!"

The woman was stunned by the comment and replied to us, "Boys, we are trying to help people understand autism."

I said, "Oh, there's no understanding them! You just got to put 'em in a closet sometimes and get 'em a new box!"

She replied, "No, boys, we are providing pamphlets, so people can learn how autism works."

Jimmy took me aside and whispered, "I think she's got the instructions or something. Go wait outside."

I went outside and watched through the glass doors. Jimmy went back inside. When the woman started talking to an old couple, Jimmy made a mad dash for the table. He grabbed a pamphlet and booked back out of the store. He told me to run, so I did. We got away clean. As we walked back home, Jimmy read the instructions while I looked for pond dragons in the ditch. When Jimmy got to the last page, he threw the instructions into the ditch, nearly hitting a frog.

I asked, "Well?"

He shook his head and said, "You've really got to stop wrinkling his Monopoly money!"

Jeremy T. Owen

The Great Jimdini

In the Spring of 1980, we were out of school on break and Jenni, Jimmy, Jarod, and I took the Greyhound bus from Seattle down to Longview, where Dad was supposed to pick us up. Only on this occasion a child or two may have been forgotten at the Greyhound station for an hour, or in this case, six hours. In this era before mobile phones, we were, let's say, given an opportunity to meet the locals and learn how to jimmy open vending machines. In our situation, the term "jimmy" was very appropriate. By the age of thirteen, my brother Jimmy was a bit of an expert when it came to freeing candy and other snacks from their little vending-machine prisons. For most of my childhood, we thought the term "jimmy" meant "without fail" or "smash if necessary," because that's how Jimmy did it. For our part, Jarod and I were the distraction for whatever sort of jimmying needed to be done, be it jimmying toys that we couldn't afford out of the toy store, or feeding ourselves when necessary. Jarod would fake a fall, and I would scream for a Band-Aid while Jarod fake-cried. The key was to cause a big enough scene for everyone to be watching you, but not so big they would kick you out entirely. It was a bit of an art form to get it just right.

The vending machines in those days had knobs that you would pull for each type of candy. If you could manage to pull enough knobs all at once, most of the candy would come tumbling out. The problem we ran into was that it took at least three of us to do it, and Jenni wanted no part of mugging candy machines. Neither did she want any part of creating a distraction with Jarod and me. We had gotten caught quite a few times while liberating the spoils from our local Astoria candy machines. But since no one knew us in this town, we couldn't pass up a chance to take a pull at all that candy, plus we were really hungry.

When we all thought no one was looking, we went for it. Jimmy put in fifty cents. We lined up side by side, spread our fingers out wide, and grabbed three knobs in each hand. Jimmy gave the nod and said, "Now!" We all pulled at once. The candy machine made a *shakunk* sound and then, like the sweetest slot machine ever, all the candy poured out at our feet. We stood there for a second amazed at our good fortune. Sadly, though, what Jimmy had giveth the Greyhound lady tooketh away. As the vending machine spewed out candy like a jackpot in Vegas, the Greyhound lady, with a blue vest and a Greyhound badge, suddenly stepped out of the bathroom and caught us red-handed. Before she could even ask what happened, Jimmy exclaimed, "Wow, it must be broken!" The Greyhound lady, not realizing that we were the ones who broke the machine, gave us two candy bars each and took the rest of it back behind the counter. We headed over and sat with Jenni, ate the candy, and waited some more for Dad.

After several collect calls, Jenni finally got ahold of Auntie Mary Alice, who was going to find our dad or come get us herself if she needed to. Only, that would take an hour if not two, and we were still hungry; two candy bars weren't going to cut it.

Jimmy got an idea and took all the money we had and went over to the all-you-can-eat fish'n'chips restaurant across the street. We watched him as he went. He paid for the all-you-can-eat fish'n'chips meal, then sat there eating for over forty-five minutes straight. Jimmy ordered plate after plate of food, packing it away like you can't believe. He ate so much fish that the waitress began watching him like a hawk to see if maybe he was stealing some. We watched him too. We watched him eat and eat and eat and eat some more. Jimmy ate so much that the rest of us were getting real mad because we were so very hungry. He was supposed to be getting us some food too! We had never seen anybody eat that much fish; neither had the waitress.

Jimmy got up, refilled his drink, smiled, and walked back across the street to the bus station. He gave us the drink. Then he went over and got some paper towels from the bathroom. He spread them out like a picnic blanket on the bench next to us. Then like some kind of magician, The Great Jimdini dealt out pieces of fish like magic cards. While we were staring at the fish, french fries suddenly appeared from nowhere. After that, ketchup and tartar sauce appeared out of thin air, then fish and more fish and even more fish. It was glorious!

I don't think this was how Jesus did it. But it felt like a miracle to us, and it was, by far, the best magic show I have ever seen. The waitress across the street was watching through the window. Jimmy looked over and smiled at her. He might have even given her a wink. She shook her head and had to laugh. When Dad finally showed up, there were still some leftovers for him. We were pretty mad at him since we had to wait so long, though, so we gave him some fish but we didn't save him any french fries.

Chapter 8

A Walk Down to the River

Sometimes when Dad wasn't playing music, he worked at the Gearhart fish cannery weighing the fish that came in on the fishing boats. He had a job there two of the summers we went down to visit him. Mostly because there was no one to watch us, we got to go to work with him for a good part of the first week we were visiting. To keep ourselves busy while Dad worked, we fished with hand lines off the edge of the pier, catching shiners and suckers. That was fun until we ran out of bait or the fish stopped biting. When we got bored we would sleep in the car, or we wandered around and just got into trouble. Dad finally realized that the cannery was too dangerous for three boys to run amuck in, so he asked if we would rather go trout fishing. We thought it was a great idea.

Before work, Dad dropped us off a few miles up the logging road that went up past the Young's River Falls. Dad bought us worms to fish with, but those were almost always gone before noon. After that we were on our own to scratch together whatever we could find to use for bait. That usually meant crawdad tails, periwinkle snails, and caddis-fly larvae.

Jimmy got to use Dad's fishing pole and reel. Jarod and I went Huckleberry Finn-style and used sticks like Dad and Grandpa Owen taught us. The three of us would fish until it started to warm up. Then we would make a bed out of the tall grass that grew alongside the logging roads, or out of ferns down by the river if we found a good spot where there weren't any bugs to bite you. We napped until it got too hot to sleep, or until we got too hungry. Most days Jimmy had built us a fire and had some sort of food ready when we woke. On a good day, we put a can of beans in the fire and had some hot dogs too. Some days we caught cutthroat and cooked them over the fire the way Dad and Grandpa Owen taught us to. On the days we didn't catch fish or bring hot dogs, we went hungry. On those days we ate what we could find—blackberries, crawdads, bullheads. We always talked about eating the snails in the river, but we didn't. We did eat a lamprey eel once; Dad said Indians ate them too. I'll tell you this: those Indians must have had a better recipe than we did, because *Blech!*

After lunch or no lunch, we would walk down the river, fishing as we went. Jimmy always went first. He would say it was to make sure we were safe, but mostly I think it was so Jarod and I didn't scare all the fish away. Some parts of the river were easy to walk, the depth never going up past our knees. Jimmy fished the foam—that's where the bugs floated into pools and streamlets and where the big fish were most likely to bite. Jarod and I fished minnow pools mostly, because we always lost our bait after only two minutes, but minnows would bite on a shiny hook with no bait at all.

Some parts of the river were too deep for wading, and the banks got to be too steep to get past. When we got to those parts of the river, we had to go up and walk along the dirt road for a bit. Most times Jimmy would start up the hill, then have to yell back to us to stop flipping rocks and catch up, saying, "Come on, there ain't no pond dragons here! Sheesh! You two got mudpuppies on the brain!" Mudpuppies are what pond dragons are before they turn into newts and before they go back to the pond and become pond dragons and do battle. They look like polliwogs with frilly gills, and kind of move like goofy puppies. I guess we did have them on our brains, and sometimes in our pockets.

We would run and catch up to Jimmy, who would teach us Dad's fishing song as we walked along the dusty roads. Really, it was a lullaby that dad wrote for us when we were babies, but we were too cool to call it a lullaby now that we were older. Eventually we would come to our favorite spot and stop for a rest. We would lie in the grass and stare up at a massive pine tree with a large hole about forty feet up. It was the Honeybee Tree. We could see the swarm of bees coming and going and the golden honey running down the side. We lay there imagining all the ways we could get to the sweet honey. We took turns guessing how many bees lived up there, if the tree was hollow, and how much of the tree was filled with honey. We would try to find the shapes of any fat and happy honey bears that might be sleeping high up in the treetops. Sometimes we thought we did.

From there we would walk back down to the river and plunge our faces into the ice-cold water to drink, coming up gasping for air. We would lie on the bank and bug Jimmy to sing Dad's fishing song for us for the ten-hundredth time. He would sing it, and Jarod and I would do our best to remember all the words.

My brother sings:

I'm going to walk down to the river
And drop my line right in
Then ain't going nowhere
Don't care where I've just been.

Soaking up the sunshine
Hoping for a fish or two
That's all I ask for
That's all I ever want to do.

Count the shadows on the water
Dream a little dream
Butterflies come flutter by
Riding on a sunbeam.

159

Fish are down there getting hungry
Hope they come my way
But if they don't, I don't care
I'll catch them some other day.

Sun's getting low again
Got to get along
Reel up my line again
Finish up my song.

Be back in the morning
When the world is new
That's all I ask for
All I ever want to do.

That's all I ask for
All I ever want to do.

By three o'clock we were at the falls or walking down the road to where Dad would find us on his way back home to the cathouse.

The Cathouse

Yep, that's right, I said cathouse! For two summers, we lived in a brothel. Only we didn't know what that word meant, and Dad got really mad at the guy who said we lived in one, so we didn't want to ask Dad what one was. We figured it was something like a duplex; it looked like a duplex, only taller. Inside it seemed like an ordinary apartment to us. When we asked Grandpa Owen what a brothel was, he said it was where the rent was cheap but the company wasn't. Uncle Bill said we lived in a cathouse, but we didn't ever find any cats, and we looked and looked.

The ladies upstairs asked us what we were doing rummaging around out back of the place. We told them we were looking for the cats. They thought that was funny. All summer the cat ladies would ask us if we had found any cats yet.

They would laugh when we would say, "Not yet, but we're still looking."

They would giggle and tell us, "Well, maybe when you're older."

Our cathouse place was small; it had only one bedroom, which Dad slept in. We got to crash in sleeping bags on the living room floor in front of the TV. That year Dad got cable. We had never had cable before, so we watched a lot of TV now that we did.

Still, we adventured too. The good part about the brothel was it was conveniently located; from there you could walk to anywhere in town you wanted to, and we did.

When we weren't trying to help the cat ladies find their cats, we headed off down to the docks to fish for whatever was biting. The tuna cannery was a mile down the road, and you could catch all kinds of fish if you could get out to the good spot under the pier where the tuna juice dripped down into the water. Mostly we used hand lines with canned corn for bait. Some days we would sneak into the Bay Shore Hotel on the way to the cannery and ask the cleaning ladies for some little bars of soap. We would cut those up and use them for bait too.

If we caught any good fish, we would bring some to the cleaning ladies on the way back home. There were salmon and trout and sturgeon and smelt and whitefish, but mostly we caught suckers and carp. Most of the time the sea lions were down under the dock with us, and they wouldn't let us keep any of the good fish, even if we did get one on the line. Jimmy would call them "fat blastards" because it rhymed with the word Dad called them. We hated them because they would sit on the floats and wait until we hooked a fish and then take it away from us. The worst part was that they only took the good fish. They would let us pull in all the suckers we wanted. But if we hooked a salmon or a trout, then those fat blastards would just slip off the float, swim over to us, and wait for us to pull the fish right to them so they could take it away. We filled our pockets with rocks and tried to scare them off, but no matter how hard we threw the rocks they didn't care.

Most days the sea lions were a real pain in the butt, taking nearly every fish we caught. Then other days the fat blastards would suddenly disappear altogether. Those were the days when we could catch the good fish if they bit. On the days when there were no sea lions at all we would pull in the fish okay, though something under the water would take some of the good fish even then.

Down on the beach we found a stick that Dad said was used for rolling logs over—he called it a cant hook, but it looked like a sea lion poker to us. The pole had a sharp point on the end and a hook part with another point on the other end. Dad said we weren't

162

supposed to take it, and that we should put it back where we got it, so . . . we didn't. Instead, we drug it out under the dock so we could smack them fat blastards with it when they came to take our good fish. It took some doing, but we got the spear thing out under the dock by tying a rope on the end of the stick part. We sort of found the rope on the beach too. When we got to the good fishing spot, we looped the other end of the rope around the big beam that we were sitting on so that if we dropped the sea lion poker, we could pull it back in again. Then we got ready for the fat blastards.

Because we were at the mouth of the river, the water was kinda salty and the tide went in and out just like on the ocean. When the tide was up high, our feet could touch the water. When the tide was out, the water was sometimes seven feet below us. That day the tide was coming in, so the water was about halfway up. Just like the day before, I hooked a little silver salmon, and just like the day before, the big fat blastard slipped into the water and came over to take it away. Only this time we were ready. When the sea lion got close enough Jimmy let him have it. He poked him right in the butt. The sea lion barked at us for a full minute, and then all at once all of the sea lions disappeared. We yelled at them to keep on going.

It wasn't long before Jimmy got a bite from what had to be a good-size salmon. As he fought to pull the hand line in, he told me to get the stick ready in case the sea lions tried to take the fish. We saw the salmon flash twice as it ran below us, and sure enough, we saw a giant dark shape cruising in after it.

Jimmy yelled, "Harpoon the blastard!"

I threw the stick as hard as I could, only my arm got tangled in the rope. There was a hard jerk and the next thing I knew I was underwater looking up. I was floating right next to the giant dark shape, only it wasn't a sea lion. There was no fur and it was bigger, much

163

bigger! I saw the side fin and tail close-up as it whooshed by, closer than you ever want to see a tail and fin. The tail was almost as big as me! Before I could even start to swim, I felt the rope pull tight and I began to move through the water fast. My arm was still tangled in the rope; I ripped to the surface and tried to take a breath. I could see Jimmy pulling on the rope as hard as he could. My ears were full of water, and Jimmy's voice was muffled. I couldn't tell what he was saying, but he was reaching for my hand and he was scared, maybe more scared than me.

The water was so cold it squished all the air out of me. I couldn't breathe, I couldn't hear, and I couldn't swim. The rope slipped down around my wrist but didn't fall off. Jimmy grabbed my arm and pulled; the water cleared from my ears. Jimmy was screaming, "Climb, climb!"

I took a breath, grabbed the rope, and scrambled up onto the beam. We both climbed as high up as we could and watched the giant shark turn and swim back underneath us. We had seen the movie *Jaws*, so we just knew it was going to jump out of the water and bite us in half at any moment. I was shivering, so Jimmy had to help me climb along the beams as we made our way back to the beach. The whole way, we were holding our breath waiting for the massive shark to jump up out of the water to get us. We left our fish, my coat, and all our fishing gear under the cannery.

When Dad came home, we told him we saw Jaws in the river, and how I almost got eaten and how Jimmy saved me.

He laughed and said, "It was a sturgeon."

We told him it was most definitely a great white shark and not a sturgeon.

He said, "Maybe it was a dogfish."

That was a kind of shark. I told him it was a Great Dane dogfish then, for sure. We didn't tell him

that we were under the dock . . . or about the sea lions
. . . or about not putting the poke stick back . . . or the
stolen rope . . .

or about losing all our fishing gear and my coat.
Dad and Uncle John made fun of us for the rest of that
summer, saying that we watched way too many movies.

For the record, great white sharks and their
slightly smaller cousins, the salmon sharks, have since
been documented many times feeding in the mouth of
the Columbia River on salmon, herring, other small fish,
and oh yeah, the occasional fat blastard!

We decided it would be less dangerous to find something else to go do. So we went back to looking for cats.

Net Weights

Just outside Astoria there is a spot where the Klaskanine River passes under an old bridge on the Olney Cutoff Road. The river, not much more than a creek at times, winds its way along the highway and eventually empties into Young's Bay. For thousands of years salmon and sea-run cutthroat trout have followed along this little path on their way home to spawn and die, passing on the spark of life to generation after generation. It was along this tiny creek that the native Clatsop people set up their gillnets to catch those returning fish. Their nets were woven of handmade twine, fashioned from the inner bark of cedar trees and weighted down with stones. Along this river and many others, they camped, made their nets, and caught these fish generation after generation. We would sometimes find the arrowheads and flint scrapers they left behind as we gathered berries and worms to use as bait to try and catch those same fish ourselves. It was common for us to find other things too. Most common of all was a thing us kids called a net weight. It seemed obvious to us children that they were made by someone long ago, so we would fill our pockets with the hardened pieces of clay to show to Dad and Grandpa Owen for identification.

Grandpa John Charles Owen was an expert on Native American artifacts. You don't find thousands of arrowheads, spear points, beads, bowls, and baskets without becoming an expert. He had many examples of what are commonly called net weights in his collection. Grandpa's net weights were rocks, usually weighing about eight to ten pounds, with a groove carved around the middle. The groove was to keep the braided cedar line from slipping off of the rock. The pieces of hardened clay we hauled back home were small and round or cylinder shaped, with a round or square hole in the center. As kids, we were convinced that these were made by the Clatsop or maybe the Chinook Indians and used as smaller net weights or even fishing-line weights.

Dad went so far as to bring some up to the college to see if the anthropologists there could tell us if they were indeed man-made. We were disappointed when we were told that they were a sort of mud ball that formed naturally around loose branches in the river as they tumbled along the river's bottom during the spring floods. In addition, they assured us that the native peoples from the areas around Astoria never made pottery, so these were surely a natural phenomenon.

Some of these pieces we found were softer and would crumble; others looked to be formed around a twig or a branch. Some were round and much harder, and the center holes were perfectly square. The man from the college told us that they were just old mud balls and nothing special. Only, we still believed they were fishing weights, so that's what we used them for.

Many years later, my best friend Mike Murray wanted to go looking for arrowheads, beads, and rolled pieces of copper like the ones I had shown him at my grandfather's house. We headed out to the old bridge at the Olney Cutoff Road, walked up the creek to the spot where we would find those clay weights as children, and once again there at our feet we found just what we were looking for. I pocketed half a dozen of the neatly formed clay spheres, but this time we only kept the ones with the square holes. I told Mike about how the anthropologist had told us that these were just a sort of mud ball, and we had no way to prove that this was an unknown form of Northwest pottery.

Mike listened to the story and said, "How about a fingerprint? Would that prove who made them?"

I laughed at his joke and said, "Wouldn't that be nice? No one could argue with that."

He said, "No, really, look!"

168

And there in his hand was a clay net weight, round and about the size of a small hen's egg. And as pretty as a picture was a thumb print baked into the clay when it was made hundreds or perhaps thousands of years ago. It was ceramics at its simplest. The holes were square because cedar-wood splits are square. Balls of clay were taken up from the streambed, rolled, slid down onto the cedar splits, and placed in the fire. The wood burned away to ash, leaving a square hole. If the clay didn't heat up too quickly or cool down too fast, you had a perfect little fishing weight. It was as simple as that.

Rocks That Talk

Dad told us lots of stories about looking for arrowheads with Grandpa in eastern Oregon back when he was a kid. I can only remember camping overnight east of the mountains once. It was mid-April, and we went east for the opening day of trout season. We were meeting up with Uncle Dave and some of Dad's friends and their kids to go fishing in what was called a canyon lake. The drive was a long one; we went out past the Cascade Locks, Hood River, and The Dalles. Eventually we turned north, driving through the foothills along the Columbia River basin. This was shrub-steppe desert, the home of whip snakes, yellow-belly racers, horned toads, pygmy rabbits, and owls so small they could fit in your pocket. The dry, sweet smell of sagebrush was everywhere. Tumbleweeds, like in old Western movies, lined the highway. Dad charged at one with the car as it rolled slowly across the road. It exploded into a million toothpicks and blew away like a cloud of smoke behind us.

We stopped a few times along the way for snacks and bathroom breaks. We passed by the Maryhill Museum, and a few miles later we pulled into Horsethief Lake State Park for a break. While he stretched, Dad said that this was where the real desert began.

It was a little bit before noon, so Dad grabbed the greasy paper bag out of the backseat that held the cans of pop and some deer jerky and our peanut butter and jelly sandwiches. We all walked down to where the train tracks ran along the water. Dad wanted to show us the petroglyphs on the rocks overlooking the river. We had heard the story of how when Dad was a boy his picture was in the paper for finding petroglyphs in a village near Sitka, Alaska. We had never seen

170

petroglyphs for ourselves, so we were really excited to see these.

Dad pointed out a few faces and some shapes. He explained how they were markers and how they told stories of the people from this place. We were looking at them when we noticed a couple having a picnic just below the largest painting. Being kids, without a thought we barged past them, ruining their romantic moment, I'm sure. Our attention quickly moved to a Western fence lizard showing off on the rocks down close to the water. He was doing little push-ups and flashing his sky-blue chest for the other lizards to see. Jimmy nearly stepped on the couple's picnic basket as he made a mad dash to try and catch the lizard.

Dad called him off and said, "Let's go eat over here," mostly to give the couple back their picnic. A bit farther down a little trail, we sat on the rocks overlooking the river and ate our lunch. With full bellies, we spent the next ten minutes chasing little gray side-blotched lizards back and forth along the railroad tracks. The lizards were too fast for us to catch, and it was getting hot out, so we made our way back up toward the spot where the couple was still sitting. We hopped down from the rocks and walked back up the same path we had come down.

Having only gone a few steps, Dad stopped short and held his hand up, signaling us to hold up, so we did. Dad had done this before in the past. It usually meant there was a deer or a rabbit or some other creature he didn't want us to scare, so that we could get a good look at it. He pointed to the path just up ahead. There, next to a boulder, was a snake lying out in the open. I didn't recognize it as anything I had ever seen before. This snake looked dry, dusty, and rough. It had a wide, flat head, and it was much fatter than any snake I had ever seen.

Dad said, in a stern, calm voice, "Stay back!"

Then we saw the rattle!

The couple noticed our abrupt stop and heard Dad's tone of voice. The man stood up to come see what we were looking at. When he got close, his movement spooked the snake, causing it to let go with a *National Geographic* rendition of a rattlesnake sound. It was a *shhushshhuhh* kind of sizzle-buzzing sound, followed by the equally startling and cinematic high-pitched scream of the woman who had been trying to enjoy her picnic just a few moments before. After the scream, the woman started to climb onto the shoulders of the poor man she was picnicking with. The man was struggling to hold her up, because the woman was kinda plump and the man was kinda toothpicky. He was trying to gather the picnic blanket and stuff with the woman riding on top of him.

She started screaming, "Leave it! Just leave it!" and the poor guy went staggering off toward the parking lot with the woman still riding up on his shoulders the whole way. All the movement made the snake coil up; it held its tail high and was rattling even louder, when about two-thirds of its rattle snapped off and landed on the path at our feet. We all backed up a few steps. Then after a minute or two the snake calmed down and crawled across the path and down over the railroad tracks, disappearing near the river's edge. We picked up the piece of rattle and Dad showed us how each segment fit together and how fragile it really was.

We could see how the rattle had worn all the way through near the end from dragging on the ground behind the snake. We all headed back up to the car, passing the man we'd seen earlier, who was heading back down to get his picnic stuff. Dad gave him a nod. The man smiled and shook his head. Dad and the man started laughing. Then we all started laughing.

We got back to the parking lot, where the lady was hiding in the car. We loaded back into the station wagon and turned out onto the highway. As we drove, we took turns looking at the rattle. One of us would give it a little shake and the others would pretend to be the lady screaming and climb over the back seat. We laughed and laughed the whole rest of the way.

We arrived at the lake three hours later. It was a canyon lake, and it seemed like the surface of Mars compared to the waterfalls, ferns, and evergreen trees back home. All the rocks were red and brown; there were no trees anywhere, just lake, desert, and rocks. It wasn't long before we saw some fish jump and people reeling in their dinner. We grabbed some poles and headed down to the water's edge while Dad set up the camp. For dinner every one of us caught a fish or two, but mostly we ate hot dogs and chips.

As the sun got lower, it was starting to get cold. I never knew that deserts could be cold, but Dad said it would get really cold at night. After dinner he took us for a walk down along the beach. He picked up a small rock that was smooth and hard, not crumbly like most of the lava rocks around us, and told us to go find smooth boulders about the size of a small cantaloupe. When we found one, we were supposed to bring it back to him.

As we ran off in all directions Dad yelled, "We're looking for rocks that talk back. Oh, and remember to roll them over with your feet before you pick them up, so you don't get bit by snakes or scorpions!"

I looked at Jimmy and said, "Scorpions?"

Jimmy said, "I think he's joking."

Dad wasn't joking about the talking rocks. Each rock we brought back to him, he would look it over and say, "Let's see if it has a voice." Then Dad hit each stone with the small, hard rock. If it made a *clackack* instead of a knock sound he would say, "Run that one back up and set it by the fire."

We did this until we had two rocks apiece. Then we went back to fishing and looking for fireflies and praying mantises. Dad sat by the fire with Uncle David, who was not really an uncle but a friend he knew from the drum and bugle corps when he was our age. Dad placed our rocks around the fire in a ring about a foot

175

away from the flames. Every ten minutes or so he would roll the rocks over with his feet, slowly turning each one. Uncle David asked him what the rocks were for.

Dad would only say, "You'll see."

After dark Dad got out his guitar, and we all sang songs around the campfire. Dad knew thousands of songs and wrote some too. One of our favorites that Dad wrote was called "Don't Let Your Finger Go." Feel free to sing along.

When I was a little boy
My daddy said to me
There are things you shouldn't do
Past the age of three.
I said to my daddy
Just what can they be?
And these are the very words my daddy
    said to me:

Don't let your finger go
Where your finger wants to go
If it starts to creep on up
You must tell it no!
Get yourself a tissue
And either wipe or blow
But don't let your finger go
Where your finger wants to go.

I looked at my daddy
And I said I understand
I took my finger out of my nose
And I went and washed my hands.
I promised him to try and be
A better little man
Then my daddy smiled and said
That sounds like a plan.

The Polliwog Fields

Don't let your finger go
Where your finger wants to go
If it starts to creep on up
You must tell it no!
Get yourself a tissue
And either wipe or blow
But don't let your finger go
Where your finger wants to go.

I went off to school
At the ripe old age of five
I'd seen some things and I've done some
*   things*
And I was feeling pretty wise.
There I met some children who much to
*   my surprise*
Hadn't learned that lesson
So I opened up their eyes.

I said,

Don't let your finger go
Where your finger wants to go
If it starts to creep on up
You must tell it no!
Get yourself a tissue
And then either wipe or blow
But don't let your finger go
Where your finger wants to go.

My daddy had to pick me up
And drive me home from school
'Cause I made the teacher cry
And that was against the rules.
When Daddy asked me what I did
I said I didn't know
I just said what you told me to

When the teacher picked her nose.

I yelled,

Don't let your finger go
Where your finger wants to go
If it starts to creep on up
You must tell it no!
Get yourself a tissue
And either wipe or blow
But don't let your finger go
Where your finger wants to go.

We laid out our sleeping bags in the back of the station wagon and in a small tent beside the car. Dad took a stack of beach towels and some old pillowcases from the car and set them on the chair next to the fire. He used a stick to roll each of the stones out of the fire pit onto a towel, then wrapped it up tightly. He placed each bundle in a pillowcase, spun it shut, and tied a loose knot at the top. We checked each bundle after ten minutes to make sure they weren't too hot. We each got two bundles. We tucked one into the bottom of our sleeping bag, and we hugged the other one like a teddy bear. We drifted off amid the sound of humming insects, nighthawks, and spadefoot toads.

The next morning Uncle David and all the other campers were complaining of the cold night. Dad gave us a wink and told us to put our rocks back by the fire. The rocks were still toasty warm, and we held them in our laps while we drank morning cocoa and waited for Dad to make breakfast. When we were done eating, we went out to look for pond dragons. Dad said we would more likely find tiger salamanders there. That was okay—anything with the word "tiger" in it was okay with us. As we hunted for the tigers, we showed the other kids, and Uncle Dave, how to find the rocks that talked back, and placed them back by the fire so they could be warm too.

Forest Smoke

When we got back to Astoria we still wanted to be camping, so we had Dad drop us off at Grandma Bea and Grandpa Roy's house out in the woods. After we ate lunch, we all got geared up and headed out into the forest to build a fort. Ricko and Jimmy grabbed Grandpa's shovel and bow saw. Matt and Mike had a hatchet and a big hammer. Shani and Badi grabbed their Darth Vader-shaped Star Wars action-figures box, which was complete minus Boba Fett, who had been lost in the high grass never to be found again. Jarod and I got Grandma's pruning shears and a small army shovel that you could chop with. We all headed up the hill like a pack of dwarfs decked out in bell-bottom pants and rubber boots.

The plan was to make a fern fort and camp out overnight when we got it done. The forest we played in was covered with sword ferns and wood-sorrel shamrocks. Sword ferns were great for making forts because they were easy to gather, and they were everywhere. We would go find lots of widow-maker branches that had fallen from large trees in the windstorms. We stuck their fat ends in the ground to form a circle all around a small tree. After gathering willow branches from down by the marsh, we would weave and bend the willow sticks in and out and around the widow-makers. We would poke the ferns in between the willow sticks to make shingles. Starting from the bottom, we would eventually cover the whole thing. It was a cool way to make a fort. It took a long time and a lot of ferns to do it, though. This meant the younger kids were always on fern detail, cutting or pulling ferns and stacking them next to where Jimmy, Matt, Mike, and Ricko were ready to put them to use.

We got the fort about halfway done and stopped to have some snacks. Most everybody was hanging out over by the fort. I sat down on a clump of ferns and started to pull at them while I munched on my animal crackers. Four or five sharp tugs later a large piece of the fern pulled loose from between my legs and flew off over my head. Dirt flipped up into my hair, ears, and eyes, and down the back of my shirt too. I looked down to try and blink the dirt out of my eyes. That's when a strange cloud of smoke began to pour out of the ground. It was thick and black and made a roaring, screaming sound as it went. The sound filled the whole forest. The smoke rose higher and higher, paused for a minute, then lashed out. It got Ricko first. When he moved, the smoke went right for him. It was alive somehow. It knocked him back over the log he was sitting on, and he screamed as he rolled on the ground and then began to run from it. It got the rest of them in quick order. Mikey, Matty, Jarod, Badi, and Shani were all screaming. Jimmy yelled something, and everybody began to scatter.

I froze, and just sat watching the smoke pour out from between my legs, trying to figure out what the smoke was exactly. I could hear the yells growing quieter off in the distance as everybody scattered in all directions. The smoke slowed, then stopped. The angry sound faded back into the quiet of the forest. With the quiet came the realization that I was now very much alone. Alone in a forest that just moments ago felt warm and inviting. Now it seemed darker and somehow farther away from Grandma's house than it was when I got there.

I wasn't lost, I was just alone . . . alone in a place where I was now thinking about the bears, cougars, coyotes, and worst of all, the screaming smoke. I stood up and began to walk through the woods, trying not to be afraid as I went. Trying my best not to draw attention to myself, trying not to bump or tickle the web of whatever monster it was that we had just awoken.

I carefully placed each step so as not to snap a branch or crunch a leaf or draw any attention. I held my breath and told my legs not to run. Slowly, I made my way to the abandoned road leading down to Grandma's house. I saw Jimmy's sweatshirt flung over the blackberry bushes on the side of the road, covered in dirt and crawling with bugs. I kept walking. I was close enough to see the house now. Dad and Uncle Jim were running hard up the hill toward me. They were calling for me. I yelled, "I'm here!" Dad ran over, scooped me up, and started taking off my shirt, and my shoes, and my pants. Uncle was checking me too. Dad's voice sounded funny and made a cracking sound I hadn't heard before.

He said, "Are you okay? Are you hurt? Are you okay?"

I told him I was okay. Then I put my pants back on. Dad carried me down to the house.

The other boys were out on the porch in their underwear. Grandma and Aunties Teri and Jerry were mixing up bowls of baking soda in water and putting a thick paste on Jimmy, Mikey, Matty, and Ricko. Grandpa Roy was heating up the Libradol; that was a kind of muddy looking plastic goo mixed with lobelia, ginger, and other plants and stuff. Grandpa used it to make a poultice that made slivers come out and other things heal up quick.

Jimmy had been stung thirty-one times by the smoke.

You see, the forest smoke had turned out to be thousands of ground hornets. Mikey and Ricko got close to thirty stings each; the smaller kids escaped with a handful of stings apiece. Because I sat perfectly still and never moved until the hornets were gone, I wasn't stung at all. We didn't ever go back to finish the fort or even to that part of the forest again. It seemed darker and farther away from home, a place where monsters lived and were best left alone.

The Siren's Call

If there was even the smallest possibility that we boys would be required to be somewhere nicely dressed, as soon as our good clothes were on we would suddenly and inexplicably be drawn by the call of the sea siren. Our siren wasn't actually calling us to the sea; instead, our siren called us to the nearest smelly, muddy, nasty thing we could find. Once there, we would be forced to run amuck! And amuck and through the muck we did run. We were well versed in mucking. We ran amuck, jogged amuck, skipped amuck; there were times when we even rolled amuck. Although exactly how much muck we could muck was always much more muck than we should muck. And it was all that muck better when we did so dressed in our Sunday best.

Now, I don't remember why we were all dressed up, or where it was that we were going looking so fancy. However, I do remember the lecture we got from Uncle Dale about not getting dirty before we had to go to wherever it was that we were all dressed up to be going to. I had on a white shirt, black pants, and shiny black shoes. Jimmy and Jarod were clothed exactly the same. Shani and Badi wore little bow ties and short pants and shiny shoes.

It was taking forever for the adults to get ready. We all pleaded and pleaded to be able to go out and play while we waited. After ten minutes of professional-level whining, Uncle Dale finally caved in and let us play with Shani and Badi's new walkie-talkies.

Uncle said, "After all, how dirty can kids get playing with walkie-talkies?"

I think the siren took that as some sort of personal challenge. We took turns talking the way people on the radio do, saying "Roger" and "Over" after everything we said. We each made up our own CB radio names like in the movie *Smokey and the Bandit*. Jimmy was Rock Star 'cause he was always singing and 'cause he was so cool. Shani was Boba Fett because he was always whining about losing his Boba Fett action figure in the tall grass, Badi went with Speed Racer because he was real fast, I was Bullfrog because I was always Bullfrog, and Jarod was The Supreme Ruler of Everything.

We tried to explain to Jarod that CB names were mostly shorter than that, but Jarod, being Jarod, insisted. So we went along with it. Rock Star and Boba Fett took one walkie-talkie and walked down the gravel driveway out toward the road.

We heard *chshhhhht* "This is Rock Star; we are at the mailbox checking for the mail. Can you hear us? Over."

Jarod pushed the button on the radio and said, "This is The Supreme Ruler of Everything. We can hear you. Roger. Over."

We heard "This is Boba Fett; you're not doing it right. 'Roger' means 'okay,' and 'over' means 'over.' Over."

We heard *chshhhhht*. Then the Supreme Ruler of Everything went on a ten-minute rant about how "over" meant "finished" and "roger" meant "received," Nikola Tesla, some French guy named Marconi, and how the words were based on Morse code. He was still talking and holding the radio button down the whole time as Rock Star and Boba Fett walked all the way back up from the mailbox.

Rock Star snatched the radio from The Supreme Ruler of Everything (who was still talking even though we were all standing right there) and said, "Yeah, we got it!"

He tossed the radio over to Speed Racer and said, "Let's see if we can hear each other talk from across the river."

Speed Racer, The Supreme Ruler of Everything, and I headed out over the Wallooskee bridge with our radio. When we got to the other side, we could see Boba Fett and Rock Star looking over the edge of the bridge into the mudflats below. They were just standing there looking at the mud. We keyed our radio and said all the CB talk we knew. We "Over"ed, we "Out"ed, we "Ten-Four"ed, we even sang some verses from the movie *Convoy*, but no one answered. We waved back across the bridge at Boba Fett and Rock Star, who shrugged and pointed over the side of the bridge. Then Boba Fett started jumping around like he was really mad. He must have said something to Rock Star, because they started to pretend they were choking each other until Rock Star got annoyed, picked up Boba Fett, and threatened to put him over the side of the bridge. We all ran back across to find out why Boba Fett was about to go swimming.

Turns out there was a dispute over whose turn it was to man the walkie-talkie. In the scuffle, Rock Star said, the radio went off the side and landed down in the mudflats below. The Supreme Ruler of Everything interrupted and said, "Over."

We all ignored him and kept talking. Then he interrupted again and said, "Over." Rock Star said, "Shut up, we're not doing that now!" The Supreme Ruler of Everything said, "Over, don't you get it? Over. The radio went *over* the side of the bridge, not *off*. You know, because it's a radio. That's funny, right, guys? Over." Boba Fett freaked out and started choking The Supreme Ruler of Everything, only for real.

Rock Star pulled them apart and said, "Look, we got to get the radio back. There's a dead tree down there. We can walk out on to it and reach the radio with a stick, okay?"

Rock Star and Speed Racer went down below to rescue the radio while the rest of us stayed up on the bridge so we could tell them where to go. Rock Star found a long branch on their way down to the water, then stepped onto the tree. He got about six feet out, only the fallen tree started to sink a bit and he had to back off. We were going to need someone lighter to make the rescue. Speed Racer was volunteered; he made a very shaky trek out on the tree holding on to some of the half-broken and rotting branches as he went. When Speed Racer got close, we all yelled, "Far enough!"

Rock Star said, "Ready? On the count of three." He motioned to Speed Racer to catch the branch he was about to throw. "One, two, three!" Rock Star let the branch fly. Speed panicked, realizing only as the branch was flying at his head that he would have to let go of the tree to catch it. But Speed froze. The branch smacked him right between the eyes and knocked him straight into the mud. Of course, we all started to laugh until it became clear that Speed was now sinking in the mud. He grabbed the radio and tried to make it back to the tree, but the more he struggled the deeper he sank. A look of panic came over him as the water started filling in all around him. We were now done playing radio.

Jimmy ran out on the fallen tree but couldn't reach Badi. Shani and Jarod ran back to the house to get help. I ran down below. Jimmy jumped into the mud and got ahold of Badi, but now they were both too far from the log to get back in. Jimmy yelled at me, "Get the stick!"

I made my way out to the end of the tree, which was by now a foot deeper underwater than before. The stick was still floating there, half caught in the branches.

185

I grabbed it and made my way back to where Jimmy and Badi were slowly sinking away. I flopped the stick out to Jimmy and held tight to both the tree and the stick. Jimmy tried to pull both of them over to the log, but it was no use; I couldn't hold on to the stick, I wasn't strong enough. Jimmy looked at me in a way that I knew we were in big trouble. He grabbed Badi and pushed him up onto the top of the mud and slid him over toward the tree. Badi grabbed the stick and pulled hard as Jimmy pushed. That worked,

Badi slid across the top of the mud over to the tree, only that made Jimmy slip deeper. Badi crawled back down the log to the shore and ran for help. Jimmy said, "Grab hold of the tree and lock your hands! Lie flat and give me your legs!"

I did. Jimmy got ahold of my foot and started to pull. His voice was starting to shake. "You can't let go!"

I said, "I know. I know. I won't let go. I promise!" Jimmy pushed the stick deep into the mud and pulled hard on my legs. It hurt, and I could hear my back crack. Jimmy heard it, too, and felt the popping as I cracked. He backed off and tried not to pull so hard.

I was crying a little and shaking. I yelled at him, "You pull like an old lady!" He knew I meant that I could take it. Both of us started pulling as hard as we could. The mud slowly began to let go, and Jimmy slid over to the tree and grabbed hold. We drug ourselves back down along the log and pulled ourselves up onto the shore. We sat up against the part of the fallen tree that was on the bank. Breathing too hard to talk, we both sat and cried for a minute until we heard people coming. Then we looked at each other and started laughing.

Jimmy said, "Hey, you got a little something on your cheek." And he rubbed mud on my whole face.

I said, "Yeah, I think you stepped in something."

We slopped our way back up to Grandma's house and met Uncle Dale as he came running toward us with a rope to pull Jimmy out of the mud. Uncle was mad; he was so mad that he expanded our vocabulary and then had to apologize to us for the expansion, even though we were the ones in trouble. Later, Mom told us that Uncle was very scared for us, and sometimes when people are that scared, they get mad and say things they shouldn't. We lined up in the driveway, and man, were we a sorry sight. Jimmy, Badi, and I were super-stinky mud monsters from head to toe. Jarod and Shani were mud Dalmatians and only a little stinky.

Uncle took the hose to us, and we were supposed to feel bad about what we did. Only, Jimmy kept saying, "Psst, hey man, you fart?" and we would start laughing.

At times, Jimmy could make people laugh so hard they would wet themselves for real. Uncle started squirting us in the heads because Jimmy kept making jokes and was pretending to talk like Uncle, saying, "How dirty can you get playing with walkie-talkies?" Then Jimmy said, "Tell him what he's won, Don Pardo." Jimmy started dancing around and the rest of us just lost it, cracking up laughing.

We all copied Jimmy, asking, "Psst, hey man, who farted?"

Uncle lost it. He started laughing so hard he had to run into the house to pee. We took turns hosing each other off and had to wear our play clothes to go to wherever it was we were going. When we got there, we all had to stay outside because we stank like rotten eggs. Sitting there quietly on the stairs waiting to go home, every once in a while, one of us would say, "Psst, hey man,   did   you   fart?"

Chapter 9

The Rubber Boa

The next day we still needed some time to air out, so we were encouraged to go play outside. It was hot out, so cousin Carrie drove us out to the lake where there was a fishing dock and a place to clean the fish you caught. We all ran out onto the dock to see if people were fishing or catching. They were mostly just fishing. There was an old guy over at the cleaning station cleaning the fish he caught earlier. Something was moving around at his feet as he cleaned his fish; it was a small black snake. We had seen many kinds of snakes as kids and called them by many names, names that mostly we made up on our own. If the snake was a fast one, we called it a racer. If it was fat, we called it a king snake. If it had checkers, we called it a bull snake, and if it had lots of red, we thought it was poisonous. It turned out they were almost always one of the three varieties of garter snake that lived on the coast—the common, the Western, or the Northwestern. They're called garter snakes, not garden snakes. They're supposed to be like a lady's fancy garter on her leg, though they're sometimes seen in the garden, where they eat slugs. They're helpful, friendly, and only smelly if you scare them.

We called the snake we saw by the man a bull snake because it was so fat. It had gotten so fat because it was eating the fish guts that the old man was dropping as he cleaned his fish. Then we saw two more snakes over by a log. We snatched them up and put them in our bucket. We were having an intense discussion about the kind of snakes we were dealing with—bull, king, or racer—when the old man asked us what we were going to do with the snakes. We told him we just liked to catch 'em, play with them, and put them back in the same spot where we found them. We told him how our Grandpa Roy taught us to always put back any boards or logs we turned over because that was some creature's house, and you wouldn't want someone to ruin your house.

The old man nodded and said he knew our grandpa and how Grandpa Roy was a hero and all, and that we should say hello for him. The old man said he used to be a game warden and knew lots about snakes and frogs and things. He was the one who told us about garden snakes being garter snakes and not the name we called them by. He told us of a creature called the Pacific giant salamander that could get as big as a boy's forearm and could eat mice if it wanted to.

Then he told us a whopper.

That's what Grandpa called it when we said stuff that wasn't one hundred percent truthful. This whopper broke my brain. You see, the old man said something funny.

He said, "You see, boys, on the rarest of occasions, things aren't where things are supposed to be, and those very things aren't always what they seem to be." And he gave us a wink.

Johnny Cash sang "Ring of Fire," "A Boy Named Sue," and my favorite Johnny Cash song of all, "I'm Being Swallowed by a Boa Constrictor." What the man told us next just couldn't have been true. He told us that there were real boas that lived in our forests here in the Pacific Northwest. They had two heads, they were bright green or sometimes brown. He said they were small snakes that looked like they were made of shiny rubber. How they were true boas, so they gave birth to live babies, and the babies were just as pink as pink could be. We thought he was pulling our legs, but he said that you could wear the small ones like a

189

wristwatch, only he joked that they didn't tell time. He was a nice man, so we didn't call him a liar or anything.

When we got back home, we asked Grandpa Roy if he knew the man, and if he was telling us a whopper. Grandpa told us that he did know the man and that if he said it, it was true.

We would talk about and look for these mythical boas for the next ten years of our lives without success.

On a hot August morning the year I was seventeen years old, my buddy Mike Murray and I drove for two hours to a spot down along the Yakima River. We had gone looking for rubber boas many, many times over the years, in various locations around the Northwest. Each time we came home empty-handed. That's not true; twice we came home with poison oak!

That day would be different. That day Mike and I would flip, roll, and turn over half the valley. It seemed all that was left to look under or in was a fallen pine tree whose massive trunk was as tall as we were. When I started toward the great tree, Mike just laughed at me.

Mike said, "There is no way there's a rubber boa in that log!"

I smiled and replied, "Well, they got to be somewhere."

We both grabbed ahold of a big piece of the bark covering the fallen giant and pulled hard. After a moment, the large slab of bark cracked free. Along with the smell of pine and chunks of bark, out tumbled an emerald-green jewel, a boa with two heads! Its tail was fat and thick just like a head. It held its tail up as if it was going to strike us with it.

All those years later, and it was true. All of it was true, just like the old man had said so many years before! In the fall, I even wore the little snake like a wristwatch to English class. Sorry, Mrs. Arnold. She was a good sport about the little snake, though; it was the five-foot-long Red-tailed boa constrictor in my backpack that she didn't like. Then at the end of summer the rubber boa gave birth, and sure enough out came four live babies, pink as pink lemonade.

The magic kept going, because I got to know these creatures very well. It's a fact that few snakes make noise other than a hiss. There are rattlesnakes that rattle, and some snakes rub their scales against each other to make noise. Rubber boas specifically *charina bottae* do something too. They make a noise I have heard no other snake make: they grind their teeth. They grind their teeth and make a high-frequency clicking sound when attacked or bothered too much. They are special, and were the most amazing find Mike and I ever made.

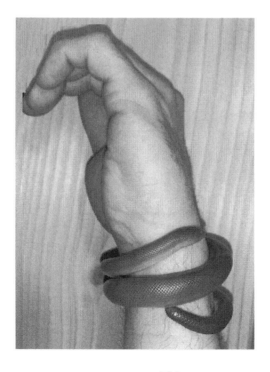

A Pony for Mom

The house Mom and us kids moved into after the divorce was a nice enough little rambler on a nice little street where all the yards looked nice and the neighbors were judgmental. Did I say all the houses looked nice? Okay, maybe our house could have used a good lawn mower. By that I mean someone to push the old lawn mower we had. Our front lawn was a tiny patch of grass, twenty-five feet by twenty feet maybe. There was a small red-plum tree in the center of the lawn about as big around as your wrist. You couldn't climb the tree and there were no plums, so the little tree was mostly just ignored along with the grass.

We were supposed to cut the grass and take out the garbage and clean our room and do our dishes and play nice with each other and not tease our sister. In other words, have no fun. There was also a never-ending chore list for each of us to complete. My poor mother must have spent a good part of her twenties creating chore charts and graphs explaining in great detail the hows and whens of the chores we were supposed to do. We could earn blue stars and silver stars and red stars and gold stars. There may have even been a star for remembering to lift the toilet seat. I don't remember. Each chart worked for a week or so until Jarod got more stars than Jimmy and me put together. We would steal some of his stars just to put him in his place or just to watch him lose it.

Rather than just do our chores, we would put in five times the amount of effort trying to figure out a way to avoid them completely. Bribery worked at first, and we got Jarod to do a bunch of our chores, but as soon as Jarod realized he wasn't getting the star count for doing our chores as well as his own, that went out the window.

The front lawn was small, but the back lawn was a big one and the longer we avoided mowing it, the taller the grass grew. Soon it was up to our knees, making the lawn mower bog down every three feet. This resulted in a very sad lawn that looked like it had tried to cut its own hair. After ten minutes of trying, we abandoned the lawn mower in favor of going on an adventure. This adventure took us past all the neighborhood houses and down to where there were still farms and fields.

We would often stop by the hippie farm to say hi and get a carrot. We called it the hippie farm because hippies lived there, and they would let us do whatever we wanted. They had a giant red rooster who was not a hippie at all. He was a mean rooster who would peck and spur you whenever he could. If we helped the hippies out a little, we could eat vegetables from the garden and ride their horses if we could catch one. When I say ride the horses, I mean we would lure the horses over to the far end of the pasture with carrots, sit up on the fence, and when a horse got close enough, jump on its back.

These horses did not like to be ridden, so they would take off for the barn and try to scrape us off on the doorway if they could. So you had to jump off before they made it there. We would ride the horses until one of us got hurt or the horses wouldn't fall for it anymore. They also had a pony there too. His name was Red, and Red was a mean pony. Not as mean as the rooster, but mean just the same.

When we got to the hippie farm, we went to get a drink out of the hose. Jimmy started talking to Mippie about our lawn mowing problem. Mippie was skinny as a rail, with long blond hair in a braid that hung over his shoulder. He was a funny guy. The first time we went to talk to him we were selling candy for our school. We had a little script card that we were supposed to read from. It was Jarod's turn to talk when we knocked on the farmhouse door. Jarod took a deep breath, held the card up, and said, "Good afternoon, Mr. Hippie. We are selling chocolate bars to raise money for school."

The man laughed hard and smiled. He said, "Mr. Hippie? Well, little man, you can call me Mippie!"

He told us that they didn't eat candy, but he gave us a dollar to help the cause. He gave us some carrots for the cause too.

Jarod and I ran and got some apples while Jimmy was talking to Mippie about the lawn mowing problem and how we couldn't get the push mower to cut the tall grass. That's when Mippie said, "That's the problem with mechanic-ery, what you need is a tried-and-true organic grass cutter. I have just the thing. . . ."

By the time Mom got home we had already come back from Mippie's and installed our new lawn mower. She pulled into the driveway, parked the car, and just sat there staring at it. We peeked out the window to see what she was doing. We couldn't tell if Mom was laughing or crying. After a minute or two, she stepped out of the car and just stood there looking at old Red, the mean pony. We had tied Red to that scrawny little plum tree, and he was just munching away on our lawn problem. We did our best to explain that the pony was better than a lawn mower, about how mechanic-ery was all unreliable, and that we could keep the pony if we wanted to. Sadly, Mom didn't even let Red finish mowing before she made us take him back to the hippie farm. I even cried, saying, "But he's a gift for you!"

Mippie said he understood and welcomed old Red back home. Two days later, Mom found the chickens we had been hiding in the backyard, and they went back to Mippie too. Mippie said, "Sometimes it's just too hard to fight the establishment."

Mutual of Astori-ha

Boys will be boys, and being boys, we liked boy things. Over the years, we drug home nearly every kind of creature you can imagine. Here is the short list: spiders, snakes, chickens, ducks, lizards, squirrels, salamanders, chinchillas, ferrets, two emus, one pony, a mess of catfish and some largemouth bass that we put in our neighbor Dennis's goldfish pond (sorry, Mr. Rogers), three bushy-tailed wood rats, an octopus named Barnacle Bill, a half dozen geckos, six kinds of tortoises, four kinds of terrapins (look it up), three five-gallon buckets of minnows, two crows, some pigeons, half a dozen quail, praying mantises (about five hundred or so when they hatched), hermit crabs (both land and sea), sea monkeys of course, a cigarette-eating goat we named Charlie, an oscar fish named Oscar, grasshopper mice, pocket gophers, voles, shrews . . . oh, and cats, dogs, gerbils, rats, mice, hamsters—a lot of hamsters—a mess of frogs, and let's not forget, about three million polliwogs.

Of all the creatures that stood out and or got out, Chester was at the top of the list. Dad's friend Mark raised homing pigeons. They were the racing kind of homing pigeons, to be exact. When Dad first told us about how the pigeons raced, I imagined the pigeons on the starting line flying around little tracks and through hoops and stuff. Dad, being a bit of a history buff, also told us how they were used in World War I. So after that I instead pictured them with little doughboy helmets and tiny rifles.

Dad had gone to work with his brothers John and Chucky on a rusty old boat called the *Mitkov*. It was a trawler boat, the same kind as most of the boats in Astoria. Dad had just come in off the water and was on his way home. As he often did, Dad stopped in to drop some fish off at his friend Mark's house, where he usually visited for a while. But not this time. This time was different.

When dad got home from Mark's, he had his coat bundled up under his arm and a big smile on his face. As he came through the front door he said, "You two grab some old newspapers!" So we did. Jarod and I got armfuls of newspapers from the recycling and followed Dad down the hall, around the corner, and into our bedroom. He told us to spread the papers on the floor in front of the bookcase, so we did that too. Dad told Jimmy to run and bring in the coat rack from the living room. We set it up on the newspapers. Dad had us sit on the bed and then, rather ceremoniously, he unwrapped the bundled-up coat.

With the sly grin of a madman, Dad threw the coat open, and as he did, he uttered the words, "Boys, meet Chester."

A pair of massive wings began to beat as the great bird rose up into the air. There was a flash of red feathers and the steely glint of black talons as it moved across the room. Its beak was pale yellow, tipped with black and covered with dried blood. It did half a turn around the room and landed on the coat rack. Dad proclaimed, "That, boys, is a North American red-tailed hawk! Now be careful, or it'll bite your fingers off!"

Only an hour before, this majestic animal was minding its own business back in Mark's pigeon coop, popping the heads off Mark's prize pigeons, eating the tasty bits and leaving the rest for scrap. Dad and Mark, hearing the ruckus, made for the rooftop posthaste. They were hoping to stem the slaughter, but it was too late. Dad quickly threw his coat over the offender, and Mark grabbed the pair of scissors he used for clipping the pigeons' toenails. Mark told Dad that he didn't care if it was a protected animal, that rotten bird had killed its last pigeon. It took some convincing on Dad's part, but he eventually talked Mark out of the execution by promising to keep the little monster locked up as a pet.

We boys slept a bit uneasily the first few nights. We were all decked out in football helmets, catcher's masks, oven mittens, and anything else we could find to keep our noses, fingers, and toes hidden from the beast. Those were some very long nights, to be sure.

Having watched a lot of TV and thanks to the old Encyclopedia Gramptanica, by the third day we were experts on all things that boys under the age of thirteen could know about red-tailed hawks. The second-most-important thing to know about hawks is that they need to see feathers or fur to know something is food. Just poke a couple of feathers in a piece of hamburger and down it goes. The first, and definitely most important, thing to know is never, and I mean never, get talked into letting a hawk land on your arm like on TV.

Jimmy felt confident that putting a kitchen towel around my arm, wrapped up with masking tape and topped off with one of Dad's welding gloves, should be good enough for hawk holding. A football helmet and a hooded sweatshirt added more than enough protection for an episode of *Mutual of Astori-ha*, our very own nature show.

I remember the host in the original TV show, *Mutual of Omaha's Wild Kingdom*, handling all kinds of animals. I don't recall the plucky assistant ever screaming the way I did when things went wrong. But after ten minutes of trying to coax Chester onto my arm with a little piece of hot dog dressed up like Big Bird (the hot dog was dressed up like Big Bird, not me), Jimmy eventually just kicked over the coat rack. With a couple of giant flaps Chester landed on the only thing left to land on, my arm!

At first it seemed like it was going to work. The giant bird gripped my arm just like on the TV. Only Chester was a lot heavier than I imagined, so it was difficult to hold my arm up. When Chester held his wings out and tried to balance, his claws started going right through the glove, the tape, and the towel, and slowly dug into my arm. I tried to lift my arm so Chester wouldn't get too close to my face and peck my eyes out, but that just made him flap more and sink his talons in even deeper. I started screaming and running around the room trying to shake the damn thing off.

Jimmy screamed over and over, "Just hold still!"

Eventually Chester flew off my arm and onto the bookshelf. We unwrapped my arm to find scratches and a bunch of little punctures that looked a lot like carpet tacks had stabbed me. Jimmy said that was what we should tell Dad if he asked. We would say we were wrestling and got stuck with carpet tacks. Jimmy found a tack strip along the wall and stuck himself just to make the lie more believable.

Over the next few weeks feeding our Chester got to be quite the chore. Hamburger was expensive—too expensive for feeding to hawks, anyway. So we took to setting rattraps out in the backyard and feeding Chester the rats, mice, and voles we caught. Unfortunately, it wasn't too long before we had trapped the place out. After that, we boys started shooting pigeons, starlings, and other small birds off the power lines that ran above the backyard.

Shooting birds off the power lines to feed our hawk would not have seemed too out of place if we had been using BB guns, but we weren't. If we had lived out in the countryside where you are allowed to shoot rifles, that wouldn't have seemed weird either. But we didn't live in the countryside. Where we did live was in a quiet little neighborhood, just up the hill from the park and the Dairy Queen. But since nobody ever called the police and Dad was the one who told us to feed Chester, we guessed it was okay.

The Silver Thaw

Four days into our winter break it happened. Snow! Yup, you heard me, there was actual snow! We had seen snow before, but in Astoria, snow usually melted before you could get the sled out of the garage. Astoria hail also melted before you could get the sled out of the garage, but that didn't stop us from trying. Even Astoria fog looked like you could sled on it, but you couldn't.

In Astoria, we had all the mailman weather that you hear mailmen bragging about making it through no matter what. Yeah, well, I bet our mailman didn't see this one coming. Then again, maybe he did, because our mailman was pretty far out there. He was a kind of groovy hippie sort of guy who wore shorts no matter what kind of weather he was mailmanning his way through. He was older than Dad and he had a long beard down to his belt buckle like the guys in the ZZ Top band.

When we woke up it was bright outside, I mean bright, brighter than the brightest day I had ever seen. It hurt my eyes to even look outside. Something new had happened, something we had never seen before. Dad called it a silver thaw. It made the whole world look like it was locked in a magic kaleidoscope.

Dad told us that after the snow fell, the temperature dropped to well below freezing and stayed there. It got so very cold, even the fog was freezing cold. Only it didn't turn to snow and it didn't turn to rain. Instead, the fog turned into ice magic. Everything the fog touched became covered in ice, and it touched everything! There was an inch of solid ice everywhere. It froze everything to everything else too. It even froze the cars to the street. It froze the mailboxes shut! Good luck, Mr. Mailman. It froze the whole town. It even froze the river. Well, it froze part of the river, the part below the house, down by the Dairy Queen. It froze a hard candy shell on top of the snow. It looked like candy, anyway. The only way you could walk around at all was to stomp holes through the ice into the snow below as you went. Then you could take a step. If you tried to walk on top of the ice you just fell on your butt, so we stomped through.

There was no milk and cereal left that morning, so Dad sent us up the hill to "Bob's little store." Jarod and I bundled up like two small winter mummies and headed off into the deep-freeze to secure provisions. We stayed over where the grass ran along the sidewalk, punching our way through the ice the entire way up to the store. It was hard work but eventually we got to Bob's. We looked around and stood next to the heater to warm up a bit. Securing the milk and a box of Sugar Smacks, we headed back down to the house. The going back was a bit more difficult than the going there. This was because we now had to cross back over to our side of the street before making our way home. We really should have walked back to where the road was flat and crossed like we did on our way up, but we didn't. Instead, Jarod and I locked arms and shuffled our feet on the ice out to about halfway across the road, when we both started to fall over. Jarod abandoned the jug of milk and made a leap for the base of the stop sign on the other side of the street. He pushed off of me, though, when he did it. For a moment, the milk and I just sort of hovered there in the middle of the street. Jarod held on to the stop sign and pulled himself up. We watched as the milk began to creep a little farther down the hill toward home. I looked to Jarod for help.

Jarod yelled, "Throw me the Sugar Smacks, man!"

I did, but that was the wrong thing to do. Turns out, for every action there is an equal and opposite reaction. We hadn't studied that in school yet, but man, was I about to get an education. As soon as I tossed the Sugar Smacks over to Jarod, I began to slide back toward the milk. The milk began to pick up speed. I panicked and sort of lunged for it, then I began to pick up speed too. I looked back at Jarod holding on to the stop sign. He leaned out and waved the box of Sugar Smacks at me and the milk as we disappeared down the hill.

The milk picked up even more speed and quickly raced away from me. There is a law about friction that comes into play here, but I didn't have time to get into it. I was doing about twenty miles per hour and was about halfway home as the milk went screaming past our driveway. I was sprawled out on all fours like a baby deer trying to stand for the first time when I myself passed the driveway two seconds later. That's when I saw the milk take the turn at the end of the block at a frightening speed.

I found myself hoping to skip up and over the curb and maybe stick in the snowbank cartoon-style. Only that didn't happen. Instead, I followed the milk.

I bounced back and forth, pinballing past the public pool. The milk was doing the same. It skipped back out into the middle of the street. I found a nice groove next to the sidewalk and bounced along for a while longer. I was passing the park below the pool at about the same time the milk got to the intersection with the highway next to the Dairy Queen. There was a little rise at the stop sign that acted as a ramp, sending the milk rocketing through the air and across both lanes of Highway 30. It landed on the other side and skidded out onto the river ice, slowly spinning into the distance until it unceremoniously *bloop*ed into the river. Now, I don't know if I was screaming when I went past the house or when I passed the pool or when I passed the park, but I was sure as heck screaming now. I kicked and flailed as hard as I could and somehow managed to pop up onto the sidewalk next to the softball field. I went a few more feet and my ankle hooked the speed-limit sign, sending me spinning off into the field below. I drifted to a stop, got to my feet, caught my breath, and now I faced the long walk back home. My ankle was messed up from hitting the signpost, so I had to pogo hop through the ice with my good leg and gimp on my bad foot the best I could. I had made it up past the park when Jimmy came sliding around the end of our block to come find me. Jarod had made it home with the Sugar Smacks and told him how I disappeared out of sight along with the milk. It took another ten minutes for us to get back home. By then I was half frozen and limping on what was now a badly bruised and swollen ankle. Jimmy carried me through the door piggyback-style, to find Jarod sitting at the dining room table with his bowl of dry cereal and a spoon. Jarod looked behind me as if he expected the milk to come limping in next. He just said one word: "Milk?"

Sleigh Rides for Busher

Snow is the time for snow forts, snowmen, hot cocoa, and if you have a Saint Bernard, sleigh rides! We had imagined many times the glorious day we would find ourselves with enough snow to harness up old Busher to our sleigh just like one of Santa's reindeer. We pictured ourselves dashing through the snow, racing snowmobiles and rescuing avalanche victims with a little wooden keg of whiskey tied around Busher's neck.

The snow stuck around for a whole week, so we found ourselves with a white Christmas for the first time ever. We begged dad to take us over to Aunt Marie's house to play in the snow with cousins Johnny and David. When we got there, we found ourselves with five boys, one toboggan, and a Saint Bernard. It took some doing, but after several attempts we managed to harness the dog up to what was left of our old rotted toboggan. I use the term "harness" very loosely, as in one large dog tied to one mostly intact toboggan using a dog leash, some baling twine, and some rotting rope we found in an old boat. None of us said anything, but this was not what we had pictured in our heads.

We went inside and asked Dad if we had a small barrel of whiskey to put on Busher's collar, the kind used for rescuing people in case somebody gets stuck in an avalanche. Dad gave us a can of beer and some duct tape, then made us promise not to open the beer and told us to bring it back when we were done. We used the duct tape and some kite string to put the can around the dog's neck. We all sat on the toboggan, and Jimmy yelled, "Mush!" Only Bush wouldn't go. He didn't want to play sleigh ride, toboggan, rescue, or any other game, really. We tried everything we could think of to get him to pull. We tried beef jerky, and that worked for about six feet. Then we were covered in slobber and out of jerky. Bush just lay in the snow, rolled over, and eventually fell asleep on the toboggan. While Bush sawed logs, we went and made a giant snow sculpture in the shape of, well, let's just say it was more "man" then snow man.

We thought it would be funny to put all six feet of the giant snow-ding-dong up next to the highway for all the cars to see as they drove by. Only, after an hour Aunt Marie told us to take it down because the old ladies from next door had called to complain that she and her church friends did not appreciate the male form as much as we had hoped.

After lunch we had a snowball fight that soon escalated into several actual fights and two fat lips. So it was a nice break when Uncle Chuck brought cousin Steven over to join in the mayhem. Steven was one of Busher's favorite kids, but not in a good way. Steven had hardly made it out of the car when the beast began to stir. At first, he didn't see the dog half-covered in white, so he made the rookie mistake of just walking right out in the open. Bush exploded out of the pile of snow, heading straight for Steven at a pretty good run. Spying their chance, Jimmy and Johnny leaped for the toboggan as it whizzed past. Bush bolted and Steven began to run in slow motion down the driveway. It was sort of beautiful when I look back on it. You could hear the sound of the crunching snow, and the huff, huff, huff of old Bush a-coming round the bend. The clapping of his massive jowls rang out as dog slobber went flying like snowflakes in all directions. I can still see that look of unbridled glee on the rosy-cheeked boys riding the toboggan, and the fear in little Steven's eyes as he ran, Steven in his little red snow suit trying to get away. All of it, silhouetted against the highway with the giant snow-wiener in the distance, is forever frozen in my mind, like a messed-up Norman Rockwell painting.

Jeremy T. Owen

The Wood Sprite

In the spring, if I wasn't out with Jarod looking for pond
dragons, I climbed trees—a lot of trees. Fat ones and
skinny ones. I climbed evergreen trees so high I could
see the entire town. Some trees were two hundred feet
tall, and some were even taller than that. Some could
even touch the sky. I would climb and climb to the very
tip top, up to where the tree was only as big around as a
small boy's arm. When I got to the top, I would lock my
legs around the tree, close my eyes, throw my arms out
like tree branches, and let the wind sway the "me tree"
back and forth and back and forth. I would bask in the
sun, watching the birds and the butterflies darting all
around me like little planes in a dogfight. I could see the
squirrels racing each other through the tops of the maple
trees so far below me; they looked like tiny mice
tunneling through the grass at the feet of a giant. I would
spend hours climbing tree after tree, mapping out the
best vantage points around our house and hiding small
toys and soldiers in the crooks and hollows of my
favorite climbs.

For a while, I carried a climbing stick with me. It
was a sturdy stick about three feet long, with a bit of a
twist, making it look like a wizard's staff or something a
leprechaun would carry. In the middle of the stick I tied
some green rope using a sailor's knot that Grandpa Roy
had taught me. He called it a bowline on a bight. It was
a tough knot that wouldn't come off the stick. Grandpa
Roy had lots of knots to teach; he knew the square knot,
the double Blackwall, the barrel hitch, and the monkey's
fist. Grandpa knew knots because he was in the U.S.
Coast Guard for a very long time. The whole time he
was there he did his job and never shirked an order.
That's what Grandpa Roy would tell us if we didn't

clean our room when Mom told us to. "Okay boys let's get this place shipshape! No shirking orders!"

My grandfather—we would always say "grandfather" when we talked about the medal he won—was a real hero and everything. Not the kind of hero that finds himself in a place and does something great. Those kinds are good heroes too. He was the kind of hero that ran into danger when he didn't even have to. He received the Gold Lifesaving Medal for saving twenty-one men off a sinking ship called the *Trinidad.*

That night the only Coast Guard power boat was off rescuing some fishermen in the big storm, so Grandpa Roy and four other brave men went out in the old open-top wooden lifeboat number 3829 to save the crew of the *Trinidad.* The wind blew over sixty miles per hour, and it took more than an hour and a half just for them to get over the sandbar at the mouth of the river. The sandbar is a very dangerous part of the river, and the Northwest has the most dangerous sandbars in the whole wide world.

The encyclopedia says, "The Gold Lifesaving Medal may be awarded to an individual who performed a rescue or attempted rescue at the risk of his or her own life, and demonstrates extreme and heroic daring." That meant we should clean our room and that my grandfather knew how to tie good knots for sure.

I don't think Grandpa would have shown me how to tie those knots if he had seen what I was doing with them in the trees. First, I tied forty feet of rope to my stick with an anchor hitch knot, then I tied the rope with snake knots at about every two feet for climbing. They were really called figure-eight knots, but they reminded me of snakes, so I called them snake knots because it was cool.

During my climbs I had my climbing rope and stick, but I also wore my special climbing gear. My outfit consisted of a long-sleeve shirt so the branches didn't scratch me too much, and a vest with lots of pockets so I could bring snacks and toy soldiers and stuff. I had a pair of pants that were hand-me-downs from my cousin Carrie. Mom told me no one would know they were girl pants if I didn't tell them. Believe me, I didn't. The pants had bell bottoms that were so big they would make a *shoosh* sound when I walked. I liked them because when I swung on the rope, they would make a sound that reminded me of a bat's wings.

When I first started climbing trees, I would just find a tree with a fork in it and throw the stick up through the fork until it caught. Then I would climb up there. That was cool and fun . . . for a while. Gradually, I got the idea of using the stick to swing from tree to tree. I would climb up a tree using my rope-stick combo, then from there I'd throw it over into another tree nearby. I would swing over like Tarzan to the new tree and climb up from there. That was really fun, too, as long as you didn't slam into the tree trunk too hard on your way over. Using my rope-stick combo, I was able to get to trees I never could before.

I was so excited I went back home to get Jarod and show him my new trick. I drug him outside to a spot down the block where the trees were close enough together. I threw the rope up into the cottonwood tree on the corner and climbed up about twenty feet. Then I threw my stick up and across at the fork of a big spruce tree that leaned out above where Jarod was sitting. It took four or five tries before I got my climbing stick to catch in the fork of the tree. I could see I was losing my audience, so I made a big show of it, making loud calls as I threw. Jarod sat on a pile of rocks below an elderberry tree on the other side of the spruce. I pulled the rope good and tight and hollered at Jarod to watch. I gave my best Tarzan call and swung hard like a trapeze artist in the circus. I could feel right away that I was moving way too fast. The sound of my pants flapping was louder than I had ever heard before. I wanted to let go of the rope as soon as I got close to the ground, but I had thrown the rope too high, so I was still at least ten feet above the ground, and I gripped the rope even tighter. I just managed to miss the trunk of the big spruce tree and started to swing upwards toward the elderberry. As I neared the height of the swing, the stick at the end of my rope shifted a bit and gave a hard jerk. That was it. The rope slipped out of my hands.

Now I was flying for real and looking straight down at Jarod, who was looking straight back up at me. I zinged down and smashed into the elderberry tree and began to tumble as I went, crashing through the branches headfirst as I careened toward the jagged pile of rocks Jarod was seated on. The ground, the rocks, and the broken glass below me were beginning to become clear as they zoomed up toward my face. I closed my eyes, expecting to be dead at any moment. Suddenly, someone or something reached out its giant hand and grabbed my leg. With a sudden jerk that made my back pop, I halted in midair. I dangled there, twisting three feet above the rocks and bits of broken glass. Jarod, still seated on the rocks below me, did not look all that impressed with my new trick. He was even less impressed when he realized I was now wetting myself. I had been scared plenty of times, but not like this—not so scared that I literally peed my pants.

Now, because I was dangling upside down, the situation started getting worse, so much worse. When you've wet yourself upside down, let me tell you, gravity is not your friend. It's important to keep your mouth closed and your eyes shut. If only I had known that then. Jarod looked up at me in disgust as pee ran into my ears, down my face, up my nose, and into my mouth. Having lost all respect for me, Jarod walked home, leaving me hanging there in the forest covered in my own urine.

As I twisted around up there, above the jagged rocks and bits of glass, I began to wonder just how it was that I was still alive. I mean really, who saved me? If ever a wood sprite saved a little boy, it was me. Sticking out of the elderberry tree was a small piece of an old broken branch no bigger than the tip of your little finger. The cuff of my hand-me-down bell-bottom pants had hooked on that tiny little crooked finger, snatching me away from death. Eventually I was able to undo my belt, unzip my pants, and use the other pant leg to lower myself down to the ground. I couldn't get the pants to unhook from the tree, so I shamefacedly made my way back home in soggy pee-soaked underpants.

Once I arrived home, I found Jarod lounging on the couch watching *Star Blazers*. I asked him why he left me hanging there. He didn't even look up from the TV and just said, "It was a good trick, but you shouldn't pee at the end. That's gross!"

Don't Tell Dad

Needing a break from the treetops, wood sprites, and almost breaking my neck, not to mention the humiliation of peeing on myself in front of my little brother, I decided to find something to do a little closer to the ground. It wasn't long before once again we were all seduced by the lady we call Monopoly. Jarod, Jimmy, and I were in the back bedroom passing the time under the sharp eye of Chester the hawk. We spread the game board out on the floor, sat down Indian-style, and started to play. Again Jarod had to be the banker, and again, in almost no time at all, our game careened toward a potential trip to the emergency room.

After only ten turns Jimmy was losing badly, mostly because he didn't want to play with us in the first place. I had to move his game piece around the board because he was too busy lighting wooden matches off his blue jeans. He struck one match after another on his zipper and then on the jean rivets, and finally ran them down his thigh. He even tried to light a few off his shoe. Eventually he had a real big pile of burnt matches in front of him and a not-so-big pile of Monopoly money. It wasn't long before he was bored with the matches too.

Jarod and I kept on playing Monopoly, and I was winning. Actually winning, by God! I had taken most of the good properties and was getting more and more hotels as we went along. Jarod just kept on banking, you know, because he was Jarod.

By now Jimmy wasn't even really playing anymore and was instead messing around with the .22-caliber pellet gun that hung on the wall of the bedroom. He had pumped it up and dry-fired it two or three times. He pumped it up again, and shortly after that he landed on my Boardwalk with four hotels on it. That wiped him out. Being a little brother and having wiped the floor with my older brother, I did what little brothers do best: I rubbed it in. I danced around and shook my little butt in his face and sang a little song that went "Loser, loser, loser. You're a loser! I'm a winner!"

While I was dancing, Jarod began organizing the Monopoly money into neat little piles to go back in the game box. Jimmy, who was getting very annoyed at my butt-shaking, dropped one of the burnt matches down the barrel of the pellet gun, pointed it at my butt, and fired! Now, I'm sure my big brother thought it would only smart a bit and teach me a lesson for being such a poor winner. Well, it smarted, all right; it smarted right through my jeans and half an inch into my left butt cheek.

I jumped up in the air like Daffy Duck and began running around the house, bawling my eyes out and screaming at the top of my lungs. I ran through the living room, into the kitchen, down the hall, around the corner, and back through the living room. Jimmy was in hot pursuit the whole time, yelling, "Don't tell Dad! Don't tell Dad!"

I rounded the credenza back in the living room again. As I did, Jimmy dove over the top of it and cut me off at the pass, or in this case the credenza.

I lay there whimpering, darted like some poor animal on a nature show; Jimmy sat on me while Jarod ran out into the garage to get Dad's needle-nose pliers to remove the matchstick. Before he would pull the match out, Jimmy made me swear not to tell Dad, saying we would all be on restriction for the whole rest of the summer. Jimmy steadied his hand, told me to hold my breath and count to three. He yanked on two. The burnt matchstick left a black dot tattooed on my left butt cheek forevermore.

Good-bye, Mrs. Brown

Great-Uncle John Van Horn had been sick for a while. Aunt Cathy called us after breakfast to tell Dad it was time for him to stop by. Dad and I did the dishes, fed the dog, and locked up the house, then drove the long way out to see Uncle. We went up past the Astor Column, around the reservoir, and past the dock where we had met Otto the fisherman the summer before. We had been to Uncle's house many times to visit, play with our cousins, and see our pet rabbits that Auntie and Uncle took in when we moved with mom up to Seattle.

On past visits, cousin Tanya would take us into the game room, where Uncle had the biggest buck's head we ever saw mounted to the wall. Tanya would tell us the story of how one day when she was playing in that room, even though she wasn't supposed to, the buck's head fell off the wall, and the antler went through her neck and poked out the other side. Then Tanya would show us the scar. We always thought that made her tough as any of us boys, maybe tougher.

It was a great place to be a kid. There was a tire swing out in the backyard that we took turns swinging on, jumping off into the grass and rolling down the hill. It was always a fun and happy place for us to visit.

We would beg whoever was driving us to stop in whenever we passed their house. If we couldn't stop in, we would always wave as if they could see us and call out, "Love you, Uncle, love you, Auntie, love you, cousins." Then we would honk twice.

This trip Tanya was at dance class, and it was just Dad and me out visiting. We couldn't have played much outside anyways because it was raining. We listened to Paul Harvey telling "The Rest of the Story" as we drove over the hill.

The announcer came on to say, "Come hear Jimmy Owen sing down at the Sunset Empire Room!" I looked over at Dad to say how cool it was to hear his name on the radio, but I could see by the look on his face that he was thinking of something else. The next song on the radio after the announcer talked was "Sloop John B." It played as we drove out past the reservoir. Neither of us talked for a long time.

When the announcer started talking again, I asked Dad a question. For a few days I had been thinking about something he'd said. We had gone to see him sing a few nights before, and just for us he sang the song he wrote called "Wall-to-Wall Love." Before he sang, he told the audience, "This is about a special house I hope to always live in."

I said, "Dad?"

"Yes, Frog."

I said, "I was wondering, the house you sing about in the 'Wall-to-Wall Love' song. What house is it?"

"What do you mean?"

I tried my best to explain. "Well, Jimmy says it's the house on Nineteenth Street, and Jarod says it's the house on Cedar Street, but then the other night you said it was the house you live in now. So I was wondering, what house is the song house?"

He gave me a sad smile. "That's a good question. The house in the song, in a way, is all those houses; in a way it's not those houses at all. The house in the song is made of wall-to-wall love. You know how it takes four walls to make a house?"

"Uh-huh."

Dad continued, "The four walls in a way are you four kids, and the roof, well, that's your momma. It's her job to keep you warm and safe and it's your job to hold her up while she's doing it. You see, the house in the song is our family."

"Oh, I think I get it. Dad? What part of the house are you?"

Dad said, "Well, your mom would probably say I'm the outhouse."

We laughed. We were still laughing as we pulled up to Uncle's. We sat in the car, and Dad told me how Uncle was real sickly and that I might not get to see him again. He asked if I understood that and if I thought I could be strong enough to go in. I said that I could if he could.

We went in and visited with Uncle for about an hour. We joked, and uncle called me Tiger one last time, and I gave him a big hug and kissed him good-bye. Aunt Cathy gave me a bag to put in the car. Dad said he needed to talk to Uncle a minute, and that I should wait outside. He'd be right there. I went and put the bag in the car. Then I walked over to see the rabbits, only when I got there the cage was empty and it didn't seem like it had been used for a while. I sat in the tire swing, looked at the river, and cried for my uncle. I saw Dad walking to the car, so I dried my tears and walked down the hill to join him. By the time I got to the car he was sitting in the front seat with the bag on his lap. He sat there for a minute; that was the only time I ever remember seeing my father cry. I got in the car and asked him if he was okay. He had always told us not to cry when we fell or skinned a knee, and I think he knew I was thinking about that.

As we drove home, he said, "You know, Frog, it's okay to cry when your heart hurts, that's how we know we're really here." That's all Dad said for the rest of the drive home.

Uncle passed away a few days later. Like everything else, his funeral was a grand affair, with a procession that spanned the length of the entire Warrenton bridge and even farther. I never found out what was in the bag Auntie had me put in the car, and I

215

never did ask Dad about the rabbits. I didn't want to know.

Chapter 10

Sweaty Betty

Grandpa Roy had an orange 1957 GMC step-side pickup truck. By the time any of us got old enough to drive it, it had some issues. The floorboards had rusted through, so you could see the road zipping by as you went along. The glove box was tied up with a piece of wire, not to keep it closed but to keep it in the dash and not in your lap. The windows were cracked and foggy. Only one wiper wiped, and there were so many holes in the sides it whistled when you drove it faster than twenty miles per hour.

Of course, us kids loved it. Cousin Daintry called the old truck Sweaty Betty; we even made up a song for when we went up long hills and the truck bogged down. We would all yell, "Sweaty Betty running steady, you can do it, Sweaty Betty. Go, Sweaty Betty, go, Sweaty Betty, go, Sweaty Betty, go!" Then we would chug up over the hill, leaving a cloud of smoke trailing behind us.

Daintry was all smiles and always happy to drive kids down to the pool on hot summer days, come pick us up and take us out to Grandma's house, or rescue us if we had a bad dream when staying at a friend's house. She was always patient with us younger kids and never got mad at us. Even the time she let me sleep in her bunk bed with her. Even though she asked me, like, a hundred times if I still wet the bed and even though I swore a hundred and one times I didn't anymore, but then I did. That's a pretty good cousin that loves you even after you pee on her. In my defense, I was having a dream where I was using the bathroom, and plus I haven't peed on her since, not even once.

We had been at Dad's for a week when Jimmy went off camping with some friends. I was too young, so I couldn't go if there were no adults going. Instead I called Grandma Bea to see if I could come out to play with Jarod and Shani, who were staying out there. She said I could, but I had to find someone to drop me off because she was busy with the senior center bake sale. I said okay and called up Daintry, who hopped into Sweaty Betty and sputtered off to my rescue.

Twenty minutes later, I heard the old truck squeal to a rusty stop. I grabbed my grocery sack of clothes and sprinted out of the house. I jumped in the cab, and with both hands swung the rusty door closed with a chomp and a clang. The door sort of dropped a little, then wobbled back open. I looked at Daintry.

She said, "Put your foot on the door jamb and pull harder."

I did, and this time it didn't wobble back open.

She said, "Stay away from the door."

We motored off down the hill, past the pool, past the park and ball field where I nearly broke my ankle on the speed-limit sign over Christmas break. We were heading past the Dairy Queen and about to go over the bump that sent the milk down to Davy Jones' locker, where presumably he got to have cereal. Daintry did a rolling stop to keep old Sweaty Betty from cutting out. There were no cars, so she gave her some gas and we took the corner out onto the highway. As we turned, I began to slide across the bench seat toward the wonky door. That might have been okay, only at that same time we hit the milk bump. Then we heard a clank, the door unlatched and swung open, and out I went.

I was floating in midair. I could even see the road zipping past below me. Just as I started to go more downways than sideways, I felt a hand grab hold of my arm. With one hand still on the steering wheel Daintry snatched me out of thin air and zipped me back inside

218

next to her. She kept driving, holding on to me as we went down the highway with my door still bouncing around half open.

Daintry looked at me with giant eyes and said, "Let's not tell Grandma about that." I gulped and shook my head yes.

She dropped me off and locked her mouth with a key. She smiled again and bounced on down the road in old Sweaty Betty.

The Bad Macaroni

The smell of bacon, eggs, and Red Rose tea would greet us nearly every time we walked through the door. Grandma would be in her apron shuffling about the kitchen, getting cookies and pouring milk. Grandma Bea was a textbook grandma. She gardened, cooked, told us stories, and crocheted afghan blankets, potholders, and hats with little yarn balls on them.

Jarod and Shani had been staying at Grandma's house for the better part of the week, running in and out and generally getting on poor Grandma's nerves. We had begged Grandma all morning to make her famous macaroni and cheese. Only, she had the senior center bake sale and didn't have time to tie up the stove cooking macaroni and cheese for three rowdy boys. Finally, she relented and sent us outside to look for pond dragons as she began preparing the macaroni and cheese. We ran down to the water but there was nothing, so we spent most of that time chasing grasshoppers and camel-back crickets, eating salmonberries, and doing all the things boys dream of doing when they aren't stuck behind a classroom desk.

In no time at all, Grandma called us in for lunch. We ran into the house, nearly knocking each other over, grabbed our plates, and piled on the macaroni and cheese sky high. We sat down at the table, said thanks to Grandma, and dug in. At the first bite we could tell that something was off. The macaroni was bitter and kind of salty. With all the baking going on around the kitchen, there must have been some sort of a mix-up and somehow baking soda got to where baking soda shouldn't be. This made the mac and cheese taste terrible.

All three of us stopped eating after the first bite. Grandma gave us a look that none of us had ever seen from Grandma before. She said in a voice that made Grandpa sneak off and hide in the other room, "Is something wrong?"

The hair stood up on the back of my neck when Jarod started to tell her. He said, "Well, Grandma, it doesn't taste quite right. I think you made a mistake."

We thought he was a goner. Grandma jammed her finger in the macaroni, gave it a quick lick, and said, "It's fine! Now eat it!"

Shani said, "We're really not all that hungry."

Grandma was now as mad as I ever saw her get in my whole life. She said, "Well then, get hungry. You can't go play until you clean your plates!"

We all looked at each other and didn't know what to do. We sat for a few minutes looking at each other and around the room. The sliding glass door was right behind Shani, and there for a minute I thought we could make a break for it. But Grandma gave me a look like she knew what I was thinking. So I took a few bites of the bad mac and washed it down with milk. Jarod and Shani did the same, but there wasn't enough milk. There was no way we were going to finish. Even if we had the whole cow for milk, we were never going to finish. By the fifth bite, I couldn't even force it down anymore. There wasn't any way out. Jarod was looking at me in the way a little brother looks at his big brother when he needs help. Poor Shani just looked crushed.

We sat for ten minutes or more pushing the macaroni around our plates trying to make it look smaller, but it was no use. We had piled the bad mac high because we were greedy little piggies, and now there was nothing we could do. Slowly, something began to grow in my brain. It was an idea—a very, very bad idea. It was wrong, and I knew it. But it was my only way out. Quickly, I sat up in my chair and leaned hard to look out the glass door behind Shani. I said, "Hey, is that a deer? I think it's a buck!" Shani, who had always dreamed of the day he would be old enough to bag a buck, whipped his head around to see the deer. When he did, I picked up my plate and swiped almost all my macaroni onto Shani's plate. I quickly sat back down before he turned around. Jarod saw the whole thing and sat staring at me in awe and disbelief.

I scooped my last two remaining bites into my mouth, held up a plate, and yelled, "I'm done, Grandma!"

I tossed my plate in the sink and ran for the door. I couldn't even look either of them in the eye as I ran past the table. I felt terrible as I was zipping up my coat. Then I heard Jarod say, "Yup, I think that is a buck!" That was followed by scrape, plop, gulp gulp, "I'm done too, Grandma!"

Jarod and I had been playing outside for over two hours by the time poor Shani made it out of the house. He was green to the gills and had to spend the better part of the next day on the toilet. Jarod and I never spoke of what we did that day, not even to each other. I finally confessed to Shani when we were in our twenties. Shani was so angry he didn't speak to me for two years. Sorry, Shani.

Salmon Seeds

The dog days of summer were a good time to go looking for beads. Polliwogs had turned to frogs, salamanders and newts were hidden deep in the forest, and most creatures of tooth and scale were preparing for the long winter ahead. The beads we looked for were extra hard things to find, mostly because they were lost. The beads we looked for were lost by Native Americans hundreds and sometimes thousands of years ago. Most times we would look on the river beaches where the pebbles make that whooshing sound when you run your hands through them. That's where we would find the sapphire-blue and the bone-white trading beads brought by Lewis and Clark on their expedition. Sometimes we found beads made from copper coins hammered flat and then rolled into tubes, or wampum beads cut by hand from seashells. We found other lost things, too—flint scrapers, stone bowls, and net weights would sometimes appear in places you had already looked more times than you could remember.

We even found beads that weren't beads at all. Instead, they were tiny, bright orange, living crystal balls filled with magic salmon fire. Grandpa Owen called them salmon seeds, but they were actually salmon eggs. He told us a story of how when large salmonberries fell into the river pools, they would hatch into baby salmon. We knew that it was just a story, but sometimes, just for fun, we would throw the biggest salmonberries we found into the deep pools and watch to see if they turned into fish. At times we convinced ourselves they did.

When we did find Grandpa's salmon seeds, he would kneel down next to the water and cup his creased and callused hand at the water's surface, holding it there to let the water run in through his fingers and back out through the crook of his thumb. He would hold his hand in just such a way that there was enough water to make a little pool in his palm but keep the water flowing and cold. He would gently place the eggs in the pool of his hand, so we could see the little creatures dancing inside.

We took turns looking the little salmon in the eye, until the tiny fish would look back at us. Grandpa said the little salmon would remember our faces and tell the other fish way out in the ocean that we were kind people. He was careful to put the eggs back in a safe, protected spot, and we would all stop looking there so we didn't hurt any of them. We were proud to be the kind of people who helped salmon and had them as friends.

Each summer we took a trip out to Uncle Ardie and Aunt Carol's farm. There we fed the chickens and rode the spotted pony that I think was really too old for us to ride anymore. But he was a good pony and liked to wander around the farm with us, so we didn't ride him too much. There was a big black dog named Joker, and he didn't like new people at all. He was over 140 pounds, and his head was as big across as a dinner plate. You could put your head in his mouth like a lion tamer if you didn't mind some dog drool in your ear.

Below the house, there was a small side pond along the salmon stream where we fished off the little dock that Uncle Ardie made. We dropped berries and worms off the dock and watched them sink until they were snapped up into the hungry tummies of our fish friends. There the big red salmon came home from the ocean and gathered in the stream below the little waterfall. Joker would chase them around until we told him not to. We spent hours watching the fish jump out of the pond and up the waterfall. Some of the fish had trouble making it. When that happened, two or three of us would go and scoop them up and walk them up over the little hill to where the stream was deeper and let them go. As we carried them, we each took a turn, and looked them in the eye.

We said, "Remember me? I met you as an egg; did you have fun in the sea? Okay, be safe." Then with a flick of their tails, *whoosh* they chattered away up the stream.

I think I have always talked to fish even when I was one. Maybe that was because my mom talked to me when I was swimming in her belly, and her momma talked to her. Maybe fish can talk, too, only people forgot how to talk back. I made up my mind to listen to as many animals as I could. I tried to catch a word or a sound that could be a bird "Hello" or a bumblebee "How are you doing?" or maybe a toad just saying "Hey." I thought about that while we watched the fish jump. Aunt Carol's place always seemed to be the kind of place where the animals would talk to you—you know, if you listened.

225

Jeremy T. Owen

Plague of Frogs

Every fall we were forced back to school, and every fall we had to listen to all the other kids brag about their summer vacations. Then year after year the teacher made us write the same old "What I did for my summer vacation" essay.

Every year, it was the same thing. "We went to Hawaii, we got to swim with sea turtles." "We went to Sea World, we got splashed by Shamu!" And the worst of all was "We went to summer camp, and we made s'mores!"

Now, growing up money poor we didn't get to go to camp. At least not the kind of camp those kids were talking about. I didn't even know what a s'more was exactly, but what I did know was I couldn't stand them or anyone that grinned like an idiot and said, "S'mores are the best!" I know I should have been happy for the other children, but we had only been to a camp once, back when I was three years old. There were no s'mores there, I'll tell you that!

Our camp was in a rain forest. I don't know who put a summer camp in the rain forest, but the words "rain forest" and "summer camp" should never go together. And yes, it rained the entire time. It was a religious family-style camp, so all of our family was there. The Bartoldus cousins shared a cabin with us kids, Aunt Jerry, and Mom. Shani, Badi, their little sister Beatrice, Uncle Dale, and Aunt Estella were in the cabin next door to ours. These cabins had bunk beds. Most cabins do, of course, have bunk beds, but these cabins had *only* bunk beds. There were two small windows, a little woodstove, and a dresser in the back corner. There was no electricity and no TV. We had a Coleman pump-style lantern for light, and we all took turns pumping it whenever it began to sputter and the light dimmed and threatened to plunge us into darkness. This would happen if anybody even mentioned a ghost or bears, or if you had to go to the bathroom. Oh God, the bathroom was bad. We, and all the other cabins, shared a real old-time outhouse with a crescent moon cut in the door and no seat, just plywood with a hole that went into the abyss. To get to the outhouse we had to walk past the other cabins and down a short path by the very swollen river. To make it worse, Mom would have to hold us smaller kids while we went so we didn't fall into the abyss.

Our camp was like Sunday school in the rain for a week straight. We couldn't go home, and we couldn't go outside. Even if we could go outside, the river was so swollen it was too dangerous for kids to go play in or around it. On top of everything else, there were no frogs or polliwogs there, and definitely no pond dragons. There were only banana slugs, eight-inch-long yellow slugs with giant black spots just like a rotten banana, and they were everywhere you went or wanted to go but couldn't go.

We got to sing some songs and roast marshmallows. That was nice, and the young adults who were teaching us were nice too. All of us kids went to class in a big log cabin and sat around a big stone fireplace and sang "Kumbaya," "Michael, Row Your Boat Ashore," and "Catalina Magdalena Hoopensteiner Wallendiner Hogan Logan Bogan Was Her Name." But Mom told us we could not sing Dad's finger song no matter what.

After the sing-along and a talk about being kind to our fellow man, we all put on our rain gear and marched off single file to the chow hall. Everybody pitched in and helped make lunch; even the kids got to help. We had potato salad, hot dogs, and all kinds of foods we had never even heard of before. Everybody had to try a little bit of everything, like it or not, to teach us about other cultures and loving one another even if some of us had stinky food. They told us the story of stone soup, and we learned about giving and sharing with all of our new friends. After lunch, we washed our plates and marched back to the classroom in the big cabin and played indoor games for an hour. Then we all lay down for our naps.

Jarod was out cold along with most of the other kids in minutes. I was on the verge of drifting off when quietly, off in the distance, I heard a small frog, and my heart skipped a beat with excitement. It was just one frog at first, then two and then three. Some of the other kids must have heard them too, because they started to cry. I told them it was okay, frogs are nice, but they kept crying. I could hear the young teachers trying to comfort them as more and more frogs sounded off.

The frog sounds got louder and louder by the minute. Kids started crying louder and louder. I started to get worried too. Now we were all awake, and you could see people running by the windows. More and more kids began to cry. One of the teachers began to cry, and then another teacher ran out of the room. The frog sounds were everywhere now. We could even hear them in the room with us. More and more kids began to cry, until they were all crying. One of the teachers began to pray, quietly at first, then louder.

He kept saying, "Oh God, oh God!"

I sat up to see what was happening. People outside were running in all directions; they were saying "Oh God" too. I heard a loud frog right next to me. It was so close I thought it had to be in Jarod's pocket, only it wasn't. He was still waking up. Then Jarod looked at me like something horrible had happened and he was shaking his head, no-ish or yes-ish, I wasn't sure this time. Jarod didn't speak, he just looked at me with his mouth open and his eyes wide and his head sort of bobbing around. Before I could ask him what was wrong, I felt a sharp pain in my tummy. It was bad, and I wanted my mom. Then, even though I tried to stop it, my own frog arrived, my own terrible, terrible frog. With a loud, long, watery *riiiiibbbbbiiiit*, it happened. Right there in front of God and everyone, I pooped a frog! I began to pray with everyone else, "Oh God, oh God, oh God, oh God."

Maybe it was the potato salad, maybe it was the Jell-O, or maybe it was something in the water. I don't know exactly. But never in the history of religious summer camps has God been prayed to with such earnest devotion.

We prayed for more toilet paper, we prayed for more toilets, and we prayed, oh how we prayed, for the frogs to stop. The next few hours were a blur of standing in line for the outhouse, running into the woods, and then getting back in line for the outhouse. That night in the cabin we played cards in between trips to the potty. Uncle Dale said we all got the backdoor trots. That was supposed to be funny because the cabin only had a front door, and any trotting would have resulted in an accident for sure. Nobody was laughing, because it made us need to run to the outhouse. The one bit of hope we had that evening was that Aunt Jerry had brought us all a treat, and man, did we need a treat.

Mom got out our big camping pot and boiled water on the little woodstove that was surrounded with about fifty pairs of underwear that we had to hand wash in the river. Sadly, that was the closest thing we got to playing in the river all week.

When a child's only hope for the tiniest bit of joy is dependent on hot water boiling, time slows to a crawl. They say a watched pot never boils, but it does. It just takes two hours and four thousand times asking, "Is it ready yet?"

Auntie had a big can of hot cocoa mix, and it smelled like heaven as we stirred it into the big pot of water. We each had our cups at the ready, like a little line of ragged cocoa beggars. After waiting what seemed like an eternity, Auntie began to scoop the liquid hope drop by drop into a menagerie of cups and bowls held by our greedy little fingers. There was still a line at the bathroom, and it was dark out now, so we had a coffee can for the little kids to pee in if there was an emergency. As Auntie dished up the cocoa, Jarod whispered to Mom that he had to go number one. She looked out the window to see where the line was but couldn't tell through the rain. So they went with the coffee can option. Jarod stood on the top bunk, where he had previously been lying due to being sick. Mom balanced the coffee can and held up a towel for privacy the best she could. Only, Jarod was weak from a full day of running to the outhouse, and he had been holding it for a long time because of his fear of falling into the abyss.

Everyone had been served their cocoa and was waiting for Jarod and Mom so we could give thanks for the miracle that was our cocoa. We all heard the tinkle begin, then something went wrong. Maybe he waited too long, or it just got away from him, we may never know. There was a crack of thunder, Jarod jumped, and all heck broke loose. It was a religious camp, after all.

The coffee can clanged to the floor. Mom tried to catch it but had to drop the towel when she did. Jarod tried to cover up and lost his balance, only he couldn't shut off his little fire hose. Everyone stood there in horror with their mouths wide open as an arc of wee-wee sprayed wild across the small cabin. It made a dotted line right down the row of us kids, splashing from cup to cup to cup, not missing one, and finally ending in the pot of cocoa itself. The room was dead quiet except for the trickle of Jarod's little fire hose running dry. That was it; we all just started to cry.

Later, after we all went to bed, there was some talk of selling Jarod off to a traveling circus. Since he was still there when we all woke up, I guess in the end we decided to keep him.

A Herd of Nerds

Jason Napolitano and I have hung out since that day we got into a fight. It wasn't with each other; we were fighting against three grade-school classes of kids who wanted to beat us up for being nerds, seeing as how we were in the nerd class and all, and they actually wanted to beat up the whole class, not just us. The problem was that our fellow nerd-mates didn't want to fight. More to the point, they didn't want to get beat up again or, in some cases, several "agains."

Somebody somewhere had decided it would be a great idea to go on a giant nerd search and then bus every nerd from the whole school district to a sort of nerd refuge. From a bully's point of view, this must have seemed like a real time-saver. It was sort of an all-you-can-beat nerd buffet. Oddly enough, they called it the Challenge Program. If anything, it was more like shooting fish in a barrel.

Seaview Elementary School had just remodeled a whole fifth- and sixth-grade wing. This was to be the first time a school in the Northwest had computers in a classroom, so it was a big deal. All the kids who went to Seaview at the time thought the new super-cool classrooms were going to be for them. The fifth and sixth graders were real upset when instead they all got crowded into the old run-down part of the school, then watched as all of us nerds got bused in from other schools to be enriched in their new digs. "Enriched" meant that we got the best classrooms, got to learn how to use the new computers, went on field trips almost every week, and had ice cream parties every other month. You know, we got to do the kind of stuff that made the other children want to beat the snot out of us. So the biggest challenge in the Challenge Program was really just to not get the snot beat out of you.

233

The Challenge Program was something most of the kids had to work very hard to get into. They had to have super-high grades and pass all sorts of aptitude and IQ tests just to be considered. At his old school Jason had seen the Challenge kids being enriched, going on all kinds of field trips and getting ice cream, special treatment, and such. He was no fool and knew a good thing when he saw it. He told me that he asked his teacher where those kids were going all the time and how he could go too. Jason's teacher told him how those kids were in the program for gifted children and that Jason wouldn't be able to join them. Jason simply said, "When is the test?"

I, on the other hand, arrived kicking and screaming. I had never heard of this Challenge Program and had no desire to be challenged. I was not what one might call academically inclined. It was no secret that I hated school, I hated classrooms, I hated homework, I hated riding the bus, and I hated getting up early to ride the bus. I was a straight D-minus student if you averaged out the Cs and the Fs, so why, oh why was I going to Challenge class? Originally, I was being placed in a class for children of the D-minus persuasion. Only before I could go hang out with the glue eaters, I had to take the placement and IQ tests to determine just how dumb I was. And how dumb was I? I was too dumb to fail the "stupid test" and save myself from being shipped off to nerd sanctuary, like it or not.

There, on the day of the fight, we all were cornered behind the handball court and out of sight of the recess teacher. It was me, Jason, and every type of nerd from every kind of '80s nerd movie ever made. We were surrounded by thirty or more kids who felt we had just snatched away the paradise they believed was going to be theirs. We were being pushed and shoved in all directions at once. The sound of wheezing from asthma and the puff of inhalers began to fill the air. All at once

234

some sort of nerd instinct kicked in. Kids started hearing their mothers calling from far away, and bit by bit our nerd horde dwindled. Soon it was five, four, three, then only us two, back to back, being shoved and taunted.

Jason called over his shoulder, "You going to run?"

I yelled, "Nope! You?"

Jason yelled, "No."

We cocked back our fists and got ready to start kicking butt. Only the bell rang, so everybody had to go back to class.

That's how we met. In life you don't always find out who has your back the first second you meet them, but with Jason I did. We were fast friends from that day on.

Jason wasn't poor like me, but he had been poor, so he knew what poor was. He didn't make fun of me or ask questions that made me feel bad if I wore the same clothes too much or couldn't get money to go do stuff that the other kids did. He was cool with doing fun stuff that didn't take much money. I told Jason about how Jimmy and I made money selling fish to guys on the fishing pier who couldn't catch fish but wanted to lie to their wives and say they could. Jason told me about his dad being a diver and going spearfishing when he was in Florida. His dad said that's how he got the biggest fish of all. His dad, Jack, said, "You just pick the fish you want, and *bang*." So Jason and I decided to go spearfishing, then charge more money for the big fish we caught.

We only had one wet suit between the two of us. We had saved, scraped, and begged the twenty-five dollars it took to buy it at the local secondhand store. You might think that with water at a balmy forty-six degrees Fahrenheit in the Salish Sea (aka Puget Sound) we would have taken turns wearing the whole suit, only where is the fun in that? Instead, we played rock, paper, scissors to see who got the top and who got the bottoms, who got the gloves and who got the boots. Not having a weight belt meant that neither one of us could swim down below the surface of the water. We could only bob along on top, looking down at the fish that swam below just out of reach. That is, you could look down if it was your turn to use the scuba mask.

Mostly the fish were surf perch, big fish up to nineteen inches long and maybe five pounds or so. Normally, the only way we could ever catch these perch was with bloodworms and a hand line, but even then it was hard. Spearing them seemed easier. We fashioned a barb from a ten-inch-long piece of wire coat hanger that we hammered flat and sharpened with a file. We bent the other end into a tight J shape, then tied a ten-foot piece of Mom's clothesline to it. The other end was tied to the middle of a ten-foot bamboo pole from a neighbor's yard. We cut the top off the bamboo pole six inches above the last joint, so we could slide the mini-harpoon into the open end. The cord provided enough packing so the barb was held tight and didn't fall out when we pointed our spear down in the water to hunt for the perch.

We took the bus down to the Edmonds beach, waited until no one was looking, then climbed over the handrail and ducked under the ferry dock. One of us manned the bucket up on the concrete structure at the water's edge. The other one swam out fifteen yards to where the water got deeper and the pilings disappeared into the darkness.

The trick to getting underwater when you didn't have a weight belt was to put your back to a piling, then wrap your legs back around it behind you. You held the spear in your teeth pirate style, and you were ready to go. Taking a deep breath, you did one monster of a sit-up—an upside-down sit-up, so that would make it a sit-down, I suppose. Then you just crawled down the pole into the deep. The barnacles and mussels growing on the pilings got knocked off as you went down; all the bits of shell fell like snow down into the darkness. The sound of the shells being chewed, cracked, and spit out was the first sign of the perch arriving. A few small fish would dart up from the shadows, followed by a few more and then even more, and a giant living ball would rise up all around you. The crunching sound of the fish eating the mussels and barnacles that rained down was almost too much to take.

You waited for the largest of the perch to swim past, picked the one you wanted, and jabbed the barb into the passing fish. You unlocked your legs from the piling and bobbed back up to the surface, being pulled around by the fish still on the line. Swimming back to the water's edge, you handed the bamboo pole to your partner, who pulled in the fish. We took turns repeating the process, taking breaks to bury ourselves in the hot sand to warm up. Our limit was six perch apiece, and that was about all the cold we could handle anyway. We took all the fish over to the fishing pier and cleaned them at the cleaning stations. Then we sold them to the men who were heading home to face their wives empty-handed. It paid way better than a paper route, and it was ten times more exciting than mowing lawns.

Respect **That!**

The alley alongside our grandparents' house on Fourteenth Street was always cluttered. It was filled with old boxes, bits of firewood, boards, barrels, and all kinds of junk a kid could flip over to find worms, salamanders, snails, and slugs. For us boys, worms were good as gold. The big worms we called night crawlers, the little worms we called bloodworms. We were always jonesing for worms, because when we got enough, Dad would take us fishing.

We spent many an hour flipping, digging, and even praying for worms. One fine morning when we had reached our quota, we were told that if we walked down to the Sunset, Dad would take us out to the Brownsmead slough to do some catfishing. We said good-bye to Grandma Mary and Grandpa Owen, packed up the worms, and started hiking down Fourteenth Street toward the edge of town. We made it all of about half a block when Jarod buckled to the ground in pain. He was holding his leg and crying out really loud. Something had hit him. It took us a minute to realize that the two neighbor boys were crouched down behind the hedge in the yard across from Grandpa's house. When Jimmy saw them, he gritted his teeth and said, "Follow me!"

We turned and walked back up the hill to where the two boys were. The bigger of the two boys let fly with another shot from his Wrist-Rocket, a very powerful and accurate slingshot. I heard the rock scream past my ear, and I ducked. Jimmy didn't even blink; he just kept walking. We were face to face with the boys before they could get off a third shot.

These were the boys Grandpa told us had been terrorizing the neighborhood all summer. The smaller and older of the two boys had thick glasses, freckles, and a '70s bowl cut. We called him the Mouth. The

238

taller and younger of the two was his half brother. He didn't say anything the whole time. Later, when we would tell this story, we would call him the Mute, and about fifty other names. So the Mute stood there being mute and pointing the slingshot at Jimmy, while the Mouth explained that this was their block and we were going to do whatever they told us to do. This was because even though his younger brother was taller, he was the oldest kid there, so we had to obey him. This was the first time I ever heard anyone except a priest say "obey." The Mouth then said to the Mute, "If either one of them moves, let them have it!" Then he said, "Respect!"

Brother Jimmy, being the diplomat that he was, said to the Mouth, "I'll tell you what; since you're closest to my age and my little brother is the same age as Frankenstein there, I'm going to kick your ass while my kid brother shoves Bigfoot's head up where the sun don't shine."

Clearly, this was not what the Mouth was hoping to hear. He glanced over to his little brother Lurch as if to say *NOW!* only the Ostrich Boy didn't get it. The Mouth still had that *Really?* look on his face when Jimmy's fist snapped his glasses at the bridge of his nose. The two pieces of glasses were still sort of hanging in midair when the Jolly Green Giant tried to pull back the Wrist-Rocket and shoot me point blank. Only when he pulled back, he fumbled it right into my hands. Suddenly he had one end, and I had the other. We were both pulling hard, only I let go. Ker-snap! It left a bright-red welt from one side of his chest to the other in the shape of a sideways question mark.

He made a loud funny *Wahhhahhrrr* sound and then came at me like a whooping crane with hemorrhoids. As the String Bean sort of fell on top of me, I tucked into a ball. He was draped over my back. Every time he tried to get up or move, I gave him a right

239

hook square in the old beanbags. A woman came out and stood on the porch and just watched the boys take the beating of their lives. Jimmy had broken one of the fence pickets with the Mouth kid's skull, and the back of his head was now firmly wedged in between two of the other boards. I had punched the Giraffe in the bing-bongs a half dozen more times already when I heard Jimmy say, "Down, hut, hut." That was just before he kicked the tall kid in the face so hard that he flew back and hit the fence that his half brother had now become a part of.

That's when the lady came down off the porch and simply said, "Okay, boys, I think they've had enough now." It turned out that the lady was their mother. I think she knew they had it coming.

Jimmy helped me up, and we walked back over to where Jarod was still on the ground. Jimmy stopped, turned, and looked at the two utterly defeated boys, cleared his throat, and said in a fancy voice, "Respect *that*!"

Unbeknownst to us, our grandfather witnessed the entire event from his big bay window. Grandma later told us Grandpa was up there shadow boxing the whole time. Swelling with pride, Grandpa called ahead down to the Sunset bar, where my Dad was waiting for us, and regaled him with the heroic tale in all its graphic beauty.

Chapter 11

Picture-Perfect Holiday

Some years our family holidays were harder than others. The Christmas Jimmy was thirteen was a particularly hard one. Mom sat us down and explained how we were going to need to make some choices. We had to choose whether we wanted a Christmas tree or wanted to get bus tickets to go see everybody in Astoria. Well, as you may have guessed, we picked the Greyhound. Mom scraped together all the money she could and loaded some things we didn't need anymore into the car. Then we headed down to the pawn shop, where we said good-bye to the old family bullwhip, a fancy clock, and some other memories I don't remember now. I was sad to see them go, but glad Jarod had never learned how to use a bullwhip. Jimmy, on the other hand, was pretty upset at the loss of our cool family heirlooms.

There was snow that year through most of December, so it was real Christmassy everywhere we looked. Jimmy's best friend, Mike Coaker, lived across from us, and his family always had the biggest and the best of everything there was to have. They had a tree that was all fuzzy and white with gold furry streamers, ornaments as big as softballs, and a train that ran on a track all around the bottom of the tree. There was a button you could push that made the train whistle sound, and little puffs of smoke would come out too. To Jarod and me, their house looked like a department-store window.

Even without a tree, we still decorated the house as best we could. We made popcorn and cranberry strings and paper ring streamers, we cut out snowflakes and Christmas angels. We even drank hot cocoa and hot apple cider with cinnamon and cloves. Even though it was the closest thing to the true meaning of Christmas I can remember, Jimmy didn't seem to care. He just kept looking out the window over at Mike's house and thinking about all they had and all we didn't.

We all wandered off to bed, drifting off to dreamland content with our love for each other and the true meaning of Christmas—well, maybe not all. Sometime around 10 p.m., I woke to find Jimmy getting dressed to go out in the snow. He slid open the bedroom window and slipped out into the night without a sound. I peeked out the curtains and watched him walk over to Mike's house. Jimmy moved from shadow to shadow, silently disappearing and reappearing as he went from one to the next. He vanished behind Mike's house for a few minutes, then came back with Mike, who had something in his hand. They walked off down the block, fading into the darkness.

Later, Jimmy told me how they made their way down to the main road, keeping to the shadows as best they could. They got to the intersection where there was a very nice house with a yard all done up with a full lawn display. They had Santa, elves, reindeer, and a baby Jesus and the whole Christmas Nativity scene. The house had a long driveway lined with different animals and the wise men that were all bringing gifts to the baby Jesus. The yard was edged with matching fir trees that looked like a perfect Christmas-tree fence. Jimmy and Mike were standing in the shadows waiting for the cars to stop passing by. As the last car motored off into the distance, Jimmy said, "Okay, go!"

They both ran and slid down into the ditch just below the row of trees. Jimmy said, "Wait here." Mike nodded. The lights were off in the house, but they had to be careful. The year before, two very similar hoodlums had glued a beard on the baby Jesus, and the family who owned the house made a big stink about it.

Jimmy belly-crawled over to Santa's sleigh and mugged two of the elves who were minding their own business. He took their clothes and threw the now naked elves in the back of the sleigh. Jimmy crawled back to Mike and gave him a coat and a pointy hat. Mike handed Jimmy the hacksaw, and they began to creep along the edge of the road down past all the yard decorations. They both froze in their best elf poses every time Mike would whisper-yell, "Car!"

Mike stayed next to the road to be the lookout. Jimmy elfed over to the row of trees, carefully inspecting each one until he found the one that felt Christmassy enough for the job. Mike whisper-yelled a warning as each car made its way past the scene. Some cars whizzed by, and others slowed down to admire the decorations. Jimmy sawed quickly in between the passing cars, and Mike continued to freeze in elf poses when the cars went by. After ten minutes, the tree began to make cracking sounds. Jimmy changed sides and sawed faster.

Mike peered into the darkness, looking for the shine of headlights, and saw a car off in the distance. He waited as the car grew closer, seeing if it would turn before it passed by them. The car slowed and stopped, then drove a bit and slowed and stopped, now only a few blocks away. Mike whisper-yelled again, "Gawkers!"

Jimmy the elf froze, but the tree didn't. It kept making little cracking sounds with the slightest breeze. As the car drew closer, Jimmy strained to keep the tree from falling over, but it was too heavy; his feet began to slide in the snow. The car slowed to just a crawl as the occupants admired all the lights and the wonder of the manger scene. It was an old couple in an old car with an old dog, all looking out the window. Just as the old woman was pointing at the two bare butts sticking out of the back of Santa's sleigh, the tree gave way and fell across the street right onto the hood of their car! The old woman looked like she was about to have a heart attack.

The couple stepped out to assess the situation, when suddenly two of the yard elves magically came to life, rolled down the bank, leaped out into the street, grabbed ahold of the tree, and began running off into the darkness. They dragged the tree four blocks back to our house, leaving a trail the whole way.

The living room of the house we rented had a vaulted ceiling about sixteen feet high. When we awoke the next morning, the snow had covered the drag trail that led from the vandalized yard to our back door. Outside my bedroom window was a good four feet cut off of the tree base. Jarod and I ran into the living room and beheld a sight that is burned into my memory forever. The top of the tree was bent over where it hit the ceiling. The branches at the bottom of the tree were eight feet across and covered half the couch and two spots at the dining room table!

In the morning, Jimmy told Mom the Boy Scouts stopped by and dropped off the tree because we didn't have one. Mom stepped out into the living room to see Jarod and me standing on chairs decorating the tree as best we could and Jenni sitting on the couch holding the Christmas angel with a look of bewilderment on her face. I think she was wondering just how we were going to get the angel all the way up on top of that giant tree. Jimmy stood next to the tree just as proud as he could be. Mom gave us all a look, shook her head, and went into the kitchen to get a cup of coffee. We all decorated the tree with every decoration we owned, and it still wasn't enough. So we just made a Christmas-tree shape on the front side the tree with the decorations we had and called it good.

A few days later, Mom put us on the bus to go see Dad; when we got there, he had a tree, too, but not as good as ours. We were glad to see dad but sad to see that Chester, the hawk, was gone. When Dad heard us talking about the old bird, he just laughed and said, "It was time for Chester to go be a hawk again. I let him go, but he's not gone." And with that he went out on the back porch and aimed his rifle up at an unlucky pigeon. With a loud *KABOOM* he knocked a pigeon off the power lines, and it dropped smack down in the middle of the backyard. Dad winked and said, "Give it a minute."

He headed into the house to put the rifle away. As we watched him go back inside, we heard a whoosh of feathers behind us. There was Chester, all fat and happy as could be. Dad came back out and said, "You see? You just have to ring the dinner bell."

We were glad to see Chester was okay. The snow began to fall, and we all went back inside to get warm.

Barnacle Bill

We bundled up in what felt like ten layers of long johns, old jeans, and bread sacks on our feet to keep them dry. Then Jimmy took me down to the Edmonds pier, where he taught me to jig for squid. This kind of fishing was done at night when it was super dark and super cold. We had to buy a special lure that glowed in the dark and was all spiky to snag the squid as it bobbed up and down in the water. Jimmy said that the squid would think it was another squid because they can light up when they want to. I laughed because I thought Jimmy was telling a whopper. But Jimmy said they really did light up and were as bright as Christmas-tree lights.

We packed some sleeping bags and a metal bucket that we got from Grandpa Roy. Mom put together a bag with aluminum foil, butter, salt, pepper, and some garlic powder. We brought some charcoal briquettes and a plastic bucket too. When we got to the beach, we filled the metal bucket with sand, hauled it up onto the pier, and tried to find a good spot out of the wind. After we dibsed our spot, we lined up with everybody else and bobbed our lures up and down for the next few hours. It was boring. I told Jimmy I wanted to fish for rock cod instead. He told me I would lose my spot if I did and that the squid would be there soon.

I kept bobbing my line up and down and complaining about being bored and being cold and being hungry. Jimmy said to shut up and eat a sandwich, so I did—eat a sandwich, that is, but I kept whining. Jimmy threw a line off the other side of the pier baited with some fish guts that we got from the fish cleaning station, and left it for a while. We lit the briquettes and warmed ourselves up on our little fire, while we kept waiting for the squid to arrive. Suddenly we heard someone yell, "Here they come!"

Next to me a little old Vietnamese lady's fishing pole bent hard as she bobbed it up. She was shaky as she reeled in the flapping, writhing creature. She brought it over the railing, and it screamed like an alien. The woman unhooked it and put it in her bucket; as she did, it sprayed ink all over her. She smiled at me and said it was good luck.

Jimmy yelled at me, "What are you doing? They're here! Start fishing."

I ran over to my pole and started bobbing it up and down. I got one, so I reeled it in. Jimmy helped me put the squid in our plastic bucket, where it squirted ink and made all the water go black. The Vietnamese lady said to me, "Good job, Jimmy!" and gave me a thumbs-up. I looked over at Jimmy, who just shrugged and kept fishing. I pointed to myself and said, "Jeremy." She smiled and pointed to herself and said, "Rông Ao."

I put my line back over the side and jigged some more. That's when I saw it.

Jimmy yelled to me, "Here come the salmon!"

Off in the distance, there were flashes of light under the water; little glowing balls raced in all directions. You could see the balls of light split apart where the salmon raced in. Suddenly they were all around us. Light was everywhere. As I stared into the water my world went sideways. I couldn't tell what way was up, and I fell back on my butt.

Jimmy said, "Are you okay? Get up and hold onto the railing; keep jigging!"

I did. The light show was amazing. The soft, glowing lights were flashing and whizzing all around us. We caught lots of squid and filled half the bucket. When the squid moved back out to deeper water, Jimmy and I checked the other line. We had a fish, a big fish! The old lady let us use her big net on a rope to pull the fish in. When we pulled it over the railing, Jimmy said it was a cabezon. That's a big fish that looks like the little

sculpins we would catch in the river. Jimmy killed it so
it wouldn't suffer any, and threw the line back out. Then
he took the cabezon to the cleaning station and cleaned
it. When he came back, he asked if I was hungry, and I
was, so we took a fillet of the fish and put it in the foil
that Mom packed. Only, the fish was green—not the
outside but the inside, the meat. I asked Jimmy if it was
supposed to be green. The old lady saw the face I was
making and laughed. She said, "Good fish, real good
fish." We cooked it up with the spices and butter. It
came out white as could be and tasted like heaven.

We gave some to the old lady, who said, "Thank
you, Jimmy," even though I still wasn't Jimmy. She
asked if she could cook up a squid in our bucket, so we
let her. Ten minutes went by and she called us over.
Smiling, she handed us each a set of crispy tentacles. I
looked at Jimmy, who knew what I was thinking. Jimmy
said through his teeth in a way I had heard Dad do a
dozen times, "Smile and eat it!" And I did.

We caught a few more squid, and Jimmy cleaned
them and put them in a bag. I went to the pay phone and
called Mom to come and get us. We started packing up
all our stuff, dumped out our bucket of sand and coals,
and folded up our poles. I pulled in the line we caught
the cabezon on; it was heavier than it should have been.

I said, "Hey, we got something."

Jimmy ran over with the bucket. We both looked
over the edge. Jimmy said it was just brown seaweed.

I said, "No way; it's heavy and it moved!"

Jimmy took the line and pulled it the rest of the
way up. It moved again.

I said, "What is it?"

The old lady said, "Ooh, octopus! Good to eat!"

Jimmy and I were amazed. We took the hook out
of its little arm and let it crawl around on our hands.
Jimmy and I said at the exact same time, "Let's keep it!"

I held it, and Jimmy went down to the beach and filled our bucket with seawater. He flipped over some rocks and grabbed half a dozen shore crabs to feed to the octopus. We put the lid on the bucket and ran up to the parking lot to meet Mom.

As we ran, Jimmy said, "Hey, don't tell Mom."

I said, "Yeah no, duh."

We had an old refrigerator on our back porch. It didn't keep food very cold but was just right for keeping our new friend, Barnacle Bill the octopus, happy as could be. Too happy, really; we had to keep taking the city bus down to the beach to get new saltwater and shore crabs, because Barnacle Bill was a pig. He would steal all the crabs out of the crab bucket and escape every chance he got. He made a mess out of everything. He wouldn't do what he was told and was a general pain in the butt.

Now we sort of knew how Mom felt raising us boys. Not much more than a week later, we decided to take Barnacle Bill down to the beach and let him go back to where he could steal all the crabs he wanted.

Have a Coke and a Smile!

My ears were ringing as I began to open my eyes. Blinking, I tried to focus a bit. Suddenly I was aware of being on the ground with Jarod kneeling over me.

"Are you dead?"

Everything rushed back. I remembered! I wrapped both hands around his throat and said, "I'm going to kill ya!"

As I choked the life out of my little brother, I could hear our cousin Andrea on the phone screaming to our moms, "They're killing each other, they're killing each other! Come home now!"

Rewind to a few minutes earlier. Jarod, Andrea, and I were at home on a Friday night while Mom and Aunt Sheryl took a well-deserved night out. We were playing Monopoly for about an hour, and as always Jarod was the banker and as usual, I was losing. I landed on Boardwalk, where of course Jarod had three hotels. The writing was on the wall and although I knew better—we all knew better, but no one knew betterer than I knew better—I grabbed the last of my Monopoly money, crumpled it in my fist, and threw it at him.

The wrinkled-up colored money was still drifting to the floor as I stood up and walked away in slow motion. I had made it across the room and partway down the hall when I heard Andrea gasp out, "No!"

I turned and immediately read the words "Have a Coke and a Smile!" printed boldly on a Coca-Cola glass that was now twelve inches from my face.

It was the twenty-four-ounce giveaway decanter that we had gotten for buying ten of something. I have to give it to Jarod, though; he couldn't hit the broad side of a barn with the dart he put under my kneecap, but man, that Coke glass was right on target.

250

I jerked my head back, which made the glass hit me square on the chin, the same way a boxer hits a guy on the chin and knocks him out cold. It lifted me up off the ground and flattened me out in midair. The glass exploded into a million tiny pieces, leaving a nice dent in my chin and a dozen little wispy cuts all over my face that looked far worse than they were.

By the time Jarod came to see if he had killed me, I was a bloody mess and out cold. I'm not sure how long I was out, but since I didn't wake up in a shallow grave, I would guess not too long. As I came to, I could hear Andrea on the phone screaming, "Get home now! No, really, they're killing each other!" When Mom got home, I was immediately put on restriction for wrinkling Jarod's Monopoly money.

Mom told me that I should have known better by now, and that it was my own fault that I got bit. Yeah, I said "bit." What Mom meant was that after all the other Monopoly episodes, I should have known that deliberately crushing Jarod's Monopoly money was the equivalent of putting your head in an alligator's mouth, so I shouldn't be surprised when I got bit by the alligator. To tell the truth, I wasn't surprised that I got bit. I was, however, very surprised that his aim was good enough to knock me out cold.

A Thing Called Hooky

As we walked to school, Jimmy began to tell me the story of hooky. Hooky, he said, was when kids ran off from school like the Lost Boys ran off to Neverland. Jimmy told me that when you did hooky you could be anything or anyone you wanted to be. Nobody could tell you what to do or where you had to go to, and most importantly, you didn't have to be in school. Hooky sounded awesome—right up until Jimmy told me about the truant officer, that is. He told me that the truant officer hunted the kids who played hooky and put them in kid-sized handcuffs and kid-sized ball-and-chains once they had been caught. I knew he was pulling my leg, but he did say that if they caught you it would be bad, worse than going to jail by far. They would take you back to homeroom, call your parents, and then make you come in to school on a Saturday, the whole Saturday!

All the way to school, Jimmy kept trying to talk me into doing hooky. He even said if I went with him, we could go to the park and look for pond dragons. He stopped at the corner just below the school but kept looking at me as I walked Jarod down the covered walkway to his class. Jarod went in and I was about to do the same when something caught my eye. I saw the big goofy black Lab that lived next to the school running and rolling around out on the school playing field. I couldn't begin to count the number of times I had watched him squeeze through the fence to run out and play with all the kids at recess, or the number of times we went back to class and I could see him still out there rolling in the sun. All those times I watched him, my little soul would float up and leap into that goofy old dog as he ran free and played. On any given day I couldn't have told you a single word the teacher said,

252

but I could have given a four-page report on everything the dog had done while I was supposed to be paying attention in class.

The sight of the dog made the thought of being chained to my desk suddenly unbearable. Little boys are not meant to be locked indoors all day. Little boys need mud between their toes and the smell of wet dogs, the way plants need the sun, the way birds need the sky, the way fish need the water.

I froze in my tracks. All the other children looked as if they had become a horde of possessed zombies. Slowly, I backed away from my classroom door, being sure not to make any sudden movements lest I get bit. I eased along the walkway staying tight to the wall, fighting the flow of all the zombie children mindlessly streaming into their classrooms. Finally, I made it down to the street corner, where I could see Jimmy off in the distance. I started running to catch up. As I ran harder, I could feel the goofy old Lab running inside me.

I was free, and it was glorious!

Half out of breath, I caught up to Jimmy and asked, "Where are we going?"

He said, "You'll see."

We walked back home and stocked up on all the things we might need for our adventure. After that we wandered down past the police station and through the middle of town until we got to Wilcox Park, where we looked for pond dragons for about an hour. I made Jimmy say the pond dragon chant even though he didn't want to. We found some leeches and saw some turtles, but the closest we got to seeing a pond dragon was some swirls in the mud that could have been anything. We didn't find any and we got hungry, so we went up to the Lynn-Mart Shop and Save. There we got a box of Pop-Tarts and some chocolate milk with our lunch money.

We sat outside the store and ate all but one silver pack of the Pop-Tarts, which we saved for lunch.

Jimmy told me to wait and went back inside the store. He came back out with a carton of cigarettes that he said he got for free. He opened up the box and told me to tuck my pants into my socks, and he did the same. We put all the cigarettes down our pants. Then Jimmy said that this was a good place to go dumpster diving, so we went around the back of the store and climbed up into the dumpster and started digging around for stuff.

Jimmy said that they threw away all the things people returned but that were too used up to sell again. We found half a set of steak knives, some perfume for Mom, and a whole box of yo-yos with the labels missing. We found bars of soap shaped like seashells and penny whistles and a Stretch Armstrong doll with the goop dripping out. We left that, even though we both agreed it would be great if we could blow it up on the Fourth of July. There were windup cars that didn't wind up anymore, a box of hot cocoa packets with four unopened packets left, karate-man rubber finger puppets, and an octopus thing that you could throw at the wall and it would walk down the wall, only it was missing some legs. We stuffed all the booty in our pants until we looked like genies. Jimmy told me to wait by the dumpster, and he went back into the store to acquire a lighter. Two minutes later, he came running out of the store with a big guy chasing him.

The man ran over and grabbed me, so Jimmy had to come back. The man said that the police were on their way, and they were going to take us to jail for stealing a lighter. Jimmy said he didn't take any lighter, and no, they wouldn't take us to jail. Then the big store guy said Jimmy did too take a lighter and the cops were going to take us away for sure. Jimmy gave me a reassuring look so I wouldn't be worried, but I was scared anyway.

The officers arrived after a few minutes to get down to the facts. They wrote down the man's story, and that he said he saw Jimmy steal a lighter. Then they asked Jimmy for his side of the story.

Jimmy said, "I went in to use the bathroom and that big fat store man started chasing me around for no reason. I don't even have a lighter. Then he came out here and grabbed my brother's arm and hurt him."

He looked over at me like I was supposed to have a hurt arm, so I rubbed it like maybe I did. The officers told us we had to empty out our pockets on the sidewalk to see if we had a lighter. The taller officer said, "Okay boys, line up what you got."

We began lining up all the stuff we had from home and from the park and from the store and out of the dumpster. We emptied our coat pockets and our pants pockets and all the stuff we had in our pants legs. We took the stuff out of our shoes, and I had to take off my socks because some of the smaller toys had slipped down in there. The man from the store was yelling, "See, see, I told you. I told you!"

We kept lining stuff up and had gone about ten feet down the sidewalk when the two officers, who were trying not to laugh, said we could make two rows instead of just one. They wanted to know where we had gotten all this stuff, and we told them that there was all kinds of stuff in the dumpster for free. One of the officers went to look in the dumpster. When he came back, he nodded to the other officer. They patted us down to see if we were holding out, then looked through all the stuff.

The man from the store said, "Look at all the stuff they stole!"

The officers asked the man if he saw us steal any of the stuff we had on the sidewalk. The man said, "Just the lighter." Only there was no lighter. The officers told the man the garbage was fair game after he threw it out, so they couldn't take us off to jail for taking garbage. The officers took one more look at all the stuff on the sidewalk, shook their heads, and chuckled. They told us to be good and got back in their car and drove away. The man from the store called us hoodlums and went back into the store.

We tucked our pants back into our socks and loaded up all our treasure. Maybe it was because the officers were laughing so much, or because they didn't want to fill out any paperwork, but for whatever reason, they let us keep all the cigarettes and the knives.

As we walked over to the alternative school, I asked Jimmy where the lighter went. He laughed and said he slipped it into the store guy's pocket when he was grabbin' us.

At the alternative school, we gave away the cigarettes to some kids Jimmy knew when they came out on their morning break.

Jimmy told the kids the story of how the police laughed and let us go with all the stuff. Jimmy did all the voices of the officers, made his cheeks puff out like the big guy who was chasing him, and did a funny walk back and forth. We all laughed so hard we couldn't breathe. After all the kids went back to class, Jimmy and I wandered back home. On our way past the police station we saw they were having an auction of stuff that got turned in or taken from bad guys.

We went in and looked around to see what they had. There in the middle of all the bicycles was Jarod's bike. The bicycle had been specially made for Jarod's birthday by a friend of the family. It had been taken from the yard two months earlier, and now the people who were supposed to help us find it were going to sell it! We went up to the desk and told the young officers sitting there that it was our brother's bike, and they couldn't sell it. They didn't believe us, and they told us that they were going to sell it anyway. We would have to bid on the bike if we wanted to keep it. Jimmy told the officers that we knew the boss of the police and if they were going to steal our bike then the man should call him right then about his job—you know, if he wanted to keep it.

After we argued for five more minutes the police chief happened to walk by and we yelled for him. The officers we were arguing with got a bit red-faced when the chief made them give us back our bike. As we walked away Jimmy made a ha-ha face at them that made me laugh.

The bicycle had two flat tires, so we had to walk it all the way back home. By the time we got to our house, there were two cop cars parked out front waiting for us. Jimmy joked that they could have given us a ride home.

They were talking to Mom about two houses that got robbed that day. They had a description of the kid who did it and were looking for Jimmy since he wasn't at school and matched the description of the robber. Jimmy told them that he wasn't the robber, and that I was his alibi, and how I had been with him the whole time when those houses were being robbed.

The police gave us a look like we were liars. Then one of the officers asked me if we had an alibi other than each other for when the first house was being robbed.

I said, "We sure do! We were with the police!"

We told them about being over at the Lynn-Mart Shop and Save and about the dumpster diving. We left out the part where Jimmy got the cigarettes. The officers radioed in to the police station radio lady to ask the first officers from the Lynn-Mart Shop and Save if we were telling the truth about being with them that morning. While we were waiting to hear back from the radio lady, the officers asked if we had an alibi for the afternoon robbery.

I said, "Yup, we were with the police then too!"

The officers thought we were messing with them, but we weren't. We told Mom to call the chief and ask him about us being with him in the afternoon and getting the bike back. Mom called, and the chief told her that we were at the auction and that we got Jarod's bike back. We were still waiting for the radio lady to radio back about the dumpster diving, but instead, to save time, the chief radioed the officers from the Lynn-Mart Shop and Save himself. They said we were in fact with them and they were still laughing about it. Then the chief mentioned to Mom how he had even seen Jimmy two days before at about 2 a.m. when he was out on patrol.

Jimmy was driving Mom's car, and the chief and his partner pulled up next to Jimmy and they waved to each other.

Mom got so mad she yelled at the chief, "He's only thirteen! He's not supposed to be driving!"

Mom handed the phone to the officers at the house, and they said, "I see, yes sir."

They gave the phone back to Mom and apologized for bothering us and then drove away. Next, I got to learn about restriction and then a thing called Saturday detention.

Hooky sucks!

Crocofamiliarisodontigluteaphobia

"Crocofamiliarisodontigluteaphobia" is a word I made up to remind me not to tease Jarod. It's supposed to be Latin, more or less. It means the fear of getting bit on the butt by the same alligator that bit you on the butt last time.

If there really is such a fear, I should have had it. But I didn't. You would think I would be as shaky as Captain Hook around a crocodile by now, *tick tock tick tock*!

Like a lot of kids, we three boys shared a room growing up. "Shared" is a bit of an exaggeration. We divided a room. Jimmy had a shelf that, like many older brothers' shelves, we weren't allowed to touch, look at, or even think about. On this shelf Jimmy kept all his cool older-brother stuff. He had some arrowheads and a big fishing weight with the groove around the middle that he got from Grandpa Owen and a glass fishing float we found on the beach down by the jetty. There were Super Sonic basketball trading cards and some Hot Wheels cars and a model of a 1971 Ford Mach 1. The coolest thing on the shelf was a big knife he got for his birthday. It was from Mom's friend whom we called Grandma Betty, but she was really a friend of the family. It was a bowie knife with a carved handle. It had a brass hand guard and was very sharp. We all thought it was super cool. Mom would let Jimmy take the knife out, but only if she was there.

We had been stuck inside again, because it was raining again. Cabin fever was starting to set in. Mom said she had just about had it with hearing us whine. She gave us an ultimatum. Actually, first she explained what an ultimatum was, then she gave us one.

We could either stop complaining and go play a board game, or we could clean the entire house. Mom

259

motioned toward the Helen Reddy album and the vacuum cleaner. We all backed away real slow like, went back to our room, and took down the Monopoly game. After a long argument over who would be the car and who would be the top hat, we got down to business.

I moved my thimble around the board, bought some properties, and collected my two hundred dollars. Jimmy did the same, and for a while we were all having fun. Jarod was bankering right along, hamsters were spinning on their wheels, and all was right with our world.

I rolled the dice and landed on Jarod's Park Place. It didn't go well after that. I just kept losing more and more money. Eventually I was overcome with that sick sort of feeling that you get from playing Monopoly when the game is all but lost. I started pretending to be bored but was really thinking of ways to distract Jarod from the bank. He was getting crafty after years of being the banker. He learned to keep his back to the wall like a gambler in the old-time Western movies. I edged over a bit and perused all the items on Jimmy's no-touch shelf, listening to our hamster Marshmallow hum on his little wheel as he ran. Another bad roll and Jarod took all but the last two hundred dollars of my Monopoly money. As he tucked it in with his own, I snatched Marshmallow from his wheel and set him on the ground along the same wall Jarod had his back to. Marshmallow waddled down and slipped himself into the crack between Jarod's butt and the wall. When he did, Jarod leaped forward, knocking the game board half across the floor. Then out ran Marshmallow, grabbing the little plastic houses and stuffing them into his cheeks. Jimmy started laughing so hard he was crying. I yelled, "You knocked the board, so you lose!" With that I jumped up, put my fist in the air, and declared myself the winner.

Remember the Crocofamiliarisodontigluteaphobia?

My first clue that I was in trouble was the look of horror on Jimmy's face. His eyes bulged out and he was shaking his head side to side in what seemed like slow motion. Jimmy's mouth was starting to yell for Mom, while at the same moment his body began to turn and run. I didn't know what we were running from, but I did know that I should be running. I got my legs to take a step, maybe two, then I saw the light! Actually, I felt the light, and the light really hurt! The light was very pointy, and it was now stuck in my ribs just below my shoulder blade.

I kept running down the hall. Jimmy caught the knife as it fell, or rather shook loose, out of my ribs. Thank God, because this kept Jarod from picking up the knife and taking another stab at it, so to speak. We all knew how Jarod liked to be thorough.

I yelled, "You win! You win!" as Jimmy and I ran to lock ourselves in the bathroom. Jimmy checked to see if I was going to be dead. He said I wasn't. Then he washed my back off and got me a bandage to stop the bleeding. We hid the knife, so Jarod couldn't find it again.

I really did see the light, because that was the last time I ever played Monopoly with Jarod. It was just too dangerous.

Did I mention Crocofamiliarisodontigluteaphobia?

Yeah, I think I did.

Jeremy T. Owen

The Kung Fu Kid

We loved kung fu! We memorized all the kung fu moves we saw, bought kung fu posters, and took the city bus down to Chinatown to look at all the kung fu weapons at the kung fu store. I even made a throwing star that stuck into anything when you threw it. I tried my best to learn kung fu from last month's kung fu magazines and from a book written by Bruce Lee that I carried around like a bible.

We stayed up late to watch kung fu movies on television so we could copy everything they did and begin to master our kung fu skills. We picked out kung fu names, and we each picked a kung fu style. Jason worked on Tiger style, and I was all about the Drunken Monkey style. Jarod got a book from the library at school called *The Art of War* by Sun Tzu. He sat inside his refrigerator box making maps of how to conquer the neighborhood once we became ninjas.

To be conquerors, we would need to master all the weapons that ninjas used for ninja-ing and such. Because we weren't old enough, we couldn't buy the store-bought weapons down in Chinatown, so we had to make our own. We fashioned what we called chako sticks or nunchucks out of some cut-up broom handles, a bit of clothesline, and a roll of black tape. They were easy to make. We just cut the broom handles about a foot long, drilled holes in the ends, and laced them together. Then we swung them around and smacked stuff. We whipped them over our heads, around our backs, and between our legs, occasionally setting back our puberty in the process.

We made throwing bolas using three of the four wooden feet off the small couch that sat outside the counselor's office at Jimmy's school. Jarod and I would run while Jimmy threw the bolas at our feet. They worked great, only we had to stop using them on each other and make up a good lie for Jarod's new black eye and what was probably a minor concussion. It was always hard to tell if Jarod had gotten a concussion or not, with him being so quirky and all.

My favorite weapon and the easiest to make was my staff. This required a trip over the backyard fence at night. I had been eyeballing a fine piece of bamboo in the neighbor's yard that was perfect for the task. The colder temperatures and shorter growing season in the Northwest meant that the bamboo grew thick walls and was just right for staff making.

I broke two of our dumpster steak knives sawing it down. We used the barbecue to fire-harden the ends by roasting the wood a bit until the natural sugars in the wood crystallized and made the whole thing tougher than it was before the roasting. It made it look cool too. Jarod copied some of the kung fu-looking words out of his war book onto the wood using his calligraphy set. Yes, Jarod was a nine-year-old with a calligraphy set. Over the whole summer, I got really good with my staff. I did wrist rolls and neck rolls and locked it in my elbow in a way cool ninja pose.

We were really excited when our local radio station had a contest to see what kinds of crazy things people would do for ten thousand dollars. Listeners wrote letters saying what their ten-thousand-dollar stunt would be. Then they read some on the radio and picked the best ones for people to do live on the air. One guy was going to climb the Seattle Space Needle wearing nothing but two smiley-face stickers on his butt cheeks. They didn't pick him.

For my idea, I took a six-foot-long two-by-four and hammered about a thousand nails through it, and walked on it with my bare feet while I swung my ninja staff around. Jenni said I should put my bed of nails up on some sawhorses, so I did. Jimmy said I should hammer long nails into the ends of my staff, so it was more dangerous. I did that too. We got two dozen shiny silver sixteen-penny nails from the hardware store. We drilled some holes to put the nails in, used lots of glue, and wrapped the end with black tape to really make the shiny silver nails stand out. I sent my name and act in to the radio station to see if I would get picked for the contest. While we waited, I practiced every day after school. I stood on the spikes in my bare feet and did all kinds of tricks. Most the time I used the handle from the push broom for safety because my staff not only looked dangerous, it actually was dangerous. I knocked myself in the back of the head twice with the spikes before I switched to the broom handle for practicing. The second time I stuck it in my head it was harder to pull out, so I only used the real staff when people were watching.

Weeks went by. I kept practicing and waiting for the radio station to call so I could win my ten thousand dollars. Eventually school started back up, and my practice time was cut short. That year Jimmy was in a new high school. Of course, Jimmy was always in a new school. Jimmy was and probably still is the only child to be kicked out of every high school and every middle school in our school district. That included the alternative school where they sent the really rough kids, and sadly, it was also where Mom worked. It wasn't long before he was in trouble at this new school too. According to Jimmy, all that getting kicked out of school wasn't entirely his fault. I can say that at least this time it may have been my fault.

I got home and went straight out to the backyard and up on my bed of spikes to practice. I had just got warmed up when Jimmy and this kid named Donny came through the gate. Jimmy threw me my shoes and socks and said, "Put them on!"

I did. He tossed me my spiked staff and said, "Let's go!"

We headed off down the road to a small patch of woods by the stop sign at the bottom of our hill. There was a clearing there in the summer that by winter was half a pond and, in the spring, had mudpuppies swimming in it. When we got to the clearing, there were five big guys in letterman's jackets.

These kids were big, bigger than us by far. Jimmy was only fourteen, and these kids were on the football team at the high school. One kid moved toward me. When he did, Jimmy gave me a look that I knew meant to start swinging my stick around. I started my routine, spinning, jumping, and stomping my feet. The nails flashed as they caught the beams of light peeking through leaves high above us. All the whirling around turned red dirt to dust, which began to form a cloud that swirled all around us. Jimmy was shouting like a preacher warning about the Apocalypse. Donny stood off to the side and back a bit. He kept yelling, "Yeah! Yeah! Yeah!" after everything Jimmy yelled.

As Jimmy went on, the light from the heavens started streaming through the dust cloud like God was on our side. I was moving faster and faster as Jimmy yelled louder and louder. Gritting my teeth, I tried to keep myself from shaking, dropping my stick, or just running away. As if I was possessed by some sort of ancient spirit, blood began to stream from my eyes and down my cheeks. Jimmy was pushing and shoving the biggest one of the high school kids, daring him to make a move. Jimmy shoved him harder and harder, yelling things that kids shouldn't yell.

Jimmy said, "You think it's funny messing with someone smaller than you? You think you're tough? You're nothing! Just a momma's boy!"

Then Jimmy said some stuff about the kid's mom that I hope to God wasn't true. After a minute, the big kid made a small step backwards and that was all it took. The other four kids looked at each other and began to crumble. Jimmy went from one to another, got right in their faces, and told them they were nothing. They all turned and walked off, not saying a word. When they were gone, I lost it. I was so afraid I began to cry a lot harder. I was sobbing now instead of just tears running down my cheeks.

Did I say blood before? I meant mud. Mud was streaming from my eyes. All the red dust was hitting my tears and running down. On the way home Jimmy got mad at me and kept saying, "Why are you crying? We won! Stop crying. We won, man. We won!"

Ghosts in the Night

We awoke to a pounding on our door. I slipped from the top bunk, landing on the pile of toys that littered the floor of our room. I rolled my ankle off to the side and landed hard on my bottom. Jarod rolled over and asked what was going on.

I said, "I don't know."

We could hear shouting, doors opening and closing, and people running. We turned on the light and threw some clothes on. It was late, maybe 3 a.m., when Jarod and I walked out to the living room to find the house empty and cold. The front door sat wide open and a red glow was coming from outside. We could hear people far away shouting in a panic. Jarod and I slowly stepped out onto the porch. It was bright and dark, all at the same time. Everything was lit by fire.

The nighttime shadows danced in a frightening red glow. We couldn't see people, only shadows of people. Two figures began to move out of the flickering darkness, slowly coming toward us. Jarod said, "Is this a bad dream?"

I told him I didn't think so. The two pale figures began to wail. Wringing their hands, they slowly approached us. Jarod grabbed my hand tight and whispered one word: "Ghosts!"

Their gowns were grayish black where they touched the ground. They had long, tangled white hair that ran down past their waists. Black tears ran down their cheeks. They floated up to us and said, "We have to go back! We must go back!"

They were pleading with us, begging us. "Don't you see? We have to go back."

They reached out to us, crying, "Can't you hear them? We have to go back!"

We could hear something. It was a kind of screaming, or a screeching maybe. It made you shiver, like nails on a chalkboard, but not fingernails. These were steel nails, and it cut your ears to hear.

The ghosts just kept repeating, "Oh please, oh please, oh please?"

From off in the distance, Jimmy ran toward us. He was moving fast through the smoke and the firelight and shadows. When he got to us he was black with soot, his hair was all singed, and he was shaking his head no. He shouted at the ghosts, "No! You can't go back!"

The ghosts wailed louder, sobbing even harder.

They were closer now, and you could see their breath when they talked.

Jimmy yelled, "You stay here with them!"

He motioned to me and Jarod. The ghosts came even closer. Jarod and I stood frozen. The ghosts said, "But we have—"

Jimmy interrupted. "They're gone! It's over! It's over!"

They listened and looked back at the fire a few houses away. The screaming sound had stopped and was slowly being replaced by the sound of fire engines coming toward us. The ghosts looked at each other, then at us, and cried even harder. They collapsed to the ground, rocking and moaning. Mom ran out of the house and wrapped them in blankets.

As she helped them to their feet, she looked at Jarod and me. "Come help."

We walked over and took their arms so they could lean on us to walk. They were shivering, frail, and felt like they would fall apart in our hands. They smelled of smoke and burnt wire and burnt hair. They seemed empty somehow, like they could float away. We brought them into the house and sat them down at the kitchen table. Mom got them glasses of water. They said, "Thank you," as best they could, their voices all but gone now, taken by the smoke and the sorrow.

One of them lifted her hand to her face. Now in the light of the kitchen, her skin was old and paper thin. She swept the soot-filled hair from her face. It was only then we could see that we knew these ghosts. These were the spinster sisters who lived in a ramshackle house half a block down from us. Milly and Katherine were in their late seventies, but now looked much older. Mom said they were Depression babies. That meant they had a hard life and because of that they kept everything they ever could keep. Their house was piled high with newspapers and books and coffee cans filled with buttons. They had jars packed with empty spools of thread, rubber bands sorted by color, and empty little perfume bottles. They were all stacked as high as they could go, and the paths in between were so small you had to turn sideways to pass.

They had a half dozen cats that ran wild through their cluttered maze of a house, a house that their father and uncles had built by hand a very long time ago. It was the house that they were born in and had lived in their whole lives. A house that was now burning to the ground as they sat at our kitchen table sipping water and mourning the loss of all they had ever known, ever had, ever loved.

The fire trucks were coming, and all the neighbors stood around outside their houses in bathrobes and pajamas watching the fire. Jimmy had seen the fire before the rest of us. He was watching TV when light started coming through the window. He knew the old ladies would be trapped, so he ran to help them. He found them in their bedroom trying to make it back through the flames to save their beloved cats. I don't know how Jimmy got the old women out the window, but he did. He tried to go back in for the cats, but it was no use. Later, he found one of the sisters' purses; it was all melted by the fire. That was all that survived.

The women went back outside and stood in the cold until there was little more than ash. One by one the neighbors went back inside their houses, shut off their lights, and went to sleep. The firemen left; it was dark and quiet. The two old women just stood there all alone in the street, staring at the ashes. Mom and Jenni walked down the block and pulled them away from their anguish. They brought them to our home, and we did our best to make them comfortable. We washed what little they had over and over, but it was no use; the smoke had taken what the fire hadn't. The woman's purse that had melted into a black glob held what little hope was left for them.

The sun came up. For most of that morning, Jimmy sat on the front porch chipping and peeling away the charred layers of the purse, freeing coins and chewing gum and bits of cash money that we taped back together as best we could. Eventually he saved the small amount of money they had. Jimmy's fingers were worn raw from the effort. When he finished, we three boys went to the house and found their cats and buried them, so the old women didn't have to see them. They had nothing now and stayed with us for half a week before a cousin from far away was able to send them bus tickets. They spent those last days wandering through the ashes trying to find anything they could and hoping that maybe a cat or two would return; sadly, none ever did.

The city bulldozed the property and hauled away all the debris. In the spring, where the house used to be, a small pond began to form, surrounded by grass and trees. Now it was a place where frogs chirped along to the hum of dragonflies, where mosquitoes buzzed, and memories faded away.

Chapter 12

Going First

We were on our way back in from the polliwog fields when we heard it. Something was falling through the branches above our heads. It landed hard at our feet, shook for a moment, and was still. It was smallish and looked like a big pink mouse. We were still trying to figure out what exactly it was when we heard a sound again.

Something began moving through the trees. There was a chattering squeaky kind of sound, and then another small creature hit the forest floor at our feet. We looked up through the leaves to see a big squirrel come out of its nest high up in a maple tree. We could see it had something in its mouth. With a flick of its head, it sent the small package flying right for us. Jimmy stretched his shirt out like a basket, and as it fell, he moved like he was catching a fly ball.

Jimmy simply said, "Move!" As I stumbled back the little creature landed in Jimmy's outstretched shirt safe and sound. We looked at it for a moment.

Jimmy said, "I think it's a baby squirrel. The mother is killing them."

I said, "Why would she do that?"

Jimmy said, "Mother rabbits do it too, sometimes; I don't know why."

Jimmy held out his shirt so I could pick the tiny squirrel up. We looked at the little guy and waited to see if more squirrels would fall from the sky.

I asked, "Will it bite us?"

Jimmy hesitated. "Um, no, I think you're good."

The little guy was pretty beat up. He had some bruising and tiny bite marks here and there, and was still bleeding a little as we walked home. I wrapped him up in my shirt to keep him warm. Jimmy named the squirrel Chipper. We took him to our room and got a small bottle from Jenni's Suzie Crawls A Lot doll. We filled it with warm milk and fed him the best we could. Mom let us keep Chipper in a cardboard box with a light over it so he would stay warm. That's the way you do with baby rabbits.

It was like magic. In a flash Chipper was outside running everywhere. Jimmy said Chipper had to go be with all the other squirrels so he would learn to be a tough squirrel. From then on Chipper the squirrel would run right up to us and we would give him treats. Every time we turned a corner, there he was, looking for peanuts.

Jimmy explained to me how to tell just which squirrel our Chipper was. Chipper grew up to be the toughest of all the squirrels. We would see him for years to come, and I was proud to have him as my little wild friend.

Over the years, I told the story of Chipper the squirrel, our childhood friend, more times than I can hope to remember. It was this story I chose to tell Jimmy's children as we all sat with Jimmy in the hospital on the very saddest of days, when once again my big brother would go first, to make sure the rest of us would be okay. Jimmy just smiled, nodded his head, and listened as I told the story of how we saved and raised our furry little sprite.

***

Many years later, my family was given the chance to hand-raise two more very small baby squirrels that had been abandoned in much the same way as our Chipper. They needed to be fed special formula every two hours around the clock for six weeks, and cleaned and bathed and kept warm like the mother would have done in the

272

wild. I took them everywhere I went, caring for them night and day in order for them to grow healthy, happy, and strong.

It was 3 a.m. in a small room on the second floor of our home. My wife, Julianne, came into the room to check on how the two little ones were doing. She found me there with tears running down my face, holding the squirrel babies in my lap. With a heartbroken look she asked if our little visitors had passed away.

I took a deep breath and said, "No. They're both doing fine."

She placed her hand on my shoulder and asked me why I was crying.

I said, "The thing is, little boys can't raise baby squirrels by themselves. It's just too hard."

It was then, all those years later, while holding those fragile little guys in my hands, I finally realized. That the battered little Chipper must have passed away the same night Jimmy and I had found him. In the morning my big brother, as good big brothers do, made up the story of how our squirrel had grown up and gone out to play with the other squirrels.

From then on, every time we saw a squirrel I would ask, "Is that him, Jimmy? Is that him?" Jimmy would say, "Yeah, that's him, that's our squirrel." And my big brother never told me any different.

Answered Prayers

Winter had come and gone. The days grew longer and warmer. We continued going out on many more adventures as we grew. It was on a day just like any other day when it finally happened: Jimmy and I really did get to see pond dragons do battle. We sat at the water's edge and said the pond dragon prayer. It was just like in the stories Grandpa Roy told us so very long ago. There, in a pond that had appeared with the coming of spring, in the spot where the old ladies' house had been just a year before, the pond dragons swam out, bowed their heads, and began to battle. They arched their backs, spread their fins, and raised their tails high as they fought. Challenger after challenger joined the fight. They fought ten at once until only the pond dragon king was left to claim his queen.

Jimmy looked at me as if to say *Now is your chance*. I had thought a hundred times about what I would say to the pond dragons. How I would ask them to please use their magic to help Jarod's differentness. Only now, standing there before the pond dragon king and queen, asking somehow seemed wrong. At that moment, it felt like I would be saying Jarod needed to be fixed. Only to me he had never felt broken. It was then I decided Jarod was just as magic as polliwogs and pond dragons put together.

I didn't ask the pond dragon king for any wishes. Seeing the battle was enough. I think Jimmy knew what I was thinking. He didn't ask for any wishes either.

The next day we brought Jarod out to see the pond dragon battles. Only when we got there, it was as if the battle had never happened. The few dragons that were left in the pond just swam off in clouds of mud. The king and queen were nowhere to be found.

Within a few weeks the pond itself disappeared, leaving nothing but an empty field of snapdragons and dandelions, bumblebees and dragonflies.

Jeremy T. Owen

Wall-to-Wall Love

In the end, most people do the best they can with what they have. Us? We had magical adventures and stories, my father's music, but mostly we had each other. I'm thankful for that. I'm thankful for all the characters I met, or imagined, or both. I'm thankful for the time I got to spend with trolls, pirates and sprites, sharks and clam bears, hawks, squirrels, and pond dragons. I'm thankful that I got to see real magic for myself, hold it in my own heart and hands. I'm thankful for my flawed, funny, funny family. But most of all I am so very thankful to have lived in our house made with wall-to-wall love.

And my father sings:

The house needs paint
Kids need shoes
I keep trying to win
But I always lose.

I know I got help from up above
'Cause God built my house
With wall-to-wall love.

Some bills ain't been paid
In more than a year
I keep telling my wife
We have nothing to fear.

When the furnace needs wood
And the food ain't enough
We must be thankful for a home
Built with wall-to-wall love.

The mail box blew down again today
Jenni wants another dog

The Polliwog Fields

She found another stray.

Jimmy broke a window
On the house just down the street
I got to tell my wife again
There won't be much to eat.

I wish my kids could have
Something sweet.

Fishin's been bad
Huntin's been worse
Even the moths have abandoned
My wife's empty purse.

I want to cry when hard luck
Gives me one more shove
But you can't cry in a house
With wall-to-wall love.

When I see my kids playing
On the living room floor
I feel guilty for thinking
I was ever poor.

Though the work is scarce
And times are rough
I'm richer than most
In a house
With wall-to-wall love.

The End?

The Tale of the Pond Dragon King

Not so long ago, in a land not so far away, there lived a pond dragon king.

He was a good king—wise, kind, humble, and proud, all the things a good king should be. He was also a magic king who ruled over a magic land, a land filled with all manner of magic creatures, places, and things.

Each year at the first croak of spring the pond dragon king held his royal court. Fairies, squirrels, sprites, and frogs would gather alongside all the other forest folk from the farthest corners of the land.

The king would sit upon his throne of beads and stone. There he would hear from all his subjects, bringing the king stories from the far reaches of his realm.

"Quiet!" commanded the king. The crowd of magical creatures began to settle down.

Clam Bear, who wasn't really a bear at all but a guardian of the forest, stepped forward on his big hairy feet. He knelt down before the king and bowed his head to show his respect.

"Rise and speak!" said the king to Clam Bear.

Clam Bear rose, cleared his throat, and spoke. "My King, I bring news of creatures seen adventuring through the polliwog fields." The crowded court gasped, then hushed once again.

"Tell me more of these creatures," said the king.

"They are on a quest, Your Majesty. They wish to see the pond dragon king."

The king smiled. Clam Bear went on. "They have bright eyes, funny smiles, and adventurous hearts. One even has pointed ears."

The crowd mumbled for a moment.

"Continue," said the king.

"They believe in our magic too. They have learned to listen as well as to speak to the forest. They have heard the stones sing, and the rocks talk back. They have fought for each other, and for others as well."

"Is that all?" said the king.

Clam Bear looked down. "No, Your Majesty. They are young, and they have learned some difficult lessons too."

"One of them killed Black Bird," interrupted Mrs. Raven. "And Spider!" added Green Forest Fairy. The crowd gasped, looking around at each other with worry in their eyes.

The king looked to Clam Bear and asked, "Does he carry their spirits with him? Does he know he will have to answer for his actions?"

"He does, Your Majesty," replied Clam Bear.

Toad moved his head to the side so as to get a better look at the king with his one good eye. "Your Majesty," croaked Toad, "they tried to save Baby Squirrel when he fell from the tall, tall tree, and they rescued Mr. Snake from being run over by the train."

"That's true. That's true," mumbled the crowd.

Chester the hawk opened his wings wide and bowed before the king, "Your Majesty, they saved me from the scissors, let me stay in their room, and fed me until I was fat." The crowd laughed at the now plump Chester.

Suddenly the ground began to shake. Mrs. Turtle fell onto her back and sucked her head and legs inside her shell. What had been a large pile of rocks a moment before began to move, revealing itself to be a very well-hidden Mr. Troll. He cracked free from his disguise and began to speak. His voice thundered over the crowd. "They could have eaten me if they wanted to, but they showed me mercy, and gave me apples and candy when I was lonesome." The king nodded with approval.

Salmon said, "They protected me as an egg and helped me up over the falls when I was old."

Mole stepped forward and laid three sparkling jewels at the king's feet. "They freed our magic stones from the heart of the mountain," said Mole.

The king admired the jewels and handed them to the queen, who held them up for all to see.

The king looked to Clam Bear. "Now tell me, Clam Bear, why do they wish to see me?"

"Your Majesty, one of them is different. They seek your magic to fix his differentness."

The king sat back in his throne, stroked his chin, and thought for a long time. Then he leaned forward and looked at the crowd. The king laughed a great laugh. The entire crowd laughed along with him.

"Just one?" said the king

Clam Bear looked puzzled and didn't know what to say.

The king continued. "Just one is different? Look around you, are we not all different?" He smiled. "You see, Clam Bear, the differentness in each of us is our own true magic." The king paused. "Have they been respectful, Clam Bear?"

"Very," said Clam Bear.

The king stood, looked out on all his subjects, and declared, "They may come before me. They may see the pond dragon battles. They may ask if they wish, but I shall not take away the differentness. Their differentness is their magic, and they will need to learn how to use it!"

The crowd cheered and looked at each other, each proud of their differentness, and began to chant:

> *So sayeth the pond dragon king.*
> *So sayeth the pond dragon king.*
> *So sayeth the pond dragon king!*

Jeremy T. Owen

THE END

Glossary of Terms

arrowheads: sharpened stones fashioned by Native Americans to put on the tips of their arrows

Astoria: a small coastal town in Oregon, located at the mouth of the Columbia River

bing-bongs: bean bags, his li'l fireman's two little friends, testicles, balls, the old nut sack, twig and berries—well, just the berries

bird point: small arrowhead used for hunting birds and small game

boob tube: television

candy drought: the entire year from five days after Halloween until the next Halloween

crib fisherman: toddler fishing from a playpen alongside the river

caddis-fly larva: nymph that lives in a small tube fashioned with sticks and stones on the bottom of the river

crawdad: small freshwater lobster (also called a crayfish)

clam bear: guardian of the forest, aka Bigfoot

crocodiliophobiaodontirectumfamiliaris: the fear of getting bit on the butt by the same alligator that bit you on the butt last time

cutthroat: native trout with red lines under its gills

dumpster diving: freeing garbage from its fate; so, recycling?

drunken marionette: little brother Jarod passed out in the car (Mom says she left the window open a bit)

Encyclopedia Gramptanica: a large set of books for looking up whoppers grandpas tell

ensatinas: see-through salamanders that ooze white goo

Eskimo ice cream: stuff that Dad ate when he was ten that he can still taste because it was yucky

fish sticks: fish pinched in a pair of tongs made from a sapling

forest folk: the community of magic creatures that live in the forest

fat blastards: thieving @$*@! sea lions

gawkers: people who are looking at something, mostly when you don't want them to.

hamster-shy: having fewer hamsters than you were supposed to have

Hide-A-Bed: a man-eating couch

iron lung: a device to help people breathe when they can't breathe on their own

iron pony: bicycle

Jarodese: the unspoken language in between the words Jarod speaks

Libradol: a compound made from the mud of Medical Lake in eastern Washington, used for poultices

newt: a type of salamander that can spend the whole day in a boy's pocket; also, can turn into a pond dragon

me tree: me pretending to be the top of a very large tree

mudpuppy: the larval stage in the life cycle of a newt or other salamander

pack donkey: Small child used as a pack animal by older siblings and paid two carrots a day

play possum: avoid chores

plague of frogs: aka the backdoor trots—in this case diarrhea caused by bad food.

polliwog: the magical little creatures we loved to catch; see *Tadpole*

polliwog fields: For the most part, mine were located in and around Astoria, Oregon. There is a nice spot just past the plum trees on Clover Lane. Yours can be anywhere adventure lies.

pog: a six-hundred-pound pig that thought she was a dog

pond dragon: A most magical creature that can regrow its parts. In the spring, newts return to their ponds, transform into dragons, and do battle.

poop lottery: taking the Saint Bernard for a walk to see whose yard he would poop in

River Sauce: Dad's recipe for fish marinade

rolled copper: coins and other bits of copper pounded flat and rolled to make beads

rubber boa: a small snake found in the Northwest that can be worn like a wristwatch

salmon fly: a large flying insect as big as your finger

scraper: stone tool used for cutting and scraping the fat off of animal hides

stealthin': sneaking up on a frog

Sunset Empire Room: the family restaurant and bar owned by Aunt Cathy and Uncle John Van Horn

split shot: a lead weight with a split in it for pinching onto your fishing line

tadpole: the larval stage in the life cycle of a frog or toad; also called a polliwog

The Club: a nonexistent affiliation designed to tease smaller children

trading beads: small glass beads, usually blue or white

trailer lion: a wherever cat

troll: a friend

twangin' it: touching yourself in a private way

wherever cats: large, mostly feral cats that would take your food if they could

wampum: flat beads cut by hand from clamshells; worn to show status or used as a sort of money

Whooack: the sound Mom made when she barfed up polliwogs

About the Author

Jeremy T. Owen was dropped on his head as a baby. That is probably all you *need* to know about the author, though other fun facts include: He used to keep a box of rattlesnakes under his bed. He has a degree in herpetology but has made more money as a singer than as a biologist. He is a prolific songwriter and poet and something of a smart-ass. He brews one hell of a good beer. He is a sculptor of stone, wood, and clay. He would rather fly-fish than work. He loves his dogs more than most people. He has a bit of an obsessive disorder, so in the end, this book was only written by accident.

Made in the USA
Middletown, DE
02 April 2020